Web 2.0 Knowledge Technologies and the Enterprise:
Smarter, lighter and cheaper

CHANDOS
INFORMATION PROFESSIONAL SERIES

Series Editor: Ruth Rikowski
(email: Rikowskigr@aol.com)

Chandos' new series of books are aimed at the busy information professional. They have been specially commissioned to provide the reader with an authoritative view of current thinking. They are designed to provide easy-to-read and (most importantly) practical coverage of topics that are of interest to librarians and other information professionals. If you would like a full listing of current and forthcoming titles, please visit our website www.chandospublishing.com or email info@chandospublishing.com or telephone +44 (0) 1223 891358.

New authors: we are always pleased to receive ideas for new titles; if you would like to write a book for Chandos, please contact Dr Glyn Jones on email gjones@chandospublishing.com or telephone number +44 (0) 1993 848726.

Bulk orders: some organisations buy a number of copies of our books. If you are interested in doing this, we would be pleased to discuss a discount. Please email info@chandospublishing.com or telephone +44 (0) 1223 891358.

Web 2.0 Knowledge Technologies and the Enterprise:
Smarter, lighter and cheaper

PAUL JACKSON

Chandos Publishing

Oxford • Cambridge • New Delhi

Chandos Publishing
TBAC Business Centre
Avenue 4
Station Lane
Witney
Oxford OX28 4BN
UK
Tel: +44 (0) 1993 848726
Email: info@chandospublishing.com
www.chandospublishing.com

Chandos Publishing is an imprint of Woodhead Publishing Limited

Woodhead Publishing Limited
Abington Hall
Granta Park
Great Abington
Cambridge CB21 6AH
UK
www.woodheadpublishing.com

First published in 2010

ISBN:
978 1 84334 537 4

© P. Jackson, 2010

Typeset by Domex e-Data Pvt. Ltd.
Printed in the UK and USA.

Contents

Preface

I didn't write this book on a mobile phone using an Internet wiki on a high-speed train from Tokyo to Nagano. Wags may well say that is obvious. Nonetheless, I got a lot of help. I would particularly like to thank Professor Jane Klobas and Dr Stuart Garner for the many discussions and reviews. I would also like to thank the organisations who opened their doors to me to look at their wikis and blogs, tags and feeds. And, of course, Christine, Tommy and Danny. The title of the book came to me in the year of the Beijing Olympics, the motto of the modern Olympics being of course Citius, Altius, Fortius – swifter, higher, stronger. The Web 2.0 tools I had been working with in organisations seemed cheaper, faster and lighter than anything I had experienced and yet were too often transformed by the dead hand of corporate tradition. So I wanted to write something that helped to realise what I saw as enormous potential. Being a social scientist as well as a computer scientist I could tell that the problems were not technological. What were missing were social and conceptual elements, ways to frame the potential applications and understand the blockages. I hope this book goes a little way towards helping resolve this.

Paul Jackson
School of Management
Edith Cowan University
Australia

List of figures and tables

Figures

Tables

About the author

Paul Jackson is an information and knowledge management specialist who has been a systems developer, product development manager, strategic consultant and academic during an international career spanning 25 years. Paul has spent his working life in Germany and Australia, working for PSI AG and IBM, and as an independent consultant. He is now a Research Scholar at Edith Cowan University in Western Australia. He has been a consultant to many commercial and government organisations and managed multi-million dollar information systems projects. He has a PhD in information systems development and has published widely on organisational information and knowledge management in highly ranked journals, books and conferences.

Using theories of knowledge from his studies in philosophy, group psychology and the sociology of knowledge, in this book he builds on his practical experience to articulate alternative approaches to making a success of Web 2.0 knowledge tools in business and government organisations. While Web 2.0 strategists focus upon the exciting potential outcomes and technologists describe the necessary skills and functions, this book emphasises the need for knowledge workers and managers to conceptualise Web 2.0 as supplying an empty field upon which they inscribe specific kinds of spaces. Each space implies a context, or frame, for enacting flows of particular types of information, constrained by the emergence of appropriate institutions and rules which match the nature of the space. It is hoped that this notion will provide a basis for knowledge workers to autonomously develop and maintain their Web 2.0 applications and satisfy the needs of management for discipline and relevance.

The author may be contacted via the publishers.

Introduction

An irregular heartbeat is a common consequence of heart attacks and can be fatal. In the 1980s a drug called *encainide* was routinely used to reduce this risk by suppressing such arrhythmia. It was logical to assume that since this drug induced a regular heart rhythm, it automatically reduced the chance of a further heart attack: in fact the opposite was true and the drug was responsible for a significant number of deaths and did not even improve the health of those who lived. This only came to light when evidence was collected in randomised clinical trials. Similarly, although there is convincing logic that it must work, the common orthopaedic process of arthroscopic cleansing of arthritic knees by washing out the joint with fluid has also been found through clinical trials to have no impact whatsoever. Both are cases where the intervention seemed 'common sense' and so the treatments were taken as the received wisdom. Both applied simple logic to a limited set of premises within a biological framework and came to compelling but wrong conclusions, conclusions that were only belatedly tested because of their apparent obviousness.

Common sense and logic tell us that the technologies known as 'Web 2.0' are destined for success in the corporate environment. McKinsey go so far as to say that Web 2.0 tools may exceed enterprise resource planning, customer relationship management and supply chain management systems in improving productivity through greater participation and collaboration.[1] They are a simple, fast, effective, cheap and useful treatment for several ailments afflicting corporations. They also appear to be the right tools to manage the increasingly fragmented, global information workplace of networked, virtual enterprises. But although there are case studies of successful implementations, generally published by vendors and consulting firms, there is still relatively little independent review or measurement of improvement. And more fundamentally, how are we to conceptualise 'success'? We need to ask ourselves whether the perspectives we are using to *measure* success actually cope with or reveal the data we need to *judge* success. When astronomical theory (largely driven by religious premises) presented the earth as the centre of the solar system, data that contradicted this (such as irregularities in planetary orbits) was catered for by the creation of additional loops (or 'epicycles') by planets circling the earth. This Ptolemaic astronomy was refined and extended until the theory was simply no longer sustainable. In our examples of failed medical expectations, biological logic told us that the knees and hearts would improve, but was wrong. In business, operational logic, which looks at throughput, efficiency, cost and productivity, may be the wrong theory to examine the consequences of the impact of Web 2.0.

So what is 'Web 2.0'? In essence, it is a mode of participatory interaction via the World Wide Web using a certain type of technology. In contrast to the posthumously baptised 'Web 1.0', which was based upon a predetermined client–server relationship between consumers and a managed website, the Web 2.0 mindset is about interactive, conversational co-production of information, products and oneself. Web 2.0 provides a platform of tools for such interaction rather than a predefined set of rules of engagement and outcomes. These tools can be taken in many directions and applied in many ways. The information content is loosely structured and conversational, in contrast to e-commerce marketplaces or business-to-business exchanges, and so Web 2.0 tools are often called 'social software'. If this is an accurate label, it follows that social theories are needed to understand and perhaps even to manage it, even within corporations. Theories other than transaction cost theory, the balanced scorecard or business process management may be needed to model the interactions between employees and the organisations to which they belong and allow new kinds of performance data to become salient.

The reason for the book

This book is about collaboration, networking and knowledge generation in the time of this second wave of Internet technology. It is based upon the premises that business interactions are increasingly, if not mostly, computer mediated and that new generations of workers find this mode of work natural, intuitive and familiar. Corporations and businesses are struggling however. E-mail, while being the 'killer application' of the Internet, is creating many problems of control, management and knowledge loss. Systems by which knowledge is created and shared, modes of authority and legitimation, are changing. The incremental is being replaced by the chaotic, the solid by the fragmented and the software programming journeyman by students and geeks. The underlying technologies are available in the home: familiar, fast, flexible and convenient. But behind the corporate firewall, IT departments and the gatekeepers of software standards, information systems policies and corporate knowledge are playing catch-up.

There are a substantial number of books about the technologies that are collected under the banner of Web 2.0. There are also books on the implications of these technologies for business strategy and in particular for certain professions, for example education and libraries. This book fills the gap between strategy and technology implementation by focusing upon the functional capabilities of Web 2.0 in corporate environments and matching these to specific types of information activity. It takes a resource-based view of the firm: how can the knowledge capabilities and information assets of organisations become better leveraged by using Web 2.0 tools?

The information technology industry is pervasive and epoch defining, yet characterised by hyperbole and failure. It must be made clear to decision-makers what the business benefits of Web 2.0 are, so that business cases can be prepared, plans written, targets defined and progress measured. The challenge in this is that these business benefits occur often at the micro-level. There is generally no specific business process like order entry or inventory management where improvements can be identified and measured. To take the analogy of e-mail: what was the business case for that? What a silly question! The improvements might be so substantial that they are not measurable using the paradigms in place within an organisation at a particular time.

Identifying the underlying benefits therefore requires the use of perspectives beyond profitability, business process effectiveness and cost control. Some of these perspectives are not in the usual business parlance, but when applied, demonstrate the role that can be played by Web 2.0 and how to manage towards these. Transactive memory systems, social uncertainty, identity theory, network dynamics, social constructivism and the demographics of inter-generational change are not normal business language but can be used to clarify Web 2.0 application and potentiality.

This book is therefore directed towards three constituencies:

- the reflective CIO, information manager or knowledge manager who enjoys a fresh perspective on information technology tools;
- the researcher who is looking for frameworks to assess the impact of Web 2.0 on businesses;

- the MBA or MIS student who, as part of the emerging generation of business participants and managers, is seeking to understand how work is to be enhanced with Web 2.0 tools.

The structure of the book

This book is an attempt to locate this new wave of technologies in two major contexts: firstly, the modern business environment of globalisation, hyper-competition, disaggregation, generational change, inter-generational knowledge loss and virtuality; and secondly, the specific social nature of knowledge construction, exchange and application. We are interested in improving the adoption of technologies which improve its utilisation as a productive, generative resource. Without an understanding of how knowledge is built, shared and institutionalised, the potential for these new tools in the business environment cannot be realised.

The technology tools available under the banner of Web 2.0 can play a substantial role in the creation, exchange and storage of organisational knowledge. This is particularly so in the case of new generations of workers with different capabilities and preferences to baby boomers, in the reduction of social and organisational uncertainty, increasing the sensing and awareness capabilities of users and facilitating the development of maps of knowledge, so that knowledge can be found, generated and legitimated by groups who never meet physically.

Given the almost inevitable passage of these new tools into the work environment, this book then presents potential applications and methodologies to support effective implementation. These applications range from building organisational encyclopaedias via wiki technologies, to knowledge capture via multimedia methods, the generation and maintenance of knowledge directories, using personal, managerial and corporate blogs to publish many voices within a firm, and the use of feed readers to reduce the flood of 'corporate spam'. But this wish-list of functionality, however, will only work if the underlying knowledge processes and constraints are understood. These processes operate differently according to the different types of communicative Web 2.0 spaces which can be created: there are many kinds of communicative space, which have varying flows and pulses, and which are governed by a variety of social institutions and purposes. The processes which build social identity as part of this human communication must also be considered. What is the self-image concept which impels particularly young users towards self-realisation through such tools? The sheer open-endedness of Web 2.0 tools introduces a need for management sophistication – a kind of 'muscular philosophy' as it were. The structure of the book mirrors the structure of this argument.

Chapter 2 explains in detail the meaning of the 'Web 2.0' and defines the various tools and technologies which are currently regarded as belonging under this umbrella term. While 'Web 2.0' has a fuzzy definition based upon a mode of interaction and participation, the respective technologies are quite concrete and recognisable: wikis, blogs and social networking sites are the key systems in which information content is accumulated. These are supported by facilities such as social tagging, really simple syndication (RSS), mashups, AJAX and REST. In this chapter I describe each technology, why it belongs to the idea of Web 2.0 and how it can be part of an overall system of interacting Web 2.0 technologies which combine to manage organisational knowledge.

Chapter 3 analyses the reasons which are commonly presented as being the business imperatives to implement Web 2.0 tools and, in a sense, the management philosophy which accompanies them. These imperatives – the global economy, generational change, network effects, the fragmentation of work and so on – are itemised and discussed. I argue that while they are all important, they are often only conditionally true and *should* not be (and indeed probably *are* not) taken as sufficient reasons to implement the tools. Furthermore, they provide only general incentives to adopt the technologies – a clearer understanding of how these tools apply to specific work activity is required.

Chapter 4 presents a framework within which to express the functionality of the tools such that a relationship to a business purpose can be defined and a clearer sense of the application developed. This helps decision-makers conceptualise how to apply the tools, what returns to expect and what constraints will apply. These concepts are those of *spaces and flows*: the space is the playing area within which certain knowledge activities, or games, with particular rules are carried out. This 'game' requires certain infrastructure and has certain formal and informal rules of engagement and behaviour. This behaviour results in knowledge flows through the Web 2.0 tools which will build organisational memory and facilitate knowledge sharing, but under a set of shared expectations and social institutions. I give examples of types of space, such as encyclopaedia, advisory or partner space, which determine what type of activity will occur, what outcomes are expected and how one should behave.

Chapter 5 discusses the movement from space to function. Once one or more spaces have been identified to support a business objective, the information flows within the space need to be identified and articulated. This is a process of analysis and design, but in contrast to traditional systems development, this can proceed with a substantial degree of emergence, autonomy and self-organising on the part of the user group. Once the flows within the space are agreed, the information to be captured and stored should be classified (prescriptive, descriptive, distinctive and emergent) so appropriate treatment of that information can be decided. The specific information objects (wiki pages, blog pages, ratings, tags and so on) need to be identified and in some cases standard layouts defined and then set up for use.

Chapter 6 is about the transition from function to use. It is quite strongly theoretical and takes the position that to get the most from Web 2.0 spaces requires an understanding of how knowledge processes within those spaces work. It may be of more interest to the researcher than the practitioner. Moving on from the notion of spaces and flows, I describe a series of conceptual frameworks with which to understand the advantages of the tools, how to implement the tools within a particular space, how to gain adoption and how to assess the benefits to the organisation. The first concept is that of organisational memory and what is involved in building it and making it accessible. I describe the different types of knowledge that organisations produce, how to manage access to them and which of these might be appropriately managed by Web 2.0. I then look at the social processes of knowledge construction in order to understand how these processes move from face-to-face conversation, meetings, e-mail or phone to the virtual environment of a wiki or a blog and what changes may occur as we do so. The social norms which govern human behaviour are known as institutions: I examine these to understand how we might manage the adoption and use of the tools. These institutions vary between groups, so the social identity of potential users helps us to understand how groups will vary in their attitude to the tools. Finally we examine the role of power in facilitating the adoption of these systems.

Chapter 7 takes the frameworks of Chapters 5 and 6 and builds a methodology for the implementation of Web 2.0 in the enterprise. As stated, the complexity and cost of the technology are not serious impediments with these tools: it is the 'technologies of the self' that are important: norms, institutions, social behaviours. And not just of users – managers, customers and partners are part of the overall institutional constellation too. This chapter moves from the definition of a space, its purpose and business benefit, the type of knowledge to be generated and stored within it, to the signposts which help to locate that knowledge subsequently. Then there is the analysis of the social institutions present in the organisation and group, which may hinder or help implementation.

Following the conclusion in Chapter 8, a detailed case study is provided in the appendix which presents lessons from success and failure in using these modern, lightweight collaborative tools.

The basic idea of the book

The tools of the Web 2.0 class, baptised by one senior executive involved in our projects as 'gunslinger technologies', are easy to use and present little or no technological challenge to most users. Yet having been involved in several Web 2.0 projects and studied many independently reviewed case studies, it is clear that there are problems with gaining adoption reminiscent of the *knowledge management* projects of the 1990s. This is even so in cases where there is direct applicability and fast payback. To explain this I would like to take a brief philosophical excursion that leads to the approaches I propose later in the book.

I have developed the view that there is an 'iron cage' constraining the participants within the environments where this toolset can be implemented. Managers, knowledge workers and technical specialists see and evaluate the world in terms of what they know, and make decisions and take actions in terms of their various constructed models of reality: *the limits to their language are the limits to their world.* If tools as simple and effective as those of Web 2.0 are not being adopted, then either they are not seen to be as simple or effective as we think they are, or there are factors in the models of reality which constrain their take-up and use. These factors are not well understood. We need to explain clearly what the tools can be used for and the barriers to productive use.

The first vehicle I use to meet these challenges is that of *space*: this is a concept derived from social theory and philosophy, but is intuitive enough to be understood and applied by intelligent laymen. It is a 'boundary object' which helps conceptualise what one wants to do with the tool and at the same time defines the modes of engagement and behaviour appropriate to using the tool within the space. Essentially, this first notion is about context setting: when we are invited to dinner with the Queen we will behave differently than at a hot dog stand or a business luncheon. We adopt different roles because the stage we are on is of a genre (tragedy, comedy or farce) that demands certain behaviour and linguistic performances: the drama unfolds according to the rules of the genre. Without this context, how is an actor to know how to act?[2]

The second vehicle I employ is a set of social theories which help to explain what it is that happens within spaces. Web 2.0 is not only 'social software' geared towards communication and information sharing, it is a set of consumer products which first appeared on the World Wide Web. Productive or enjoyable use is not a technological issue: the software is easy to learn and use, familiar to many and generally intuitive. Effective use in organisations is constrained or enhanced by 'technologies of the self', the embodied social institutions which govern our social behaviour, our production of ourselves as individuals. We need useful theories to understand what it is that this technology is contributing to the organisation's ability to act and learn: its memory in other words. We need to explain how this memory is created, stored, classified and found by people when it is needed. We need to understand the processes that transform ideas and solutions into shared social structures and worldviews. We need to understand the institutional impediments and prerequisites which make organisation members participate in creating themselves and knowledge through this set of tools, what social groupings are prone to adopt or reject such tools and how they can be influenced (or how they influence others). The focus of implementation in Web 2.0 moves away from the technological almost entirely to the social realm – so muscular social theory is required. This is the second key argument of this book.

Using Web 2.0 tools is *easy* and it is my experience that the applications lie on the street, waiting to be picked up: there seems to me to be little potential for breakdown at the level of usability and at the level of functional applicability. But there is breakdown happening in the adoption and sustainment of these tools. I hope that by framing the use of the tools in this way, a method for envisioning, planning, justifying and implementing these eminently useful tools can evolve. I also hope that these notions provide an evaluative and analytical framework for investigating and researching their value.

Notes

1. Chui et al. (February 2009) write: 'Web 2.0, the latest wave in corporate technology adoptions, could have a more far-reaching organizational impact than technologies adopted in the 1990s – such as enterprise resource planning (ERP), customer relationship management (CRM), and supply chain management.' This is an extraordinary statement given the impact of enterprise data management systems on company efficiency and business models, and is

also extraordinary given the cheapness, ubiquity and immature nature of this software in firms. But McKinsey are not alone: the Gartner Group writes: 'Many enterprises are adopting new Web 2.0 technologies and methodologies, but others are struggling with basics such as value propositions and justification. Despite some difficulties, 2008 will be the year that Web 2.0 enters Type B (mainstream) enterprises. Understanding the future directions of the Web and how it can be leveraged in the enterprise are critical success factors for IT organizations' (Phifer et al., 2007), and further: 'Web 2.0 is one of the most hyped and misunderstood concepts in IT, yet it will have a significant impact on technology architectures, application content, communication, collaboration and business services' (Smith, 2008b).

2. Lemert and Branaman (1997).

Web 2.0 tools and context

This chapter describes some of the key tools within the Web 2.0 suite which have potential corporate applications. These tools are essentially knowledge tools: they support knowledge creation, interaction and collaboration, networking and sharing. One can use them to mediate interaction between the personnel within an organisation, with the organisation's customers or with business partners such as suppliers and vendors. This is not the intended function of these tools, which have their genesis in the role they play in the lives of Web users. It so happens that they have characteristics that make them useful for the management of working knowledge, knowledge which is a key productive resource for the delivery of industrial production or services.

We shall discuss a number of tools: some provide functionality which is used directly by users, such as wikis, blogs, social networking and RSS readers. Others provide underlying capability to the end-user tools, improving the usability of those tools: AJAX, REST, the semantic web. The tools we discuss offer a complete and mutually complementary suite for the management of knowledge in the corporate environment.

This is a key point of this chapter: that the Web 2.0 tools, although individually useful, should also be seen as a set of configurable components which, when working together, provide strong functional support for the production and exploitation of organisational knowledge. This platform of tools provides open-ended, highly flexible support for knowledge transformation activities and, I believe, wherever possible should be left to the devices of self-organising, dynamic groups and individuals to design, use and combine according to their requirements and capabilities. This is not only an emancipated and ethically correct approach, but I suspect that this is also the most likely way to achieve success.

Web 2.0 – the concept

The expression 'Web 2.0' emerged as part of a conference workshop conducted by O'Reilly media and was coined by Tim O'Reilly and Dale Dougherty as they discussed the aftermath of the 2001 dot com collapse.[1] It was mooted that far from being over, the potential impact of the Internet was as great as ever but taking a different form. This form was exemplified by moves to new types of website, product or service, for example:

- from static, carefully designed personal websites to a blogging stream;
- from file downloads on mp3.com to peer file-sharing using Napster;
- from online malls and third-party directories to the social tagging of content by shoppers and users;
- from the Encyclopaedia Britannica to Wikipedia.

These shifts contained some underlying principles which at least warranted the claim that a qualitative change was taking place. The 'meme map' in Figure 2.1 shows the major elements in this transition,[2] but in essence the change was from a 'Web 1.0' which was predicated on the provision of data or services via a 'server' to a 'client', to a 'Web 2.0' which provided a platform for users to participate on an equal footing. A platform is a toolbox of capabilities which are open-ended, adaptable to many purposes and contain low levels of inbuilt constraint. Software tools and websites were appearing and constituting a Web toolbox platform which enabled any non-technical, low-budget user of the Internet to create, use and control information and information exchange as they chose. This context of user-driven, user-managed Web participation led to a rise in the provision of services (rather than finished products), which users could configure and mix, and enabled users to themselves provide 'services', even if that service was a stream of their own opinions in a blog.

These services could start cheap, small and simple, but were infinitely scalable in both volume and function. One did not have to invest big to have an impact and it became possible to start a long Internet journey with a single step: the functions of the website could be upgraded in increments as a 'perpetual beta' (or stream of prototypes) without big-bang risks and costs. The speed and simplicity of communications products led to the development of interactive conversations (as opposed to just shouting into the void), allowing participation in persistent, prolonged conversations around shared areas of interest. Solid, dependable information and other forms of digital products, such as

Figure 2.1   Meme map – the gravitational core

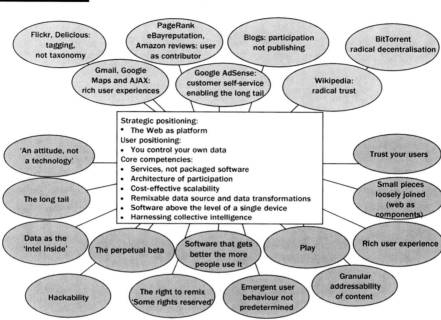

Source: http://oreilly.com/web2/archive/what-is-web-20.html

software, bookmarks, recommendations and reference works, emerged, based upon the collective intelligence of many participants. These outcomes became a service to others.

These tools were not invented to manage knowledge and information exchange in corporations. But they are tools which are integral to the system of knowledge creation and sharing which now dominates the Internet. They emerged because they play a role in capturing, exchanging, storing and classifying information symbols in a form which is persistent and shared by users across the physical and temporal ranges reached by the World Wide Web.

So is the expression convincing and durable, and are there essential characteristics in the definition of Web 2.0? There are certainly some tools in the Web 2.0 suite which existed before the expression appeared and even before one could imagine talking about Web 2.0. Other tools considered to be in the Web 2.0 set, such as Twitter's microblogging technology, have emerged since the term was coined. And one needs to be ever mindful of sales hype in a rapidly moving marketplace of ideas in which the participants are constantly seeking points of differentiation in search of profit or acclaim. But there does seem to be a use for the concept, which embodies a new paradigm of interactivity, collaboration and self-service. This piece of language can be used to convey a message to corporate decision-makers, marketing personnel, designers of websites and e-business marketplaces, namely that forms of information exchange and generation are changing and that a product catalogue with secure credit card transactions is not enough to make a successful website, indeed that control over the future use of that information will restrict its generative power and the return on its investment.

The expression Web 2.0 provides an umbrella term which can be used to strategically harness the existing and rapidly multiplying tools into coherent yet responsive organisational strategies for interactions with customers, partners and between people within the corporate firewall. The elasticity and usefulness of the term are reflected in the emergence of terms such as 'Library 2.0', 'Enterprise 2.0' and 'Government 2.0' to reflect the same attributes of networked, interactive, accessible and participative information creation.[3] Charles Leadbeater even talks of 'Art 2.0', in which the artistic avant-garde of the twenty-first century develop mechanisms and a culture which encourage people to create common works across the Internet.[4] But we need to bear in mind, that the tools are a necessary, but not sufficient, part of the definition of Web 2.0. The way the tools are used is also definitive: using a wiki as a corporate intranet content management system, in which content is only allowed to be added by a certified administrator, is not Web 2.0.

Blogs

A blog is simply a sequential log of writings or, more recently, video expression, published in reverse chronological order, such that the newest entries are at the beginning of the log. 'Blog' is an abbreviation of 'weblog', a form of personal record or narrative that first appeared on the Internet in 1997. It allows personal publishing with no editorial intervention or review. Blogging software became available in 1999 and since then has exploded as a form of expression and personal website management. The 'blogosphere', or collective community of all blogs, contains anything up to 180 million blogs in the English-speaking world alone (and over 70 million in Chinese). Almost all mainstream media publishers use journalist blogs and the most popular ones are overwhelmingly theirs.[5]

Blogs are generally personal in that they are owned by an individual (who may be representing a firm) and the blog is a vehicle for the expression of their views. But a blog can also be a 'normal' high-function website containing multimedia content with sophisticated presentation capabilities. A blog entry can be commented upon by others and responses can be built upon to form a cascading chain of comment and response. Each of these blog entries has a 'permalink' which is an individual web address, simplifying access to and distribution of a particular entry. For example, you may have read an insightful and particular comment in a blog: so you simply copy and send the permalink URL to a friend who may be interested. Blogs are often personal or political opinions, commentaries, news items and corporate announcements. They can become open forums for discussion and collaboration, but they still retain personal ownership. Blogs also generally provide subscriptions, creating RSS syndication feeds which can be subscribed to by others who will be notified when a new comment is made or responded to. 'NightJack' for example is the depressing but compelling blog of an anonymous policeman who won the Orwell prize for journalism. Unfortunately, NightJack (see Figure 2.2) was 'outed' in 2009 and forced by his employer to cease blogging.

There are several ways to obtain and use a blog. There are hosting services, such as Bloglines or blogger.com, which allow one to set up a personal blog on the Internet and use the various blog functions for free. One can download free blogging software to run on a web server, a typical

Figure 2.2 The NightJack blog (now unavailable)

Source: http://nightjack.wordpress.com

example being Wordpress, which uses the open source MySQL database management software. Or there are blog functions existing within corporate products such as Microsoft Office Sharepoint Services, the Confluence or Socialtext wiki products, or as an extension in MediaWiki.

The blog is a powerful broadcast mechanism with many corporate applications. A personal blog can be used to communicate with co-workers, a collaborative blog to communicate between teams (for example at shift change) and a corporate blog can be used to broadcast newsworthy events to the enterprise.[6] As an outward-facing medium, it can be used by nominated business specialists to post information about products and services, plans and directions, and general chit-chat. The first famous corporate blogger was Robert Scoble (see Figure 2.3), who gave Microsoft a human and sometimes critical face; he now blogs independently of that company. In a recent interview he noted that corporate blogs seem lifeless because they are like press releases, 'new, friendly, cuddly press releases'.[7] Authenticity, the representation of a true, personally held set of beliefs, seems an important component to a successful blog.

In organisations whose core business is information, such as entertainment, news media or lifestyle programming, blogs take on an operational hue: their production *is* the product.[8] But Blogs are not just a

Figure 2.3   Robert Scoble's blog

Source: http://scobleizer.com/

product for the media; they also support other journalistic processes. In one survey, 60 per cent of journalists use them for research, 51 per cent to create opinions and 46 per cent to discover themes which interest the public.[9] Further research into the impact of blogs on product decisions demonstrated that although 8 per cent of Internet users use blogs for information, of these, 54 per cent have built an opinion on a blog entry.[10] Of course, as Dan Gilmour points out, these tools and more are available to everyone, not just to professional journalists.[11]

Blogs can be used in the monitoring and management of issues and emerging problems. Koller and Alpar analysed the use of Internet blogs in issue management in the public sphere: they cite two examples of issue conflagration through blogs. The first cost the Kryptonite bicycle lock company over $10,000,000 and considerable reputation when an expensive lock was shown in an uploaded video to be opened using a Bic pen.[12] The second example was the ringtone vendor Jamba, whose staff attempted to defend their pricing model against a critical, but amusing, blog entry which was becoming popular with young people. When this was discovered, it led to a 'blogstorm' and the original critical blog appearing (because of the increase in the number of links to that offending blog) on the first page of search engines. The loss of reputation to Jamba was significant. The bottom line for companies is that although cases like these are rare, and the cost of blog monitoring can be relatively high, certain industries (particularly automobile, retail, telecommunications and transport) should pay attention to blogs and their criticisms (34 per cent of firm-specific blog entries are negative).

Although numbers are perhaps starting to plateau, Internet blogs are now an established part of much personal and professional information sharing and mainstream product information management. Blogging will become increasingly important, although its form will change as new modes (such as real-time microblogging) become available.[13] If only for defensive purposes, firms need to monitor Internet blogging activity. In a time where information warfare and rumour conflagration represent a new set of hazards, the ability to defuse destructive waves becomes increasingly important. If Web 2.0 allows greater participation and influence by outsiders, responses by organisations to possible misinformation must also become effective, convincing and appropriate. Responses to outside feedback which are not honest, open or transparent will simply lead to greater mistrust and the erosion of a company brand.

Given the acceptance of blogs and the use of Internet blogs for corporate purposes, the move to blogs for internal information-sharing purposes seems a natural progression. Consider again issue development and escalation, but within the company, not just beyond it: there is a discernible unfolding of issues from latency, emergence, diffusion, maturity to reduction and closure. A firm might manage exceptions using excellent issue management and tracking systems, but firefighting is often a symptom of poorly designed processes, incompetence, bad product design and bad management. For a well organised, well run company, with a well functioning issue-management system, further business improvement can be gained by moving issue management to an earlier phase in the issue-management process. Blogs and forums can be used by experts and non-expert staff to raise issues (or monitor conversations for anomalies) while these are latent and isolated and have them brought to the attention of management. A specific example might be safety – noticing that a particular conveyor belt does not have a mesh guard – or trends with certain types of machine under certain circumstances – a machine from a particular manufacturer might have an exposed gearbox and be prone to wear and tear from dust. Blogs and forums provide a simple avenue for identifying and objectifying issues so that preventive action can be taken before accidents and breakdowns occur, in a sense providing a virtual 'suggestion box'. And issue management is only one of many potential internal applications for blogs.

In cases where a firm produces goods or physical services, the company bloggers announce and discuss corporate wares and are often called 'evangelists', as the blog offers a kind of pulpit for their deliberations. Because these blogs can be linked to and commented upon, they exemplify the interactivity dimension of Web 2.0. Instead of organisations being closed shops and their designers, strategists and marketeers insulated from direct interaction, corporate blogs pull in ideas and comments from the entire congregation of interested parties. Although these corporate forums often provide a tightrope suspended over heresy, they are nevertheless aligned to and constrained by what the blogger chooses to articulate. Much of the language one reads in replies to blogs and discussions indeed suggests familiarity and virtual closeness: one part 'the usual suspects', one part 'true believers' and one part 'concerned dissent'. Angela Merkel, the Chancellor of Germany, has an official video blog, but some students found it too unresponsive, so they created a website 'direktzurkanzlerin.de', where questions can be put by text or video and voted on by the public. After early resistance by the Chancellor's Office, the demand became so strong that the top three questions are now answered each week (see Figure 2.4).

A similar function can be performed within an organisation. Formal and acknowledged experts can be given a blog, as can managers and administrators, from which events, concerns, product announcements or

Figure 2.4 The student website which collects and rates questions for Angela Merkel

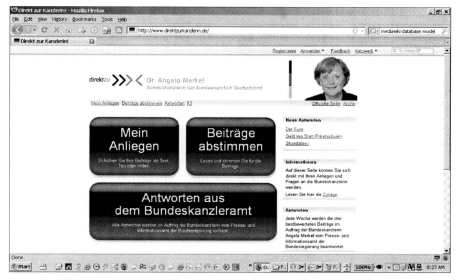

Source: *http://direktzurkanzlerin.de/*

improvement ideas can be distributed and feedback received. While it is tempting to view this as just another broadcast channel for personal and managerial blogs in particular, the expectation in the time of Web 2.0 is that such communications be two-way, personal and authentic.

Microblogging

The next generation of blogging is so-called microblogging. This is the capability of blogging small amounts of text to a website in much faster cycles, typically from a mobile device. The site first credited with this innovation is Twitter.com, which allows text of up to 140 characters to be blogged. There are a number of functions available within Twitter which allow you to 'follow' a person by subscribing to their 'tweet' via a mobile phone, invite comments from people to your twit, and reply to tweets and so on. A Twitter.com address, like a standard blog, is generally personal, but there are interesting applications when the Twitter address is a theme, an event, a university course or some other 'situational' object. A lecturer could tweet their thoughts or delays in getting to a lecture: a mobile maintenance company could tweet news to its mobile fleet: a health programme in any large organisation could tweet reminders to its members to exercise that day. The Web 2.0 company Socialtext has a twitter-like product called 'Socialtext Signals' as part of its social software suite Socialtext 3.0 which is designed to provide this kind of contextual constraint to messages, allowing rapid, interactive communication while reducing the amount of signals and requests actually received by an individual.[14] While interesting, however, this capability is already present in many standard applications which provide event-notification as part of standard workflow.

Wikis

Web pages are written in the Hypertext Markup Language (HTML) – this is the language that web browsers understand and can render onto a computer screen. The resulting display might contain text, entry fields, videos and images and be formatted to any level of sophistication and interactivity. The responsiveness and usability of web pages can be enhanced by using an extended version of HTML called XHTML with Javascripting, animated images and videos placed in strategic positions and with the video controls embedded into the overall page's script.

The HTML language standard was first conceived by Tim Berners-Lee, a British researcher employed at a European nuclear research centre. Working at the CERN laboratory, he was seeking a way for scientists to better share information and research results. He opened the world's first website on 6 August 1991 at the address *http://info.cern.ch* (see Figure 2.5). As Attali says, many major innovations come from the work of publicly funded researchers who actually look into something utterly different to what they are commissioned to do.[15]

A simple HTML page looks like Figure 2.6, where the words enclosed in diagonal brackets < > are called 'tags', which are interpreted by a web browser like Internet Explorer, Firefox or Google Chrome as commands to make a line appear as a heading or a particular colour.

But this language is not easy to learn and write. Tools have evolved to simplify the web page programming process and develop more sophisticated results. So instead of programming using this language directly into text editors, we use WYSIWYG (What You See Is What You Get) toolkits. Standard office products such as Microsoft Word or Powerpoint let you save a document as HTML, thereby allowing it to be opened and presented by the web browser. No HTML coding skills are required. Then there are sophisticated products like Dreamweaver and

Figure 2.5   The first Internet website

Source: http://info.cern.ch

Figure 2.6   A simple HTML page

```
<html>
   <head>
      <title>Hello HTML</title>
   </head>
   <body>
      <span>Hello World!</span>
   </body>
</html>
```

Websphere which are specifically intended for the development of powerful web applications. Although tools like this are a major productivity advance, three things are notable:

- The process of publication is still document or file centric – the web page source is an object of some kind. It is developed and this developed instance has to be moved to a location where it becomes accessible to web server software
- The process requires at least some level of skill which is not part of the portfolio of the normal knowledge worker. This includes page design at the very least and knowledge of stylistic standards, not to mention the mechanics of the products used to actually develop the pages.

- The process of 'promotion' to a live web environment requires some form of administrative rights or privileges. It is usually not in the range of authorities for anyone to be able create and publish web pages at will.

In response to these barriers, wiki pages were developed in 1995 by Ward Cunningham, an American computer programmer, to allow the immediate creation and editing of web pages. A wiki user usually just clicks a function to request a new page which they can then edit and format. Typically, the user can create headings, tables or change fonts, upload videos and images and create links to other web pages or other wiki pages.

The wiki system produces the HTML code required by browsers, but generally stores this in a database rather than in individual text files. The HTML page is constructed and sent at the moment it is requested by a user at their browser from the data stored in the database. Changes to the page are stored in the database, along with previous versions of the page and the identity or IP address of the user who changed the page.

There are usually a range of standard functions in wikis for editing, linking, formatting, undoing changes, viewing the history of all changes, managing security and so on. In the final analysis, a wiki is a website (such as that in Figure 2.7) that can be dynamically constructed by users who have no knowledge of programming, but who do know, for example, how to do basic text processing. Early versions of wikis used a simple but nonetheless offputting wiki mark-up language to format wiki pages but most now provide a reasonably comfortable text editing system.

An important standard function within wikis is the ability to define templates for different types of content page. When a new page is created, the template can be automatically inserted into the page with standard headings, boilerplate and even input fields with drop-down lists of allowed input values. This is extremely useful in corporate contexts: where consistency is important, direction for content creation should be provided, and although certain tasks might be routine, scope must still be allowed for variety. For example, a template for collaborative authoring of proposals and responses to tenders can automatically pull in company information, provide headings under which standard phrases are presented and so on. These templates provide important guidance to users and can themselves be adapted and enhanced by users.

Another notable wiki function is that of categorising (or tagging) pages: any page can be labelled with a tag which can represent an information category. When the category is searched for and found, all pages tagged with that category will be presented in a list. This resembles a keyword search with the added advantage that these categories can also be linked

Figure 2.7 A simple wiki page using Mediawiki freeware

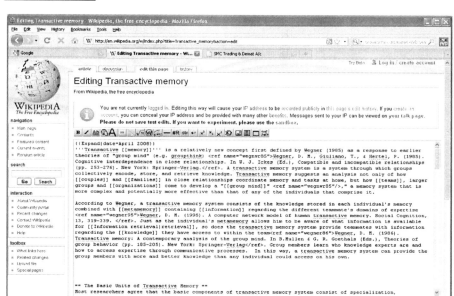

Source: http://en.wikipedia.org/w/index.php?title=Transactive_memory&action=edit

to each other in a meaningful way to reflect relationships in the real world. The category of hub cap might belong to the category of wheel which might itself belong to the category of chassis. But categories might also be less abstract: the category of Barack Obama might be useful to sort all wiki pages with some or any information about the president, but might also be linked to the category of Michelle Obama so that information about concrete instances of concepts can also be easily collected together and linked to information about other real-world entities. In Figure 2.8 we see how a conceptual hierarchy of category pages 'Event', 'Machine' and 'Design Parameters' can integrate information on a number of wiki pages, without those wiki pages 'being aware' of each other. A user will find these through navigating the category pages and then drilling down from a category page, such as Machine, to find relevant content pages, for example about the specific machine.

There are continual refinements to tagging in wikis: the Semantic Mediawiki group, for example, enhanced the base Mediawiki code to

Figure 2.8 Marking up pages using a category page hierarchy in Mediawiki

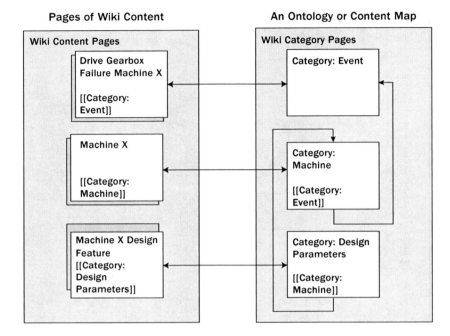

allow parts of wiki pages (as opposed to the whole page) to be marked up with metadata such that SQL-like queries can be run against the database. I might mark up a word in a page as a 'German City' and be able to ask the wiki how many German cities there are or to list all German cities mentioned in the wiki. A wiki page marked up like this:

> Shakespeare [[class:author]] was born in 1564 [[author 'Shakespeare', property:dob]] and died in 1616 [[author 'Shakespeare', property:dod]]
>
> Shakespeare [[class:author]] wrote [[relationship:is the author of]] Hamlet [[class:play]].

will allow queries across the wiki like:

1. Find all authors
2. Find all plays that Shakespeare wrote
3. Find all authors born in 1564

There are dozens of wiki products available and most are available free to download or use directly as a service on the Internet. They vary in the power of their function, their scalability, whether they use a database, the integration of user enhancements and the brute number of users supported by the system. Some are more reliable than others, many are quirky (and proud of it) requiring users to be a little tech-savvy and prepared to rough it. To help the overwhelmed, there are several useful sources for comparing functionality and reliability.[16] Some significant providers in the free wiki arena are Mediawiki, Wikia, PBWiki, Drupal, Twiki and Moin Moin. Most allow some level of HTML coding within a wiki page, but most also restrict this to prevent the possibility of malicious or dangerously incompetent code being introduced into the wiki.

If there are dozens of wiki products, there are literally thousands of public wikis on the Internet now. Special interest groups use them as a way to create collective knowledge and resources and generally have very low barriers to entry and contribution. There are several wiki *indexes* of public wikis, pointing to sites about law, philosophy, education or politics.[17] Figure 2.9, for example, is a collective 'Tax Almanac' wiki which is not just itself an information source, but points to other wikis and information sites pertaining to taxation.

Figure 2.9   The Tax Almanac wiki

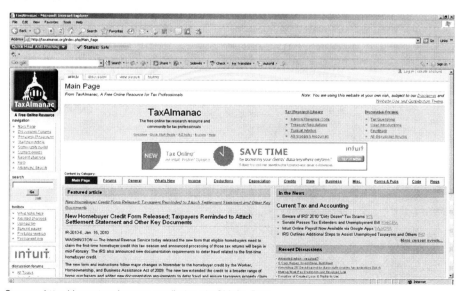

Source: http://www.taxalmanac.org/index.php?Main_Page

The technology behind wikis is simple: the Mediawiki product, for example, consists of only about 35 data tables, although this has evolved over time to accommodate new functions (such as history, logging, content validation), enhanced performance and the growing volume of aging content. Unlike business process software, wiki technology supports general information sharing. It generally does not manage structured user data – the level of data granularity is at the page level, so there are no complex data relationships or minute adjustments continually required as business processes change.

One can divide the rest of the wiki products which cost money into two general groups: products which are available as stand-alone solutions and wiki functionality which is made available within broader-ranging products. These can be installed on a local server or hosted on a provider's server and accessed as a service via the Internet.

The first set of products is exemplified by Confluence from Australian software firm Atlassian, and Socialtext. These are both highly rated by the Gartner Group and the information industry. In a nod to the open source origins of the concept, both make free versions available to individuals and offer a discount to community groups. Confluence resembles Mediawiki in its range of function, but is more robust, more user-friendly and corporate in its professionalism. It is also relatively cheap and has over 5,500 installed customers. Socialtext offers the usual functions of a wiki, but adds the ability to access it from mobile devices and to develop content offline and then upload this when a network connection is available again. It is also installed for corporations only as an appliance, that is as a physical server to be rack-inserted.

The second set of products covers those included in existing collaboration products or content management systems. Microsoft Office Sharepoint Services includes blogs, wikis, tagging and RSS feed capability as part of its overall collaboration and file-sharing suite. ECM, a leading supplier of content management systems, also includes blogs and wikis in its Centerstage Pro product. This uses the underlying versioning, security, information lifecycle management, archiving and retirement facilities of the Documentum product as a key selling point: the advantage of flexible, lightweight collaboration tools with the robustness, integration and control of a proven content management system. It is to be expected that any content management system will introduce the Web 2.0 capabilities into their function and that furthermore these will be 'free'. Most companies prefer Web 2.0-type products to be integrated into existing content management systems.[18]

So we see three classes of product: freeware, stand-alone products and products integrated into content or web management systems. The Web 2.0 components are inexpensive in all these options.

In the corporate context, wikis are used or intended to be used as knowledge and information repositories.[19] They are flexible yet structured, persistent yet dynamic. They are particularly suitable for communities of practice who are developing knowledge or are sharing information pertinent to a discipline, but also have application as an intranet content management system, with the bonus of immediacy and interactivity. They are particularly useful for the distribution of answers to frequently asked questions and user manuals. Where blogs have a role in pushing emerging information, particularly to customers, wikis are most usefully the result of considered knowledge interactions and so not as suitable for customer exchanges, although they can be used for interaction with known suppliers and partners to exchange unstructured information in place of e-mail and telephone calls.

Corporate wikis will almost never be anonymous: any page created or changed will be associated with the user's login identification. This of course will influence most people with regard to what information they are willing to enter into the wiki. Corporate wikis will also be user-constrained: the volume of people involved will generally be far less than if the entire Internet population could theoretically contribute: the 'wisdom of crowds' might be more like the wisdom of the one or two as firms generally keep specific expertise to the minimum necessary.

While case studies available on the intranet tend to provide success stories, these generally should be taken as demonstrating use-cases for potential application and not taken for granted as out-of-the-box applications. Organisations vary widely in their needs and in their ability to implement. McKinsey warn against the expectation that these systems will simply work. Indeed they record that about half of all adopters are dissatisfied and recommend a number of critical success factors, including leadership, support, integration into workflow, non-financial rewards and clear risk-balancing.[20] Some early research analysis of corporate wiki use is also not exalted, although the evidence is limited. Blaschke found at an innovation agency which introduced a wiki to enhance collaboration that when a social network analysis was developed to account for indirect links and interaction on any specific page (rather than parallel wiki monologues), the amount of collaboration across authors was actually very limited and had to be judged a failure: he concluded that 'the central concept of Web 2.0 was not to be found in the company'.[21] Most interactions went through the main project manager who was also the wiki administrator. In seeking wiki-metrics, Ebersbach et al. found that in the first year of operation at Robert Bosch that a wiki, although producing many pages, showed little evidence of true integration or collaboration. For example, the low number of internal and external links and the different authors, versions and changes indicated that the pages were not being used with the fluidity and dynamism of which wikis are capable.[22] Perhaps this is because in travelling lean, most organisations have as few duplicate specialists as possible so there is a dearth of conversation partners. Their conclusion, on the other hand, was that this revealed the 'uncertainty and inexperience of the users' (p. 153). Both these cases emphasise the need for further qualitative data to understand the reasons why wikis do not just 'take off'.[23]

Social tagging

One of the miracles of the World Wide Web is not that we have so much useful information at our fingertips but that we find any of it. Amid the dross, the trivia and the nonsense, we still seem to find what we need. If you enter 'IBM' into Google, the first result delivered is the IBM home page. If you type in 'Web 2.0', the first result is a very useful introductory Wikipedia page. As you type in more keywords, so the result sequence homes in on your need. It is important to realise at this point that Google (or any other search engine) must maintain its integrity and deliver search results sequenced on an objective basis which has not been interfered with by Google (the famous 'Do No Evil' company motto). The first position or first page on a Google search is of enormous financial benefit and a whole industry of 'search engine optimisation' has been spawned by the need to make Google rank your pages higher than those of your competitors. Nonetheless, if users thought that Google could manipulate search results, for example to benefit a particular company, the search would lose credibility and usage would probably decline.

The miracle of search is due to the brilliant search engine logic which crawls all publicly accessible sites on the World Wide Web, indexing every meaningful token that differentiates one page from the others. Google's patented page rank algorithm is of particular interest, as it is one of the key inputs to working out the relevance and anticipated likelihood of a page meeting your needs. As the web crawlers send back their information from all over the Internet, the indexing logic also records how many other sites link to this page. The more links coming into a page, the higher it becomes ranked in the search sequence. This is a manifestation of the 'wisdom of crowds' phenomenon – the more people consider a site to be worth linking to, the more likely it is to meet your needs too.

Finding what you need has become supported by increasingly sophisticated means, with search engines now building histories of personal and group searching in order to anticipate what result would mostly likely satisfy a request, building taxonomies on the fly which the search engine then applies to web pages to help you find them within 'categories' and so on. But finding pages is still challenging and if you have been researching a certain topic for more than a few minutes, even finding the pages you have already visited yourself can be difficult.

The phenomenon of social tagging emerged to address the difficulties of classifying and finding information. Put simply, it allows users to 'tag' or mark up a web page or document with a name which classifies that page in some way. These tags are formally called *metadata*, or data about data, which has been used to manage content in database management systems and information management circles for many years. They are social because they are available to others to use. The tags can be used to find information in future. You might create your own private tags or you might use the tags used by others. You might create a tag to describe web pages containing entertaining malapropisms or a tag called Beach Holidays for when planning your next getaway. These tags are created and kept in social tagging websites like digg.com or delicious.com. You simply go to one of these sites and enter your tag, which then becomes available for others to use too (hence it is *social*). You can search for the tag at the website, link it to other tags and add a web page address to that tag. When you look at the tag web page, it will list all the web pages and their links which belong to that category.

Physical objects described by physical labels are restricted by space, but digital signs are not and digital information can be described in many ways that do not interfere with each other. The classical methods of carving reality into 'natural' hierarchies (or taxonomies) which reflect an underlying essence are too restrictive, even if many categories do describe natural 'joints' in nature. Much of the world is in fact arbitrary and socially constructed and the capability of the Internet to allow people to tag, mark-up and share tags according to their various purposes is a useful advance in managing everyday information. In the same way as tagging, cooperative knowledge creation and information ratings lead to signage about the value of content. This is particularly important on the Internet, and to a degree in modern enterprises, where knowledge is a constant work-in-progress. Most significant news sites, for example, have a list of social tagging websites at the bottom of each page to help you note interesting articles for future reference. This has the useful side effect for the newspaper of making the articles more findable by others. In Figure 2.10, we see how *The Australian* newspaper, by offering readers the opportunity to tag articles, is simultaneously raising the connectivity of these articles and the likelihood they will be found by others. *Die Bildzeitung*, a German newspaper, offers social bookmarking and integration of their news pages with your personal blog (see Figure 2.11).

Here we see the 'many hands make light work' axiom in operation – but instead of many people creating information content (as is the case with Wikipedia for example), one is categorising web pages (working with information about information). And the more people do this, the more convergence and sense can be made of the vast quantities of Internet information. However, does this mean the categorisations are accurate or even correct? Some researchers take issue with social bookmarking in arguing that it not only degrades truth in classification, which is a normative act, but that it is philosophically unreliable: according to Aristotle, a thing can only belong to one category. If we take classification as an isolated, truth-functional process, this would seem to be correct: 'Fido is a dog' is true if and only if Fido is a dog. However, Fido is also brown, cute and the kind of dog I would consider buying: I could tag a web page about Fido with all these tags which serve my own purposes, and all can simultaneously be true. Further, classification is a final act on the way to making judgments: the construction of concepts is a social and permanently ongoing process. The consistent application of certain tags in clusters may lead to the development or recognition of new constructs. Tagging becomes a behavioural proxy for conversational *objectification*. Tagging overcomes the inherent 'miscellaneousness' of the Internet, allowing as many tags and sets of tags as there are points of view and purposes to which the Internet will be put.[24]

A particularly interesting component of tagging is 'tag clouds' which are increasingly a feature of search engines and large websites. These clouds consist of a display box of tags. Tags which have most referents or which have been most accessed recently ('hot tags') are displayed larger than less-used tags. Further, the tags which are displayed might be conceptually related to each other, so users can click on tags which they might not otherwise consider searching for. Figure 2.12 shows a tag cloud on the Blogscope website called 'Hot Keywords', where popular tags are displayed and magnified according to popularity.

Tagging has very interesting implications for organisations. It is an advance on document and content management systems which carry a

Figure 2.10 Referring readers to social tagging sites in *The Australian* newspaper

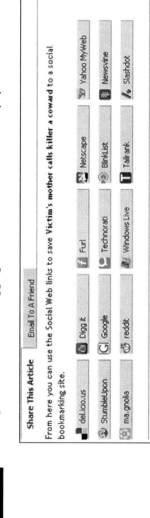

Source: *http://www.theaustralian.com.au*

Figure 2.11 Referring readers to social tagging and blogging sites in *Die Bildzeitung* newspaper

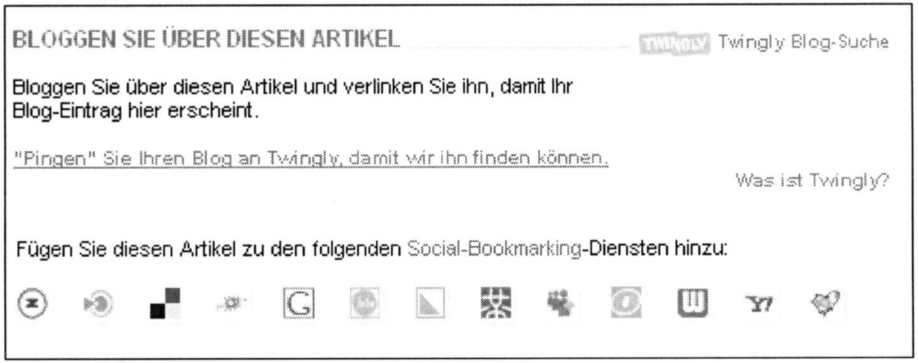
BLOGGEN SIE ÜBER DIESEN ARTIKEL
Twingly Blog-Suche
Bloggen Sie über diesen Artikel und verlinken Sie ihn, damit Ihr Blog-Eintrag hier erscheint.
"Pingen" Sie Ihren Blog an Twingly, damit wir ihn finden können.
Was ist Twingly?
Fügen Sie diesen Artikel zu den folgenden Social-Bookmarking-Diensten hinzu:

Source: *http://www.bild.de*

Figure 2.12 The tag cloud on the Blogscope.com website

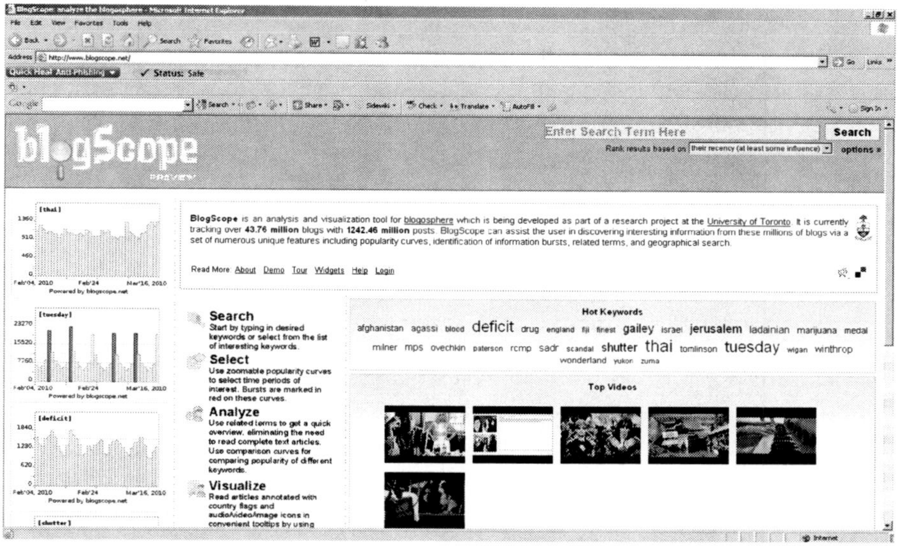

Source: http://blogscope.net/

'folder structure' philosophy. According to this, a company department like Finance might have a document management structure which has a folder for correspondence in and one for correspondence out. But it would be useful to differentiate correspondence out to debtors, creditors, suppliers of raw materials and suppliers in a certain country: correspondence might belong to two of these categories but can only be in one folder. A single folder has as much meaning as the standard document management system can provide. But any number of tags can be applied to a document, as documents and web pages, by their very nature, often cover multiple topics and cannot easily be pushed into one category. These documents and web pages within companies become far easier to locate and retrieve when tags, and tag groupings, begin to emerge as part of business workflow. Personnel in different departments may know a document by a different name, or as a different type, or use it for a different purpose, or even use different sections. Tagging allows each group to mark the document using the appropriate vocabulary without affecting the location, structure or internals of the document or web page in any way. Furthermore, as user-created tags become highly used and institutionalised, they can be harvested and used as standard keywords throughout the organisation.

RSS

Syndication is a way of multiplying the impact of, and revenue gained from, information without a corresponding increase in effort. A syndicated news columnist, for example, writes an article once and it subsequently appears in many newspapers to which the columnist is syndicated. The same applies to television programmes, cartoon strips, lifestyle articles, horoscopes and recipes. RSS stands for 'Really Simple Syndication', a technology which uses the Extensible Markup Language (XML) to allow Internet syndication.

This system is a format which makes article headings, summaries and link information available on the Internet to any feed reader, a small and simple piece of software which runs in the background of Internet-attached personal computers. A person might be interested in current affairs and finance for example, and regularly browse the BBC and the Economist websites. These sites provide RSS feeds in special areas to publicise 'what's new' to people who wish to subscribe. Users create topic areas in their personal RSS readers for news, sport or finance or whatever interests them and gather the web addresses of their favourite sites' feed in these topic areas. The software then goes to websites at periodic intervals the user nominates and inspects whether any new articles have appeared. If they have, it displays a discreet message to the user and will download the overview, or header, information. If so configured, it can download the whole article or any embedded files such as video or audio. This latter capability is the basis of Apple iTunes for example, which will download podcasts from websites for music, language learning or radio series into the iTunes file system and then copy those to the iPod device.

There are several benefits to this approach:

- A site user does not have to keep returning to a site to inspect it visually to see what is new.

- The site pre-sorts items of interest into categories on the user's behalf.

- The user does not have to reveal personal information in order to receive a notification.

- The information which the user needs to process to decide whether the article is worth reading is condensed.

- The notifications do not clutter up e-mail in-boxes.

Well-known free RSS readers which can be downloaded to run on your personal computer include RSS-Owl and FeedReader. A popular

Internet-based reader is FeedBurner.com (now owned by Google), which gives you an account in which you set up your own feed reading preferences and publish feeds for others. Many related information management products include an RSS reader: Microsoft Outlook 2007 has a feed reader as a standard component, as do all commercial wiki products.

RSS is the glue that holds together the content systems such as blogs, wikis and web pages. It raises information to the level of salience, distributing targeted notifications to people and again overcoming the miscellany of the vast information resources of the Internet. At the enterprise level, some products (such as certain Mediawiki extensions for example) even allow subscriptions via RSS to a social tag or information category, such that any changes to any information in a certain class cause a notification to be sent to subscribers.

RSS helps to overcome the problem of information overload in organisations by allowing staff to receive notification of information about specific areas. So an engineer in a maintenance department might subscribe to the department manager's blog for administrative announcements and to the local maintenance schedule page on the enterprise wiki. The engineer might also subscribe to the CEO's announcement blog, the health and safety wiki page and the social club pages. The notifications contain links to information which is stored and maintained on a server. A job role, such as engineer or scientist or works supervisor, can be equipped with a default set of RSS subscriptions which tailors information notifications to those required by the role.

RSS is also of use at the project or ad hoc level. Notifications of changes to project pages in a wiki can be picked up by team members' RSS subscriptions as can updates to discussion pages and special subject pages in which an engineer is interested or an expert. Every person sits in the centre of their personal information hub, and can tailor the information they are notified about to their own needs and according to their own work preferences. Notifications from an RSS reader can be inspected immediately or once a day, without disturbing a person's concentration or work habits or clogging up their e-mail in-boxes.[25]

Social networking

Since about 2005, there has been an explosion in the usage of computer websites which provide functions centred on the social self. Sites such as MySpace, Facebook, LinkedIn and Ning work from the inside out; that is, they provide facilities for people to describe and define themselves as a prelude to forming relationships, alliances and relationships using their self-constructed models of the self. Web 2.0 tools amplify the sociability of computer-mediated interaction through permitting interactions which resemble conversation: they are quick, they are easy, they are minimally structured, they are immediate. When a friend logs in it's like they walk into the room. You can meet friends of a friend, pursue a chance meeting or just watch and listen.

Computer-mediated communities have existed since the beginning of the Internet in the late 1960s. Howard Rheingold describes the emergence of genuine groups brought together by shared interests and values in online conferences, bulletin boards and e-mail lists.[26] The number of participants moved into the tens of thousands in the 1990s and although the Internet allowed the formation of relationships across the world, the patterns of communication and interaction were basically the same as those in the physical world, although the Internet is particularly strong in its support for the formation of 'weak ties'.

The key tools of social networking are the social networking sites which act as hubs of activity. Self-disclosure is the first act, creating a profile of yourself which projects your personality, likes and dislikes, your interests and experiences into the common pool. You can then be found by others, usually your physical friends first, or you can invite others to become part of your network and sense their presence when they log in. Your network will grow or shrink, you will converse with some and not others and will discover new people who may or may not ever meet physically.

LinkedIn (with about 35 million members in 2009) is the pre-eminent hub for business and professional networking. Applying the same logic as social network sites, in LinkedIn, professionals can describe themselves, their professional background and qualifications, be recommended by colleagues or customers for further projects and join or form special-interest groups (see Figure 2.13). Interestingly, in the wake of the 2008 finance crisis, LinkedIn and Facebook both experienced greatly increased use as job-search mechanisms, which of course erodes their function as social sites and professional networks for knowledge exchange and partnership development.[27]

A highly-hyped platform for social interaction is Second Life, in which 'avatars', or graphic animations, can be used to represent an individual persona and conduct conversations in a kind of cartoon virtual reality. Use of this space is not restricted to entertainment: companies such as IBM and Ernst & Young, have set up shop fronts in this environment,

Figure 2.13 The Special Interest Group function of social networking site Ning

Source: http://www.classroom20.com/?xg_source=ningcom

and NASA have established a collaboration environment where scientists and team members can meet and converse. However, the use of this particular platform, in spite of the intriguing possibilities, already appears to be stagnating.[28]

There is a sense in which all tools which provide computer-mediated interaction can be characterised as social software, as the term 'social' applies wherever humans create and exchange meaningful messages based upon language and shared social structures. In a sense, asking Fred how many widgets were in stock was the face-to-face precursor of 'social' inventory management software ('Stockbook'?). It is therefore useful to differentiate the Web 2.0 social tools from the conventional tools like e-mail or electronic forums, which have been used for thirty years or more. These tools can be characterised as 'weak' social networking tools, as they generally follow the patterns developed in non-computer-mediated interactions. E-mail, for example, will usually build upon existing patterns of communication and sustain roles which are developed in meetings, conferences or pubs. Similarly, electronic forums tend to be restricted to forum purpose (a professional project managers' network of interest in German shepherd dogs for example) and so is constrained to these informational exchanges, albeit with humour and personal asides.

Strong social software allows the emergence of new patterns of behaviour and the definition, adoption and assertion of new roles that are not foreseen or constrained by the software itself. Strong social software provides an environment for the development of context over and above the exchange of information. The nature of this context (hostile, subservient, friendly or purposive) evolves through the use of the software.

Gartner define some useful characteristics of social software:

- It is an open social context that reflects what others are doing and saying by capturing and revealing the content of interactions.

- It provides functions to define, capture, gather and reveal patterns of interaction between individuals: this can be done explicitly, on the basis of common interests or friends in common.

- Decisions about how, when, where and with whom to interact are individual and personal and express individual needs or desires. The less the decision is personal, the less social things become.[29]

The personal data entered become hostage to the intentions of the social networking site, intentions which usually involve the generation of profit. These intentions are constrained by a judgment of how far one can go with this data before the users object or feel exploited. Given that many people publicly document intimate details of their lives, one might assume that privacy, as previously understood, is unimportant. For example, in 2006 Facebook introduced an application called News Feeds, which automatically sent a message to a person's friends when that person updated their personal data. Some 700,000 complaints later, it became clear that the problem was not about privacy, but about visibility – being in a mass of non-private individuals is fine until one is somehow lifted out of the mass. This may be analogous to the fact that while everyone knows that enormous amounts of information about oneself are stored, shared and collated by enterprises and governments, most people only care when it actually affects their next purchase or passport application. Or perhaps, as Montaigne wrote over 400 years ago:

> Many things that I would not care to tell any individual man I tell to the public, and for the knowledge of my most secret thoughts, I refer my most loyal friends to a bookseller's stall. (*The Complete Essays III*, Essay 9)

Similar applications introduced by Facebook in 2007 were Social Ad and Beacon. The former enabled Facebook to automatically send positive comments made by a person about a product to their friends and the latter revealed on the person's public profile that they had bought a certain product. Both applications were implemented without consulting users – and the objections to these products were less about privacy and more about the unendorsed use of the information. This also seems to indicate a change in what privacy means, perhaps that the rights to a person's information are now the main game – not the mere existence of the information somewhere in cyberspace.

In enterprises, there is also great scope for the application of social networking at the professional level and at the personal level. There are a number of software products which supply social networking functionality for use within corporations, and even one called WorkBook, which uses the functions of Facebook but stores the personal data on the enterprise's servers within the firewall.[30] Many organisations already use Facebook itself for their social networking, and there is much unsanctioned use by employees. This carries grave risks of breaches of security, disclosure of confidential information and the legal liability for publishing information purporting to represent the firm.

Large enterprises would probably benefit the most from internal social networking, as there are more possible configurations of groups and potential members who might not find one another other than through technologies which support group formation and connection building. Natural communities can form but, more importantly, personal connections can be maintained. Strong and sustained relationships are often formed, for example, between people in the same-year groups who are hired and inducted together but who subsequently disperse to other areas of the company. A company 'Facebook' allows these relationships to be maintained or at least rekindled when there is a need. People will often seek advice or help from people they have some affinity with rather than the official expert (who may be anonymous or even unpleasant), or ask their personal acquaintances for information on where to find an expert. A personal acquaintance will give information about a potential information source which is not necessarily publishable in a Yellow Pages directory of expertise.

An enterprise social networking site is not just a skills directory; it is for the enactment of discretionary personal relationships. Social software is a platform for enacting the sociability of the individual. If it is mandated, it just becomes a glorified business process or workflow management software. This is one of the institutional barriers that need to be overcome by new management approaches. Baby-boomer managers reject the very idea of pursuing personnel relationships using corporate technology at work, in the same way that baby-boomer parents cannot understand how their children can simultaneously chat on Instant Messenger, listen to their iPods and do their homework. Where wikis and blogs allow the publication of information or opinion to an open forum without management approval, social networking sites allow the formation of relationships independent of management fiat and of groupings which transcend organisational boundaries; this may threaten the power base of uncertain or vulnerable departmental managers.

Semantic web

The concept of the semantic web originated with the founder of the World Wide Web, Tim Berners-Lee. Recognising the rapidly growing volume of accessible information on the Internet, Berners-Lee proposed that a framework of machine-readable meanings had to be constructed to assist navigating and searching through the volume of documents, files and pages. He says the '... Semantic Web is ... an extension of the current one, in which information is given well-defined meaning, better enabling computers and people to work in cooperation'.[31] The intention is to allow searching, navigation and information retrieval to be performed by machines. HTML, the current dominant language in which web pages are written, is intended to allow a browser to present the information in a form which is easily readable by humans independent of the software platform: HTML mark-up tags are provided to highlight text, make headings and include images and so on. What are needed are mark-up tags which allow a software program to extract meaning from the information, not just the format.

The semantic web is an initiative of the World Wide Web Consortium ('W3C'), the body which governs the standards and protocols of the World Wide Web. It specifies certain technologies for the task of creating and publishing 'meaningful' metadata (hence the expression 'semantic' web) which are designed to encapsulate all or part of the content of web pages, using tags which reflect meaning rather than format. These tags function as labels, as social tags or as bookmarks, but they allow a program to specifically interrogate a web page or document to see if it matches the desired criteria. XML (the 'Extensible Markup Language'), while being a relatively mature technology, forms the basis of the tagging language.

RDF, the Resource Definition Language, is a modelling language based upon XML, which allows tags to be related to each other to form a data model which describes concepts, the relationship between concepts and the properties of concepts. OWL, the Web Ontology Language, is a more expressive modelling language than RDF and is proposed as the standardised ontology language of the semantic web by the Web Ontology Working Group of the W3C. OWL allows other features such as restricting the scope of the properties of a concept or the possible values of a property.

The essential outcome of the semantic web is rich, interconnected, standardised metadata which can be used to tag and add structure to documents, linking specific parts of their content to semantic maps or 'ontologies'. An ontology is a conceptualisation of a particular domain of activity (such as dog breeding or conservation biology for example). The World Wide Web can itself be navigated by people or software programs until a target domain is found, at which point one 'drills down' to find concepts within the information objects in this domain. Shopping bots are an example of this: you may be searching for an ice-cream maker. A shopping bot site provides software search agents which scan the Web looking for this item. Within relevant web pages, standard XML data tags are found. For example, the price for the item, country of manufacture, guarantee period and delivery time are extracted and presented back to you, along with the result for other brands or stores, and you can then make a selection.

Alternatively, the objects, through association with the concept, are able to be filtered more effectively to provide a smaller subset of results from a search which more closely matches the searcher's intent. For example, a semantic search could differentiate and filter results for 'Jaguar' based upon whether the search was for a cat or a car. This judgment can be made by a search engine based upon a user's previous information behaviour. Having found the car, the user can find not only documents about the car, but also about motor cars (the class to which the Jaguar belongs) or wheels, chassis and engines, the parts of which a Jaguar consists.

The integrated knowledge map within the semantic web envisaged by Berners-Lee is an 'ontology', the network of related concepts which describes some domain of human reality. There are several ways to construct the semantic web or the analogues of it. One can deliberately create maps of concepts (such as taxonomies, glossaries or ontologies) which become a kind of controlled vocabulary and authoritative knowledge map which is used to classify information (for example by librarians). One can allow these maps to develop via organic growth and contribution, which is the approach underlying social tagging: groups of people unrelated in any way other than that they are interested in similar meanings can create or nominate 'concepts' and then begin to attach these tags to information. Concepts can also be created by software programs, which scan databases, documents and web pages and establish profiles of words, their context of usage and their relationships. Some search engines allow searches to be constructed and used by other users, effectively creating new shared concepts.

The notion of *meaning* is critical in the search function. An optimised search engine matches what the user 'means' with what the document 'means'. Search engines now routinely construct user profiles from stored information (such as previous searches, browsing history, e-mail history and workgroup affiliations) and prioritise search results based upon the match of likely user intention with the meaning of the Internet or intranet information it has previously analysed and indexed. Indeed, through the use of agent technologies, users can be informed of the emergence of information which matches the users' 'meanings'. These agents monitor the Internet (or intranet) based upon previous searches which are either concepts or nascent concepts. For example, a search for uranium and Siberia in a sense is an instantiation of a new cluster of attributes which may be a formative concept (i.e. Siberian uranium): this 'concept' is then used (and even shared) by others to search or monitor changes in the information environment.

Meaning is measured by relevance within a domain of intention and action. So the fundamental intention of the semantic web is to lift information from the mass by its meaning and context. One application of this is that of 'attention metadata', where key elements are lifted from the mass to catch the eye of the user.

Within the corporation, metadata have been used for many years to describe database structures and documents. Increasingly, retailers use XML to make their databases available to shopping bots or even other companies to use in business-to-business e-commerce. But the semantic web moves metadata to an evolving, global platform. Specifically within the context of Web 2.0 'social software' (as opposed to routine transaction processing for example), the notion of linked, navigable, searchable metadata relates to any content created in wikis or blogs or Twitter or the like. As we have seen, using some wiki products, such as Mediawiki, one is able to define concept wiki pages called 'categories'. These categories are used to mark-up other wiki pages, allowing a search for a category to reveal all pages in that category. Further, these category pages can be linked to each other to form an ontology which defines an activity domain within the organisation.

So it is possible to build a map of the knowledge in an organisation using wiki categories and use this, at least, to mark-up wiki pages. Starting from a top-level concept like 'Our Business', one decomposes into the top-level business processes, sub-processes and then concepts which are relevant within the sub-processes. This tree can be displayed using standard wiki functions or placed within standard wiki information pages using the Mediawiki *CategoryTree function*.[32] This is an example of a local 'semantic web'.

Tagging is of course not restricted to documents. On discovering that 40 per cent of employees had not updated their personal pages in the previous nine months, IBM developed a social system called 'Fringe', which was based upon the data from the standard personal pages with some enhancements: in particular, it allows IBMers to tag their colleagues in much the same way as social bookmarking tags websites. This increases the specificity and currency of metadata about a person's capabilities by using the 'wisdom' (and energy) of crowds.[33]

Proponents of the semantic web themselves remain agnostic about the prospects for its success. A semantic web for an already rigorous and normative area such as medical science or geophysics is strongly facilitated by the momentum of the discipline. But as Antoniou and van Harmelen say '... the greatest challenge is not scientific but rather one of technology adoption.'[34] Who will write the ontologies, who will authorise one ontology over another and where will the semantic mark-up of documents come from? This is particularly pertinent for ontologies to be used by business-to-business transactions, web services and search engines. These authors surmise that 'the first success stories will not emerge in the open heterogeneous environment of the WWW but rather in Intranets in large organizations ... we believe that knowledge management for large organisations may be the most fruitful area to start.'[35]

But the business case for such detailed mark-up is ambivalent. The precursor technology to semantic mark-up called SGML (Standard Generalized Markup Language), which allowed organisations to create their own tags, has enjoyed moderate but not resounding penetration. To generate a return on investment for semantic mark-up that goes beyond high-level tagging or categorisation of documents, an organisation would have to generate a very large number of (probably) complex yet structurally consistent documents. The general mode of processing those documents would have to rely upon a high level of specificity (for example, find me all financial documents where the County = Devon and the revenue from dog licences was greater than 500 pounds). Hansard (the proceedings of Parliament) is a good candidate for semantic mark-up, as are insurance claims or the documents created by journal publishers.[36] But until the cost and effort come down (which of course they will), most organisations would likely be satisfied with a higher level of granularity, that is being able to navigate through an ontology and find documents which fall within a category.

Mashups

A mashup is a composite web page, one that consists of parts drawn from information facilities on another web page or provided by services on a website. Individual websites usually have a competency in a certain type of content or a mode of presentation. Real estate agents know where houses and apartments are for sale, government land planners know where new highways will be built, the police know the distribution of crime and house burglaries and a bureau of meteorology has the weather statistics of the past 100 years. These are examples of where the core competency of a group becomes explicit in the form of structured data. Google Maps is an example of a competency in representational form, namely two-dimensional mapping as well as three-dimensional image rendering of streetscapes. An example of a mashup is to bring housing, crime and planning information from different websites into a geographical layout using Google's mapping facilities, such that people can make informed decisions about where to buy a house using specific data to answer the questions people usually ask.

Such a product might be for a particular niche of users and not be worth the effort of data collection, organisation and programming. However, if the effort is limited to building dynamic interfaces to those websites and then combining that information with standard Google maps, then one has a cheap-to-build service that may generate some revenue or sufficient social benefit. A neat example is the 'unfluence' website, which is a mashup that maps political donations to congressmen (see Figure 2.14). (For a similar idea, see muckety.com, which is a website that publishes schemas of relationships between individuals and institutions along with its news stories.)

The key to mashups' capability, particularly in enterprises, is the construction and publication of web services via a services-oriented architecture (SOA). An SOA is a blueprint for how an enterprise will deliver data using new, powerful techniques of programming, design, networking and networking standards.

Figure 2.14 The Unflence mashup of political influence on US politics

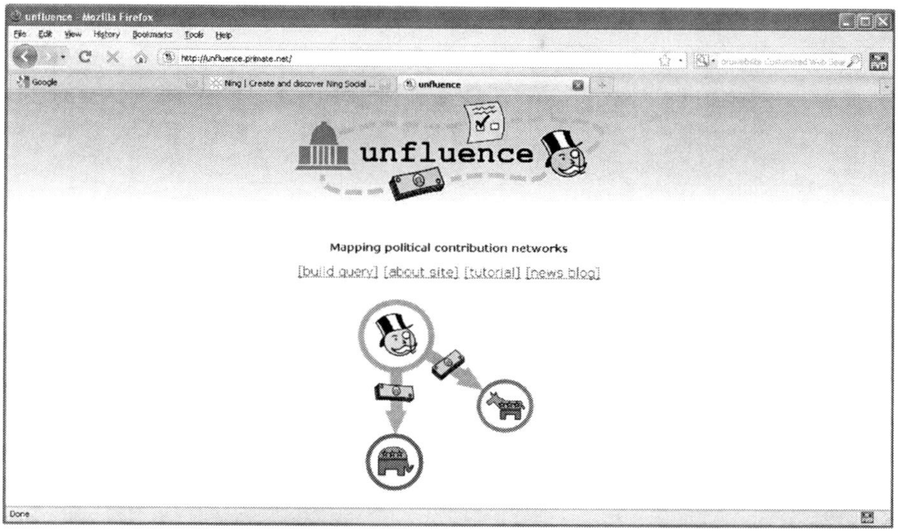

Source: http://unfluence.primate.net/

A cursory examination of the limits of conventional programming structures is apposite. Using standard relational database programming methods and languages such as the Structured Query Language (SQL), data can be retrieved from databases and presented to both users and programs for display or processing. One can easily combine data, filter it and perform basic calculations using SQL. However, this is a low level of 'value add' to the data and corporations need more complex processing involving validity checking, combination of data across different systems, sophisticated calculations and so on. This is currently solved by application programs for accounting, finance, works management, logistics and so on, which deliver 'screens' of information and which are driven by user functions to add an order, enquire on the levels of widgets in warehouses across the organisation or in a certain area, or compare the budget versus actuals for fuel and the transport of goods. These applications are delivered overwhelmingly via commercial off-the-shelf packages and often integrated as modules into enterprise resource planning suites. The best known of these is SAP's R3. While these are powerful systems that are flexible and configurable, there are some disadvantages:

- Not all required data is presented on one screen, requiring navigation and swapping between applications, for example if one wanted to see the number of widgets in the Spandau warehouse, their financial value and the value of those on order.

- To redesign screens, even slightly, to fit in data which is required by a new business process requires reprogramming (which only the package supplier or the information technology department can do). For example, a sales screen might need a field which states the creditworthiness of the customer, but this simple Yes / No might be the result of a complex process of combining previous history with Dun & Bradstreet credit data.

- Any project which is seeking to develop a system for a different business area and which uses portions of the existing data must develop its own programs to access and process the data for presentation. For example, a product support system for a new call-centre will need to access existing customer and product data, as well as warehouse data.

The underlying conundrum here is perennial in information systems: reuse of data and programs, and how to design, package and deliver software which, like Lego bricks, can be combined to build whatever structure the builder requires: *write once, use anywhere, use often.*

SOA is an approach to building reusable program components which deliver data and make them part of an organisation's infrastructure.[37] The components are discrete, visible, documented and have a clear, single purpose. They must be written in such a way as to be easily orchestrated into an ensemble which fulfils a business need. And the data services provide a single point of truth – there are no competing versions or combinations of data where different programmers have performed slightly different operations on data to attempt to achieve the same goal. On the Internet, SOA services are better known as widgets and a good place to observe these is in iGoogle, where a user can decide to place SOA components which deliver the joke of the day, the time of day or a favourite news feed.

From a set of SOA artefacts one should, with little effort and possibly no programming skills, be able to construct a screen which supports a particular business act. This capability can accelerate the construction and delivery of new information systems and applications but also fill a niche for what IBM calls 'situational applications'. These are applications which may have a shorter life span than usual (a few weeks or months even), for which scarce and expensive IT programming resources are unavailable and which perhaps do not generate a sufficient business case.

Currently, many large organisations have recognised the potential productivity gains from this kind of programming 'holy grail'. Now that this is technologically feasible, SOA generally exists as a plan, or program of works, which revolves around enterprise architecture and the disciplined design, deployment and exploitation of the data services. Many large packaged software providers (such as SAP) have promised to deliver their functionality as SOA components so that customers and users of their packages can use them directly for new systems or situational applications.

This sounds of course like software engineering, not Web 2.0: why is this mentioned at all in the discourse about Web 2.0? The reason is that Web 2.0 exemplifies the consumerisation of SOA applications: mashups based upon the ability to easily combine functionality into a single screen are an example of how modern Internet users interact with and drive the systems themselves rather than passively accepting whatever is available or served up by the IT department. SOA will be a driver of business information productivity, whether or not Web 2.0 exists, but making it available and easy to configure at the user interface will be demanded by users – and will indeed accelerate productivity increases based upon information use.

A good illustration of SOA meeting Web 2.0 is QEDWiki, or Quick and Easy Development Wiki, first developed as a product prototype by IBM and now existing as LOTUS Mashups. This integrates wiki technology (immediate page writing, discussions, tagging and so on) with the ability to compose business screens by combining SOA component services. This is a non-technical process, supported by a drag-and-drop interface, for 'power users' or business analysts. Significantly, this screen is then available to any other users of the wiki, so a team can create and use for a brief or extended period the wiki part for information interactions and the SOA parts for data provision and processing. This screen can be used by others in the future, creating a powerful network effect as word about the screen functions spreads. Security is not the concern of the user, because this is managed within the SOA component as it accesses relevant databases.

Sandy Carter, an IBM Vice President of SOA, predicates the implementation and success of Web 2.0 in enterprises on flexible yet standardised data services provided by SOA, and certainly routine business processes where structured, accurate data are provided are where the rubber hits the road. She cites a survey in which 80 per cent of CEOs identify rapid response to changing conditions as a major competitive priority, but only 13 per cent rated their organisations as 'very responsive' – indeed the majority of CEOs perceive their IT departments to be inhibitors of flexibility.

This is indicative of perhaps two things. Firstly, those business transactions are at the heart of commercial activity and that data is a primary driver of business transactions. This is what needs to be managed first and foremost in order to deliver products and services according to a controlled regime, but it needs to be managed flexibly. A McKinsey 2008 Web 2.0 survey showed that the most important 'Web 2.0' technology for business users is web services, the use of SOA to deliver packaged business function. Fifty-eight per cent responded affirmatively to this technology (oddly down from 70 per cent in 2007) compared with the next most used technology, blogs, at 34 per cent. This suggests strongly that delivering specific, data-driven business functionality is the focus of organisations and has a higher priority than free-form information exchange made possible by other Web 2.0 technologies.

Secondly, it is perhaps indicative of the interests of companies like IBM who are providers of programming services and technology. Web 2.0 products like wikis and blogs are not going to generate much wealth, either in software or consulting fees.

Combining Web 2.0 tools into a system for work

Web 2.0 implementations in the enterprise usually involve individual products or several products together to achieve some sort of coherent and synchronised informational flow. Indeed, it is no accident that most products offering wiki capability also contain blogs, RSS feeds and tagging as a minimum. It is quite simply because these products complement each other in knowledge management:

- The use of one leads naturally to the other – an entry in a blog or wiki should trigger an interested party to go and have a look (RSS). An interesting post in a blog should be recommended to others and an article about bird manure fertiliser should be tagged 'guano' even if that word is not in the article.

- An environment in which one of these tools is used implies fertile ground for the application of others. Consider the extensive use of Web 2.0 tools by the USA's top 100 newspapers in Figure 2.15. These facilities are combined to provide readers with a complete functional environment for interacting with the newspapers' information.

A convergence of many forms of software is taking place; as the overlaps between document management, forums, wikis, blogs, RSS and e-mail become clearer, so vendors will offer all these functions in a single suite. But why do these products converge? It is because knowledge processes

Figure 2.15 Use of Web 2.0 facilities by US newspapers

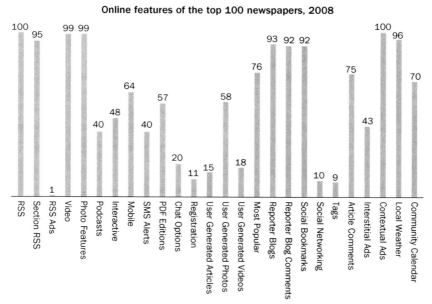

Online features of the top 100 newspapers, 2008

Source: http://www.bivingsreport.cam/resources/2008.gif

cannot be constrained to a single form of interaction. Any one of these tools on its own does not suffice – taken on their own, they will lead to fragmented and undisclosed stores of knowledge. That is why the products must be viewed as supporting an overall system of knowledge transformation. Further, these products operate at two levels of meaning. Where wikis, blogs, mashups and social software contain or present content, social tagging, recommendations, ratings, the semantic web and meaning-based search operate on *metadata*, making the content salient and visible.

When implementing or designing structured business applications, one usually develops business process models and flow charts which represent business activities and tasks. Then one identifies what pieces of information or knowledge are required to accomplish the specific task. But with collaboration and exchange of unstructured information, the paths are not always formal and predetermined. Sometimes exchange and collection of information can be steered using so-called workflow products which will route documents or text from one designated person to another (for example, via e-mail), capturing their changes, reviews and approvals. But when it comes to collaboration and innovation, big ideas can come in small packages and progress is often dynamic, non-linear, recursive and complex. Small interventions can create huge opportunities (a single brilliant word) or destroy them (the manager entering the room). Value in collaboration and knowledge sharing is not related to quantity, duration or routine.

Figure 2.16 shows how the Web 2.0 technologies can be combined to deliver a suite of open-ended services to an individual information worker. The worker will adapt these to suit their own purposes: the services are common, general-purpose infrastructure and can carry any type of information to any required level of detail or granularity. These services include:

1. Expressing managerial or expert information via a blog.
2. Subscribing via RSS to the manager's daily blog.
3. Searching and navigating via the semantic web to find wiki pages.
4. Using social tagging to mark-up wiki pages for others (or myself) to find.
5. Linking from wiki pages to other systems such as document management systems.

Figure 2.16 Combining Web 2.0 components to create a work system

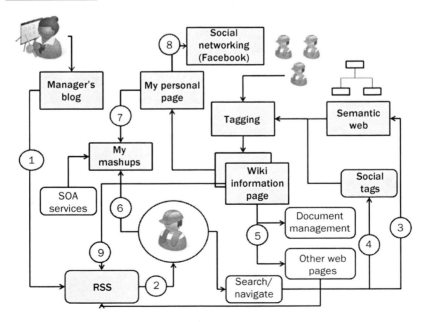

6. Using SOA services to create personalised mashups.

7. Placing my personalised mashups in my personal page.

8. Making the mashups obvious to others in my group via social software.

9. Being informed via RSS of changes to wiki pages, documents or other web pages.

Figure 2.17 shows how individual knowledge workers, through the intermediation of various Web 2.0 components, are linked to each other and have facilities to capture, describe, find and share knowledge through wikis, blogs, social and 'semantic web' tags, RSS, social networking services and mashups.

Figure 2.17 Sharing using Web 2.0 facilities

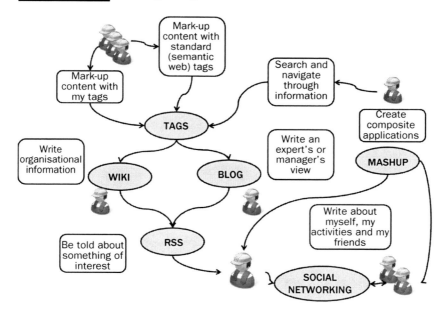

Notes

1. O'Reilly (2005).
2. O'Reilly (2005).
3. Enterprise 2.0 is the term coined by Andrew McAffee of Harvard University (McAffee, 2006). It has gained prominence as a term building on the concept of Web 2.0 to describe enterprise use of Web 2.0 technologies according to a

certain profile. While this book is about this theme in general, I have preferred to steer clear of using the name, as it has spawned its own controversy and taken on a trajectory of its own. For an excellent review, see Buhse and Stamer (2008), which describes the use of Web 2.0 tools in organisations.

4. 'The Art of With', a seminar held in Manchester on 24 June 2009.
5. The Technorati website tracks blog use and activity and their blog survey is available at: *http://www.technorati.com/blogging/state-of-the-blogosphere/*.
6. See Charman (2006) and more generally Bruns and Jacobs (2006).
7. See 'Robert Scoble on Corporate Blogging' at: *http://www.cioinsight.com/c/a/Foreward/Robert-Scoble-on-Corporate-Blogging/*.
8. For example, according to the Bivings group, 93 per cent of the top 100 US papers have reporter blogs (*http://www.bivingsreport.com/2008/the-use-of-the-internet-by-americas-largest-newspapers-2008-edition/*).
9. Welker (2006: 162ff.).
10. Walther and Krasselt (2005: 13ff.).
11. Gillmor (2006).
12. Koller and Alpar (2008).
13. For the latest numbers and trends see the Technorati website: *http://technorati.com/blogging/state-of-the-blogosphere/*.
14. For more on this see: *http://www.cio.com/article/452115/Socialtext_._Bringing_Facebook_Twitter_and_iGoogle_to_the_Enterprise*.
15. Attalli (2009: 90).
16. Several websites exist to help compare and decide upon a wiki product, for example: *http://www.wikimatrix.org/*.
17. For example, wikiindex.org and even wikindex.com which shows usage statistics.
18. Anonymous (2009a). Further, integration into current suites of content management software increases manageability of unstructured and semi-structured information and documents and increases levels of control and oversight.
19. Chui et al. (2009).
20. Chui et al. (2009).
21. Blaschke (2008: 201).
22. Ebersbach et al. (2008).
23. For an excellent overview of wikis see Klobas (2006). For comprehensive concrete implementation methods, see Mader (2008).
24. See Weinberger (2007).
25. Some studies show that e-mail arrivals, even when corporate spam, cause a significant loss in concentration and work momentum.
26. Rheingold (1993).
27. 'It's a safe bet that if the economic downturn grinds on, we will witness further conflict between the nonrational instinct to connect socially and the rational calculation to build social capital for professional reasons. If so, it may put further strain on the notion of an online friend. We may find ourselves asking more frequently that age-old question, "What are friends for?"' (Dutta and Fraser, 2009).
28. Anonymous (2009c).
29. See Drakos et al. (2008).
30. From the company Worklight – see: *http://myworklight.com/*.

31. Berners-Lee et al. (2001).
32. This is described in the section on wikis in this chapter.
33. See Farrell and Lau (2006).
34. Antoniou and van Harmelen (2004: 9).
35. Antoniou and van Harmelen (2004: 225).
36. For example, the Canadian government makes up its proceedings of parliament using semantic mark-up, as do many other countries now.
37. The definition of SOA from IBM is as follows: 'A business-driven IT architectural approach that supports integrating your business as linked, repeatable tasks or services. SOA helps today's businesses innovate by ensuring that IT systems can adapt quickly, easily, and economically to support rapidly changing business needs. It is a flexible architectural style that enables customers to build a set of loosely coupled services for automating and streamlining business processes' (Carter, 2007: 288).

3

The modern business environment

'To someone with a hammer, the whole world looks like a nail.' This is a proverb one might readily apply to information management and communication tools. To IT specialists, salesmen and web evangelists the world is pieces of information waiting to be processed, tagged and stored, such is the hype that has surrounded successive waves of technology product announcements over the past 30 years. An evidence-based database juxtaposing claims and disappointments for the IT industry would make interesting reading. Are we standing before a similar mountain of hype with Web 2.0?

There does seem to be a lot happening. A young woman of about 25, an administrative assistant at a Chinese university I visited, writes a blog for women, about their lives, their pain and their joys. She writes short stories into the blog of things that women tell her, in particular about the sadness of their marriages and the disappointment they begin to feel the day after the ceremony. She has 500 readers, people who she says return regularly because she catches their sadness and frustration. It is impossible to read a newspaper online without seeing the social tagging links to websites like digg and delicious. Stories are rated, linked, blogged about and classified. I read about Richard Branson twittering on his Virgin flight to Orange County: 'Arianna Huffington and I chatting on Virgin America's inaugural flight to OC. Have put my trousers back on. 2:11 PM Apr 29th.' And of course the use of Twitter.com in the disputed Iranian presidential elections of 2009: 'RT @hughdeburghRT @iran09 To world press in Tehran: People have died tonight, B a witness at least. Don't let them die in the dark#iranelection.'

'Web 2.0' was deliberately so baptised to contrast with 'Web 1.0': it encapsulates an evolution from client–server relations (where there is an implied master–slave relationship) to peer–peer (where partners stand on a equal footing), from one-directional broadcasting of information to conversations, from formal specification of products and objectives to iterative collaboration, from planning to evolving. The Amazon.com of the 'Web 1.0' era allowed a person to search the Amazon books and music database catalogue and buy their products. The 'Web 2.0' Amazon.com allows a person to write a review of the products, rate a book, discuss their views with others and even merge the Amazon product catalogue into their own product database using Amazon functions. Web 2.0 is a platform of possibilities, allowing people to construct and arrange information according to their needs and tastes rather than predefined rules for interaction. Indeed, we probably shouldn't talk of 'users' of Web 2.0: one is a partner, collaborator, participant or co-creator.

This language resonates strongly with modern business rhetoric, which emphasises speed, dynamism, unpredictability and flexibility – 'virtual, adaptive and contingent'. IBM calls this the 'flex-pon-sive' corporation:

> ... it is the description of a company that responds with lightning speed and agility to rapidly changing business needs. This company must have a focus on processes that are enabled for change through IT.[1]

Corporations have changed – and continue to change – their underlying organisational models to cope with the unpredictability that has accompanied technological, economic and structural change. They constantly reconfigure themselves, their partners and their processes for new projects, adaptive services and demanding customers. Castells describes this as the networked enterprise, a '... lean agency of economic activity, built around specific business projects, which are enacted by networks of various composition and origin: the network is the enterprise.'[2] These 'networked enterprises' succeed because of their ability to create competitive, desirable commodities by sharing information signals with customers and suppliers.

The tools of the Web 2.0 suite, with their emphasis on equality of participation, openness and ease of use appear to offer compelling arguments for corporate application, within and beyond the firewall. Indeed, most knowledge workers expect to be able to use the tools they use at home on the World Wide Web at the office.[3] But in contrast to the personal sphere, what counts is getting work done or adding some value for some future time. By work, I mean the production of the main outputs of any organisation, the primary value chain of marketing, production, logistics and sales, and, in support of this, the secondary value chain of human resource management, finance or IT services. Information systems are intended to support these functions, but often do so inadequately and sometimes hinder and constrain them. Active adoption of systems that appear to offer strategic, tactical or operational benefits is driven by human institutions and perceptions of value, not just of value to production, but of corporate acceptability, personal taste, trust and managerial control, compatibility with existing production norms, authority, fear and egoism.

We need to ask of Web 2.0, therefore, not only how it can be used in enterprises, but will it be really adopted and useful or just of marginal interest? Indeed, will it be real 'Web 2.0' or some conventional shadow of it? Will it satisfy the 'fast return at minimum cost' principle which dominates IT decision-making in many corporations today? If Web 2.0 technology is potentially useful, are there other more useful tools? In whose interest is it that it be used or not used – management or operations – and which are the stronger institutions in an organisation – hierarchy and authority, regulation or professional dedication? Who will use it more, who will use it less? A 2008 survey by Gartner of Japanese firms' use of Web 2.0 Internet facilities found a decline in use, which they attributed to increased concerns about compliance to Japanese Sarbanes-Oxley legislation and security of intellectual property.[4] So, in short, not everything in the business world is a nail. Indeed, it isn't about the hammer, it's about the carpenter, the house, building codes and even the weather.

In this chapter we look at the factors which are often cited as compelling evidence for the impending success of Web 2.0 in enterprises: information overload, knowledge management, network effects, generational change, globalisation, the 'strength of weak ties' and the 'wisdom of crowds', for example.[5] Generally these appear to be strong macro-level arguments favouring a broad-based take-up of the technologies. In the main, these theories argue why Web 2.0 tools are the right solution for our time. However, this is quite a different thing to making an adequate business case for investment and then making it work (let us keep encainide and knee arthroscopies in mind here). In a later chapter we present theories of knowledge and human behaviour which we think provide a more appropriate framework for understanding the power of these systems and the impediments to their implementation and adoption. We will review the research to the present moment in these areas and examine what factors may influence the adoption of Web 2.0 in business.

We also need to consider the timeframe for the adoption of these tools – the impact of technology has often been overestimated in the short term and underestimated in the long term. Immediate feedback may show that there is little or no benefit, but over time (like telephones and electricity), as tools become systemic, pervasive and familiar and work processes adapt to and integrate the capabilities, a more typical response may be 'how did we ever work without this?' So there may be several different time dimensions at work: the structures and patterns which influence short-term adoption of technology, such as immediate productivity gain or unique functionality, may in the end be less significant than the momentum generated by evolving social habits and new mindsets. Patience may be needed.

So this is the key message of this chapter: there are many systemic and environmental arguments to consider in the adoption and use of Web 2.0 technologies. But although these factors should attract the attention of senior management, they are usually not arguments which suffice to make a specific business case for investment or give a clear idea of concrete applications. Further these general arguments do not apply equally to all companies in all types of industry. It is not a fait accompli that the acquisition and implementation of these tools leads to the successful adoption of new ways of working and appreciable returns to the business.[6]

Mobilising knowledge assets

The primary purpose of business is to make a profit – and *stay* in business. Unlike the personal sphere, where these malleable technologies can be adapted to a multitude of private uses, Web 2.0 as business tools must offer a more productive, compelling alternative to accomplish a business task than incumbent methods: or they must facilitate the introduction of new value-adding activities and services. Designing products, taking orders, planning maintenance, resolving complaints and filling in holiday applications are repeated processes which contribute to the success of a streamlined, running business. In general, new information tools need to support these kinds of activities.

The fundamental challenge in business is of course to be competitive and to generate returns from the assets of the firm, creating profits for shareholders each quarter. Productivity is the cornerstone of this, the ability to generate optimal returns from all assets at your disposal. Improvements to productivity occur insofar as profit is generated. Many of those generative assets are intangible and reside in the capacity of knowledge workers to generate new products, new services and better ways to manage the value chain from conception to delivery.

Therefore optimising the capacity and the motivation of those knowledge workers becomes a crucial strategic requirement of competing firms. What hinders this? Much of this can be traced back to complexity. Of 7,900 global executives surveyed by McKinsey in 2005:[7]

- 64 per cent noted a significant increase in interactions compared to five years ago (e-mail, meetings, voice-mail);
- 25 per cent stated that communication was unmanageable;
- 40 per cent stated that their company does not manage information and knowledge well;
- 35 per cent found it difficult to find knowledge and information to make decisions.

As interaction costs have decreased through digital networks and communications software, great opportunities have been created, but the ensuing complexity has generated problems of a different kind. While reduced interaction costs have meant that global outsourcing and inter-firm collaboration allow it to be cheaper and more effective to move work to other locations and organisations, the volumes of e-mail and mobile phone use have exploded.[8] But although useful for specific interactions, these are highly individual, fragmented, non-persistent and unavailable to the enterprise: the only records left are scattered throughout individual memory traces and massive personal e-mail in-boxes.[9] This makes it extremely difficult to learn from previous interactions and decisions, and further means that interactions adopt individual options with their own nuances, leading to greater 'ad-hocery' and complexity. Managing this has become much more difficult say 60 per cent of the surveyed global executives.

Digital technologies have also increased the volume of what is called 'virtual work', which is the distribution of work across barriers of time, space and the firm. This brings many advantages: access to the best resources and talent, use of all 24 hours in a day, close proximity to customers and the ability to 'punch above your weight' by finding business partners with key skills that complement yours. Virtual work takes many forms: telework, mobile virtual work, customer frontline work, virtual teaming and the virtual enterprise. But it also involves risks: miscommunication, loss of trust, loss of managerial control over performance and productivity, a longer working day and impaired coordination and cohesion. How is a unified and positive organisational mindset to be maintained in the face of such workforce fragmentation?

The fundamental proposition is therefore that tools are needed for knowledge workers which reduce information complexity, which minimise unproductive e-mail and one-to-one interactions, and which build up corporate knowledge for others to use in the real-time, digital environment of the modern workplace. Where possible, these tools need to maintain a sense of cohesion and work against the risks and disadvantages of isolation and distance. Properly managed, the Web 2.0 tools we saw in the previous chapter such as *wikis* and *blogs* are excellent vehicles for the capture of knowledge within the context of workflow rather than as an additional (and therefore ultimately doomed) data entry step in routine business processes. Add to this the classification of that information through the use of an organisational *semantic web* augmented by *social tagging* and the issues of information management begin to improve. Corporate *social networking* tools (exemplified by the functionality of Facebook or MySpace) offer the ability to disclose information about the self and facilitate group relationships, enhance affective relationships and strengthen cohesion. A coherent and consistent 'single version of the truth' may begin to emerge, not because of rigid controls by the few, but because of the attention of and contribution by the many.

Generational change

Web 2.0 tools are often said to be the implements of the 'net generation', who have grown up surrounded by the Internet, mobile phones and computer games. Web 2.0 capabilities first appeared on the Internet and were quickly adopted by young people in particular for social, special interest and non-commercial interactions. It is anticipated that this generation will expect and demand similar tools at the workplace and will indeed be able to use them to improve organisational performance by working at Internet speed.[10] But the world does not fall neatly into 'digital natives' and 'digital immigrants'. Depending upon the psychosocial attributes of individuals, there are always people who have the characteristics of both generations: some digital natives are disengaged and some digital immigrants are 'naturalised' and fluent participants. As the factors that cause changes in attitudes and behaviour evolve and spread, so there will be people who absorb these attitudes and behaviours at different rates and in different proportions. There are also intergenerational flows from younger to older, as children influence their parents and teach their grandparents how to watch YouTube (and even vice versa).

But even with these caveats in mind, we can nevertheless generalise about shifts in attitudes and behaviour in a generation that is hitting the workforce now, and whose characteristics will become more pronounced and dominant. Enterprises will need to implement tools which match their expectations and patterns of interaction and enterprise technology departments will be judged on their success in achieving adoption in new and evolving enterprise information tools. The net generation, so it seems, are the people for whom we need to start designing and implementing technologies – and Web 2.0 tools are natural candidates for a range of knowledge work activities.

Increasingly, young people moving from university and higher education institutes do so having had ubiquitous access to computing, to smart mobile devices and Internet broadband. The provision of these facilities has given them a level of expectation about what constitutes an acceptable level of service and connectivity in their education and in their leisure time. But of course it's not only about the technology: technology must be seen as one element embedded within a set of social norms, values and expectations.

In anticipating the demands on workplace computing, we therefore need to look at the social and historic context of the emerging generation of workers and what has shaped its expectations. A comparison with a previous generation, the baby boomers, will help us here. The boomers were born into the postwar optimism of the Anglo-Saxon and European countries. Birth rates increased until the mid-1960s, when they declined to a low point in about 1975 (the Germans affectionately called this the *Pillenknick*, the bend in the population graph due to the contraceptive pill). The baby boomers delayed parenting and prolonged their youth. As the biological clocks continued to tick down, however, the birth rates took off again, producing the 'boomer echo' generation, from which we are deriving the current and future crop of knowledge workers.

Baby boomers were brought up in a time when the dominant information technology was television and the mode of transmission was a unidirectional broadcast style. The formation of public opinion and personal taste tended to be along broad lines. There were left and right, mods and rockers: there was little or no interactivity with technology, diversity was restricted and collaborative co-creation of knowledge and ideas was low. This is not to say that people passively accepted content or didn't have choices: indeed, there was an explosion in the 1990s of television and radio providers catering to a wide variety of market segments. But as Neil Postman points out, ownership of the means of transmission gives the ability to set the thematic spaces and agendas for discussion for society at large.[11]

At the same time, however, we cannot assume the attitudes and capabilities of baby boomers are cast in stone. A survey of baby boomers by McKinsey showed that 40 per cent of them are ready to 'change my life as I age', that 77 per cent are on the Internet and that 'this generation's experiences ... have generated a real openness to change'.[12] The Gartner Group argue that more differentiated criteria than age are required to account for propensities to use or not use Web 2.0.[13]

But certainly in contrast to baby boomers, the children and grandchildren of the boomers in the USA were confronted with the personal computer and, from the early 1990s, with the Internet. They have inherited outsourcing, downsizing and a cooling of affections between employers and employees. They are more inclined to use 'I' than 'we' and their social role profiles tend to be personal rather than group oriented. They are generally wealthier than previous generations, well educated and, compared with previous times, are raised in environments which encourage curiosity and openness. Since the widespread affordability of broadband, features of the Internet such as interactive chat, video streaming, search engines, infinite numbers of websites, news, culture and sports subscription have become commonplace and changed information behaviour. They seek information rather then passively watch a limited number of TV channels, they observe diversity every day, and they engage regularly with a wide range of previously inaccessible opinions and viewpoints in communities that *they* actively choose. Practical objectives are achieved online: banking, booking holidays, submitting university assignments or observing surfing conditions. In a nutshell, the social context and the technological capabilities have changed radically since the boomer days and co-evolved to create the mindset of what Don Tapscott characterises as 'The Net Generation'.[14]

There are some grand dangers in simplifying the characteristics of generations, but let us persist, as these generalisations are widely used to justify the need for new workplace information tools. Tapscott orders these into ten themes: they are open, inclusive and independent. They are used to open expression, they innovate freely and naturally, they are sceptical, require evidence and reasoning, and expect immediate gratification. They are sensitive to the image of the corporations they work in and have a need to be taken seriously. These characteristics are generally echoed by Rigby who in writing about the potential for Web 2.0 tools to engage young people in political and civic activities describes them as politically involved, critically active, technology savvy and influential.[15]

Utrecht observes the potential of Web 2.0 in education and describes current students as the 'customisation generation'.[16] At a basic level, students customise their Windows desktop, settings and menus. In a more sophisticated process, students customise their approach to learning, taking what they perceive they need to succeed according to the rewards and constraints of the system. This mirrors the logic behind the introduction of IBM's Common User Access architecture for Graphical User Interfaces in the 1980s: that instead of the users being driven by rigid menus and transaction codes, the users of systems would multitask and themselves drive the sequences of work on the computer.

John Seely Brown describes several dimensions of current schoolchildren whom he observed as part of work at the Xerox Palo Alto Research Center.[17] Their literacy is in navigation, multitasking and sorting multiple informational medias (not just text); they learn by finding and sorting information from a vast, available array, not being spoon-fed by figures in authority; they put this information in purposive yet original ways to achieve specific goals ('bricolage'), rather than using analytical, deductive methods; their learning is largely action-based rather than being derived from an internalised theory or body of knowledge.

If these are plausible generational characteristics, the outcomes of social, ethical, economic and technological currents, it is clear that expectations at the workplace will also change. Instead of being hierarchical, command and control, routine and constrained, segregated and clinging to their jobs, this generation will bring entirely new characteristics to the workplace and therefore to their demands for tools. These tools are not only what this generation demands, they are an orthogonal fit between their characteristics and the self-organising, emergent behaviour required in the workplace.

But there are reasons to qualify the need for new information tools in the workplace based upon the needs of the incoming generation. Firstly, as demonstrated, it is not only only Generations X, Y and Millennium who are responsive to systemic social and technological change. Baby boomers are also capable of appropriating and using new techniques and tools.

Secondly, if information tools are to be successful they need to satisfy a range of criteria, not just resonate with the feelings of the current younger generation. They need to be ready at hand, providing accurate, precise, timely information relevant and applicable to a task. Customisation and informality is fine, but much of work is uniform requiring coordination and coherence.

Thirdly, in a workplace characterised by outsourcing, high unemployment, short-term work and contracting, career change and individualism, attitudes at home or to society may be quite different to those of the workplace. If the objective of information tools is to renew or generate organisational capital, it may be that the new generation has even less interest in contributing to the organisation's intellectual assets than the previous one.

Finally, young people take developmental trajectories and develop preferences which are only partially influenced by global factors such as materialism and technology. National, cultural and economic factors are also determinants of the expectations of generations. Where young Anglo-Saxons use the mobile phone to talk, the Catalans use them to arrange to meet face to face.[18] Such cultural preferences co-determine the use of technology; technology is not adopted uniformly in all contexts.

The loss of baby boomer knowledge

As baby boomers head for retirement, there are fears that firms are losing a key generative asset, limiting their capability to make effective decisions, solve problems and continue the relentless cycle of competition, innovation and adaptation. Wheels will be reinvented, lessons will be forgotten and mistakes repeated at great cost. Relationships with employers for baby boomers have tended to be longer term, containing relatively high levels of mutual commitment and a personal identification with the firm, although job tenure and security varies widely from country to country. The boomer generation was highly educated and have learned much on the job, and as this generation moves into retirement, the tacit knowledge gathered over decades of work experience will be lost. This is already posing a problem as some of those boomers with adequate wealth seek to retire. The effects of this knowledge loss vary between industries and type of role played. It is expected that oil and gas and healthcare, for example, will be more affected than manufacturing and technology. There is greatest concern at the senior management level, but firms are also worried about losing middle-manager expertise as well as specialist knowledge. There are a number of strategies to ameliorate this: phased retirement, job redefinition, mixed-age teams, mentoring and flexible 'at call' working arrangements. Indeed, the concept of retirement will undergo change as a nexus of corporate knowledge loss, personal financial need and the boomers' refusal to 'grow old gracefully' coalesces.

But although a genuine and significant challenge for many western economies, the disappearance of the baby boomers may not be as abrupt as is expected and the 'lockstep' retirement of entire cohorts is probably a myth. A McKinsey survey revealed that 62 per cent of boomers 'worry that I have not planned sufficiently for retirement'.[19] This is confirmed by a Bucks Consulting survey of 480 American enterprises, in which 86 per cent of mature workers said they would prefer to continue work for financial reasons.[20] Another McKinsey study prior to the financial crisis of 2008 showed that baby boomers, although having earned more than twice that of the previous generation at the same age, have saved poorly, with only 2 per cent of income being put aside (in 1985 10 per cent of income was saved). The ratio of debt to net worth is 50 per cent higher than the previous generation at the same age and 69 per cent of baby boomers are unprepared for retirement (about 50 per cent of baby boomers are ignorant of this exposure). Thirty-eight per cent say it is extremely likely that they will have to work longer than the normal retirement age and 85 per cent say it is at least somewhat likely. The reasons to postpone retirement are mostly to meet expenses (35 per cent) and maintain their lifestyle (24 per cent).

But the financial crisis of 2008 has led to devastating losses in retirement portfolios. Hits of 25 per cent are not uncommon and two trillion dollars was wiped off the value of US retirement savings in 2008–9. Retirement ages are being pushed out even further still.[21]

Taken from this perspective, the disappearance of baby boomers from the workplace in the near future has been perhaps exaggerated. They will have to work longer, reduce their draw-down on savings and therefore continue to have managerial control over policies, budgets, strategy and attitudes for some time to come. A 2009 Gartner report states that as recession bites, baby boomer CIOs (according to HR reports more risk-averse than their business peers) will first lay off Generation Y IT employees on the last-in first-out principle, valuing experience rather than potential. In this process, IT service providers will lose 'access to Gen Y's strengths ... These digital natives often help more experienced peers understand and appreciate new ways of using and applying new technologies.'[22]

In the USA, between 1977 and 2007, the number of people employed over 65 years of age (these are not baby boomers) rose by 101 per cent, compared with 59 per cent for the total employed population. Since 2001, in a trend starting in 1995, most of these older workers are working full time rather than part time. As mass layoffs take place as a consequence of the global financial crisis, Figure 3.1 suggests older workers, far from being disproportionately retrenched, are being retained.

But in a significant survey of 4,000 firms in Germany entitled 'Farewell to the Obsession with Youth', Commerzbank found that 85 per cent of the participants focused on educating younger employees as a method of managing demographic change and only 44 per cent educated their older employees.[23] Indeed, one-third sees no possibility of keeping their employees until 67 and 12 per cent only after extensive adjustments to work processes. Companies with more than 250 employees in particular focused on winning over younger hires in the war for talent rather than educating mid-term and older employees. But at the same time, they recognised that the aging of a wealthy and choosy

Figure 3.1   US labour force participation by age

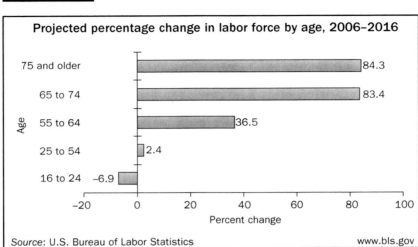

Projected percentage change in labor force by age, 2006–2016

Source: U.S. Bureau of Labor Statistics   www.bls.gov

Source: US Bureau of Labor Statistics (*http://www.bls.gov/spotlight/2008/olderworkers/*).

society meant that they needed older employees in order to remain responsive to the market's changing demands for products and services. In spite of their current strategies, 77 per cent of the respondents said a move away from the obsession with youth was necessary and over three-quarters demanded a longer working and learning life. This would only work if all stakeholders – government, states, industry confederations and unions – worked together.

So there is a varied and complex picture of the impending retirement of baby boomers. In the US, with voluntary retirement being delayed and the preparedness of older workers to remain, the boot has moved decisively to the other foot. Under the more social European model of greater state-funded retirement, the picture is different but in a state of change. Ultimately, corporations will decide which workers go or stay, depending upon regulatory and institutional criteria and the national-cultural models of capitalism in place. They will make decisions based upon what they deem important for their business at that time.

Network dynamics

Web 2.0 is a phenomenon based upon networks: networks of computers overlaid with software capabilities which facilitate the creation of linkages between the people who use that software. This introduces the peculiar mathematical properties and powers of networks, which are increasingly argued to be foundational arguments for the use of these technologies in commercial contexts.[24] The development and usefulness of links between nodes in networks follow certain patterns which underline how the networking technologies of Web 2.0 create value.

If each node in a network of things has an average of one link to any other node, a network cluster forms which exhibits particular properties, particularly in the transmission of information. The more links we add, the less probable it is that any part of the cluster is isolated, meaning that once in a network, the probability of missing information reduces according to how the links subsequently develop. This is not a simple linear reduction.

In networks where links do not form in a random manner (which describes most networks) and where links between nodes can be consciously navigated, the number of links needed to transverse the network to any other node, without knowing the path in advance, becomes quite small quite quickly. This is reflected in the concept of 'six degrees of separation', which stems from an experiment performed in 1967.[25] Stanley Milgram asked residents of Wichita and Omaha to send a card to a particular person in Boston. If they knew the person they should send the card directly, but if not, they should send it to a person who is more likely than themselves to know that person. The average number of letters sent turned out to be 5.5, or 'six degrees'. In 2001, Duncan Watts performed a similar experiment with e-mail, again finding the average number of intermediaries to be 6.[26] The implication is that the distance between any two people between whom some link can be imagined is actually far less than we might expect. It is a matter of providing a means to identify the best next step towards the target.

Far from being uniform, networks have asymmetric properties. Some parts of networks are denser than others, having strong interconnections between all or most nodes in that particular 'sub-network' (you and a group of close friends for example).[27] But the other less common links between your dense network of friends and other dense clusters can be very useful; indeed they can be more useful and more wide-ranging than the strong ties within your own dense network of close friends. Granovetter's famous work on 'The strength of weak ties' found that links to acquaintances, rather than close friends, are more likely to lead to a wider range of social advantages.[28] For example, they play a critical role in getting jobs. The general structure of social networks is therefore of strongly tied clusters with links to other groups facilitated through weaker links. It takes only a relatively small increase in weak links to radically increase the average closeness of nodes to each other in a network. Strong ties, between committed friends for example, are not used nearly as much, often because close friends, having a similar profile, do not offer each other capabilities which the other does not already have. Simply put, this reflects the fact that much social activity, of which business interaction is a type, occurs through finding and exploiting people through a 'weak tie' (a friend of a friend or someone who went to the same school).

It seems to be a common occurrence in networks of all types that some nodes have a considerably higher number of links than others: these nodes are known as hubs, and most systems appear to fall into a pattern in which a small number of nodes have a disproportionately high number of links to other nodes. Some web pages within websites (or even over the entire World Wide Web) have a huge number of links while the others drop away to ten or less; some people are tremendously popular and facilitate relationships between many others; a few airports have a huge number of incoming routes – the next level of airport far less; profitability is often concentrated in a few customers or customer types and a few products often account for the most sales. Power, wealth, attention, complaining customers or productive workers are concentrated in 'hubs' rather than being evenly distributed across populations.

Networks are not static: they grow, and as they grow they demonstrate certain behaviours, in particular preferential behaviour, by means of which new nodes will tend to link to the most popular existing nodes. Clusters form as nodes become linked, and they lead to hubs, which have a larger number of links than most nodes.

This information about networks is relevant to the adoption of Web 2.0, because Web 2.0 technologies link people and ideas across the entire Internet or corporate intranet. A node in a computer network is not just a computer with an IP address. It might be a person, an event, a discipline or area of knowledge or just a web page. The links between nodes are given through the hyperlink path information and signposts to those nodes which are retained and in many cases automatically managed in wikis, blogs, social networking sites and so on. Figure 3.2 illustrates how the network effects influence communication and access to knowledge resources within the linked enterprise.

So, because there are several levels at which we can specify node granularity, there are many forms of interconnectedness which can be supported by Web 2.0 tools. Through simple hyperlinks in web pages, the Internet is already a network of linked page-nodes. Then there are people-nodes, individuals who may have previously been isolated experts, who

Figure 3.2 Network effects and their impact on resource access

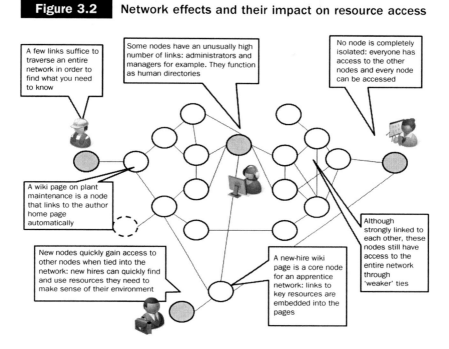

are made visible and connected as authors of wiki pages or members of social networking sites: they become informational hubs, their knowledge elevated and leveraged, and they become members of networks with common interests. At the group level, people work together and collaborate based upon a common interest or objective and will have strong ties to each other, interacting on a regular basis. On occasion they go outside of the group, using the weak ties, and sometimes the generative expertise of their group will be needed by others. Web 2.0, through making nodes and their competencies more visible, enhances 'weak ties' and the subsequent network traversal. Web 2.0 facilitates the automatic addition of network pathways across cluster boundaries, thereby multiplying the capability of the whole according to power laws rather than linear laws of growth.

At a business level, the number of nodes-as-organisations is increasing as value chain disaggregation and outsourcing occur. A firm may analyse its value chain and find it can do better outsourcing product design and support or information technology and manufacturing. Firms emerge and specialise to provide these services: the average size of corporations decreases as the vertically integrated concern is abandoned for the network.[29] This means more nodes exist, but some nodes will continue to grow at a faster rate, as they have more links into others. The growth of nodes is preferential, favouring some nodes (i.e. firms) over others. Managing the connections into and out of your node, as well as navigating the network to find a specific node or node type, cannot be defined in advance due to the volatility of the network and the fact that you cannot anticipate in advance which node you require. Therefore firms require systems which can take advantage of the laws of networks to locate nodes (such as other people who might offer specific and complementary skills) both within the firm (if it is large enough) and beyond: the strength of weak ties, the exploitation of hubs, the power laws which lead to the small degrees of separation between you and your target, even though you do not know your target in advance.

The rapid establishment of transparent information exchanges with transient partners in the modern, semi-anonymous digital marketplace requires shared network capabilities and is itself a network creator. The Internet has provided a simple, universal, robust platform for connecting many buyers to many sellers. E-marketplaces and hubs which provide shared repositories to exchange enterprise resource planning data have proliferated for vertical integrated and horizontal industries. But not all information can be structured and inserted into databases. Where abstract thought and unstructured discussion dominate work activities, Web 2.0 capabilities allow network interactions to happen earlier in the value chain: requirements definition, designs, quality standards and collaboration around marketing strategies can be supported through Web 2.0 tools, where the downstream ERP systems support structured, repetitive and defined transactions.[30]

The power of the crowd

Where groups of people are physically or formally separated, the development of knowledge and solutions to everyday organisational problems becomes fragmented and localised. Islands of information develop and local experts evolve who embody and legitimate these local solutions. As groups make local decisions and assessments, fragmentation and deviation occur within organisations, even when desired methods are initially codified and distributed as policies and procedures. Furthermore, local optimisations are not shared with other groups. Web 2.0 tools allow an incremental pooling of knowledge which facilitates input and review by others. Information can be scrutinised in open public forums and its validity and relevance assessed.

There are many such instances on the Internet of dispersed groups with a common interest in developing a body of knowledge, a product or accomplishing a job of work: Wikipedia and the open source software movement are examples of contributions of knowledge, brainpower and critical capability to a common cause. There are sites where professional groups of scientists, educators or librarians make opportunities available to develop their discipline. And there are project sites where people within organisations construct common knowledge.[31] But what is the quality of this information? How reliable, accurate or even 'true' is it? What level of remuneration or recognition is required to stimulate worthwhile contributions? In this section we will first examine the process of information gathering in networks before moving to decision-making processes regarding or based upon this information.

Networked collective intelligence

Many hands make light work and many people engaged in doing a little bit can add up to a lot. The connectivity of the Internet and the fact that it is an information-based network means that a vast number of people can contribute a part of a whole, can look at the contributions of others and improve what others have created without having to commit substantial personal time or resources.

A powerful example of this is open source software, which is software made available for free and for extension by others on the Internet. Linux, for example, is a computer operating system developed by Linus Torvalds, a young Finnish programmer. In 1991, he shared the source code of a simple operating system he had written with other programmers via an Internet bulletin board. He invited them to improve the system, placing it under a general public licence, so there were no fees to pay or licences to acquire, but others were not permitted to make money from it themselves and had to make their improvements available to others. Now Linux is a major product for managing large computers and co-developed (for free) by IBM at a cost of around $200 million per year to them (but saving them money overall through the contributions of others) and freeing capacity to offer higher value, less imitable consulting services. Other open source software products are Firefox the web browser, Open Office, Joomla and Apache (a freeware product which runs most web servers in the world). Mediawiki, the leading free wiki product, is constantly augmented and enhanced by programmers contributing extensions they have created for their own use. The SourceForge site for the Open Source Initiative lists thousands of products which can be downloaded for free.

The motivations to contribute to such product development are varied, although perhaps they all boil down to *money, love* or *glory*. Certainly, motivations other than the financial are at play – self-actualisation, reputation enhancement, recognition and genuine pleasure are some of them. Free software can be an inducement to use associated (but not free) products and services. But the bottom line is that for large-scale open source products, no single participant has to do a lot – thousands of interconnected programmers, each writing a few lines of code, can result in a large, sophisticated product. The overall design, architecture and coordination of systems (as opposed to snippets of code) require dedication and should not be taken for granted. But these are driven either through 'true believers', indirect state funding (i.e. research institutes and universities) or discretionary donations which cover some basic costs.

The Internet allows access to the vast intellectual and physical resources around the globe. Of the billions of people connected, there will be enough to participate. For example, the Galaxyzoo project is a collaboration between researchers at Oxford University and Portsmouth University in the UK and Johns Hopkins University in the US which began in 2007.[32] The aim is to recruit Internet volunteers to visually classify large volumes of images of galaxies taken by the Sloan Digital Sky Survey II. It now has over 100,000 active volunteers who not only classify the images, but who also engage actively with astronomy, sharing particularly beautiful or quirky photos. As Daniel Thomas of Portsmouth University says: 'We now have the world's largest computer working for us, through the combined power of all these human brains.' A similar project is NASA's 'clickworkers' project, which uses volunteers to visually classify Mars craters. The website Patientslikeme[33] allows sufferers from around the world to exchange stories about their ailments, adverse reactions to drugs and feelings (see Figure 3.3), leading to what the think-tank the California HealthCare Foundation calls a body of knowledge which 'may rival the body of information that any single medical school or pharmaceutical company has assembled in this field'.[34]

This harnessing of public capability and enthusiasm has extended into application development in the form of *mashups*. Some governments, for example, encourage the public to develop mashups using existing government datafeeds. One might combine maps, schools matriculation data and crime statistics and make this web page available to the public so young couples can decide where to buy a home for example. The productivity benefits for government agencies can be substantial: the public is better informed and the degree of democratic participation is increased.

Figure 3.3 The Patientslikeme portal

Source: *http://www.patientslikeme.com/*

The office of the technology officer of Washington, DC published a public competition in October of 2000 which solicited the creation of web pages to use the datafeeds of the state of Washington, DC.[35] The entries by the public included mashups for bringing data and maps together for car-pooling, historic tours of the city and building permits for certain parts of town.

Mass contribution is not restricted to information creation: it extends to the creation and application of tagging metadata as well, the descriptive data which helps make sense of the information that is out there. The more people tag pages with whatever tags they find important, the greater the scope for other users to find a page and also for intelligent software to make automatic links between tags based upon the coincidence of labels and the sorts of words in the content. Networks of concepts and ideas evolve that can present the underlying information from many angles and for many purposes. *Networked collective intelligence* applies to the *classifying* and *ordering* of the mass of information on the Internet as well as the *building* of that information content in the first place.

Web 2.0 technologies are in a position to harness this 'wisdom of crowds' through providing easy-to-access, wide-scope tools like wikis, blogs, social tagging sites, quality ratings and widgets. Much of the Web 2.0 literature suggests that the ability to network and reach the minds of the many will lead to new forms of extended collaboration, which will threaten the 'traditional' integrated, control-oriented development/production business models, in particular product design and co-creation with customers.[36]

But the proportion of commercial activity which will be subject to volunteer input is not yet clear and the degree to which it happens depends upon the motivations and capabilities of contributors and the willingness of firms to open up their product development processes to outsiders. It will be interesting to observe the sustainability of volunteer models in the immediate future, as competing models of pay-for-small-service evolve and hard times begin to bite due, for example, to the global financial crisis of 2008. In July 2008 Google announced Knol, an online encyclopaedia in which users can write articles on any subject, much as in Wikipedia, but gain income from the resulting traffic generated to the page. It remains to be seen how this will disrupt the volunteer basis of competing knowledge bases like Wikipedia, which was in fact not founded as an experiment in mass democracy but to be a world-class encyclopaedia. Nevertheless, with or without direct remuneration, networked collective intelligence appears to be an area of substantial and growing activity.

In particular, it remains to be seen how influential the phenomenon of collective intelligence will be within the firm. Firstly there is the question of numbers: commercial firms usually try and minimise redundancy and overlap in knowledge – will there be sufficient potential contributors with the right kinds of knowledge to achieve the desired effects? Secondly, there is the question of motivation: whereas contributors on the Internet seem to be mostly (but not always) driven by enthusiasm for the subject matter and the desire for recognition, workers within the corporation may be more driven by financial incentives, which are largely associated with how well they do their own job, rather than whether they contribute to the firm's general stock of knowledge. Indeed, there even may be norms in the firm which militate against contribution. Thirdly, the efficiency gains of collective intelligence are not clear: the distribution of work over an unmanaged network may be lead to remarkable outcomes on the Internet, but it may also lead to great waste. Personnel (possibly unqualified) may spend company time following blind alleys and creating unnecessary work products – anathema to the philosophy of management which has encouraged specialisation and efficiency. Finally, even where networked collective intelligence is required within the firm, it may well be that conventional methods and technologies suffice. Perhaps e-mail, project e-rooms, Intranets – even meetings and conversations (!) – are enough.

Networked collective decision-making

So collecting information from many participants at low cost is all very well, but what about its quality and reliability? How do we assess this? How do we arrive at good decisions and evaluations? In the previous section we discussed *descriptive metadata*, which gives an idea of the meaning of web material. There is also metadata which is evaluative. There is a type of tag called a *rating* which provides the participant with an opportunity to express an evaluation of web content or general products. This is usually visible as a set of stars which express a consolidated assessment by readers of the material. There are now an increasing number of opportunities to review and vent an opinion about material and products, opportunities which can either be provided by the website owner or are placed by people with an opinion onto a general-purpose subject website. So Amazon.com and youtube.com, for example, allow customer to review and rate products and content, and tripadvisor.com allows anyone to share experiences about hotels, travel destinations and airlines. In spite of the potential for information warfare and sabotage, this information generally proves to be a useful indicator, as long as one realises it is in fact from a source whose reliability is not known in advance. The sheer number of people who have watched a YouTube video, for example, is some kind of indicator of its quality and attractiveness.

There are several ways to develop assessments of content, decide upon courses of action and arrive at conclusions about quality. There can be authoritarian and hierarchical approaches, by which a legitimated leader or expert, informed by subordinates or colleagues, decides upon the right course of action, or mandates a value or a process to be followed. This leader or expert can be selected by various means – a strong (or overbearing) personality, 'superior' experience or intellect or simply the prevailing social norms – but once anointed, the right to make decisions is also assumed.

When searching for a correct answer, one might elicit information from a number of people and take the statistical mean of the responses in the belief that the average will be closest to the truth. This kind of information gathering and assessment works well for information and decisions where there are definitive answers based upon estimates and facts. Research shows that judgments such as guessing the number of jelly beans in a jar or the weight of an ox at a county fair are best arrived at using this method.[37]

One might elicit information, discuss ideas and develop options and decisions cooperatively in a group. The consensual, deliberative approach (of which brainstorming is one variety) is intended to take the best ideas and perspectives and meld them into an optimal solution. This is the mode of idea generation which appears to be most favoured in modern organisations, as it implies a contemporary democratic orientation towards the best knowledge in the group, an aggregation of the best partial knowledge towards a more complete knowledge, and the availability of critical review to weed out bad ideas and develop good ones. However, there are multiple potential distortions in this mode of decision-making.

Firstly, in groups people read information signals from others. If the prevailing views contradict their own, they are more likely to doubt themselves than the group, leading to a failure to dissent.[38] Furthermore, homogenous groups tend to become more pronounced in their views, leading to more extreme positions than those held by the individual participants.[39] This is compounded when others are known to be authorities and is widely known as the 'groupthink' phenomenon.[40] Famous examples are the disastrous assessment of Iraq's weapons capability,[41] the failure to prevent the ill-fated Columbia space shuttle flight[42] and the surreal Bay of Pigs fiasco, in which 1,200 American-trained insurgents were to invade and overthrow the well-trained army loyal to the popular Fidel Castro. Indeed, most of us have probably participated in meetings where something like this has happened, albeit with less dramatic consequences.

Secondly, people in groups are not only information processors, they are social agents. If they feel that their statements will be ridiculed or lead to sanction, they will not speak out. If they feel of lower social status, they may not volunteer information. Conversely, other research shows that some people routinely overestimate their own knowledge, a phenomenon known as 'illusory superiority': if they are considered an 'expert', they may well believe that they know more than they actually do, meaning that the social certainty and authority they project will cause a disproportionate degree of influence on a group's decision.[43]

Thirdly, arriving at the best decision is simply not always in everybody's best interest. A decision in the best interest of the firm may mean more work or less resource for a set of individual departments who, in the service of rational self-interest, withhold information or ideas which may lead to this decision.

So how does one reduce the distortion in decision-making? It may be possible through leadership and culture management to create standards and behaviours which protect dissenters and the vulnerable, and which construct 'the ideal speech situation' in which people are socialised into institutions which create the best conditions for discourse and decision-making.[44] Further, Suriwiecki demonstrates with several case studies and experiments that group deliberation can be efficient and more effective than the smartest individual within the group, but only if there is adequate *diversity* and when there is some method to *aggregate* the knowledge of group members.[45] But the norm in organisations is that informational, social and power pressures may distort collective decision-making in deliberative groups.

Finally one method of decision-making which tries to gather opinions from many while minimising the distortions of social presence is the anonymous vote (of which ratings are a basic form). The veracity of knowledge or the best course of action can be decided upon statistically, for example when a group is asked to rank ideas or to vote for the best ideas and do so anonymously. This can now happen over distance and include vast populations, increasing the statistical probability of arriving at the truth. As long as voting members of a group have a probability greater than 0.5 of being right, then the greater the number of voters, the higher the probability of the decision being correct or the knowledge 'true'. This removes the distortion of face-to-face situations while gaining the feedback and assessment of participants. The number of these so-called 'prediction market' scenarios on the Internet is increasing and their accuracy appears to mirror real-world events.

An example of this in action is Google's 'market system'. Google give their staff 'money' to invest. The price of an event as a 'stock' reflects the probability of it becoming true (i.e. 10 cents is 10 per cent probability). The value of events in internal Google markets subsequently predict with good accuracy actual events, that is events which were predicted to have a '10 (per) cent' chance of occurring actually occurred around 10 per cent of the time and, further, the decisiveness of predictions increased as an event approached. While this is a useful confirmation of the prediction market approach, research into the internal Google market revealed some biases. There is a tendency to optimism, for example when Google stock happens to increase, and there are distortions due to close social and physical proximity, where people sitting close together share opinions. This suggests that people will be influenced by incidental factors even when they are anonymous.[46] A nice operational example of such an anonymous market system is in project management, a discipline which is often subject to the informational distortions of pressure from above to deliver and restricted information flow from below: a Microsoft software development project was deemed by the project managers to be on time and on budget. When 'floated' on the internal market, the project shares went to a value showing a 1 per cent probability of success – the project came in three months late.

But some kinds of judgment are even more delicate than this. Collective judgments about commercial entities, institutions, people or products may lead to severe difficulties which challenge and erode traditional notions of quality, truth or depth. Websites such as tripadvisor.com for hotels and travel destinations, docinsider.de for the quality of medical practitioners and meinprof.de for university lecturers give Internet users the ability to express an assessment as well as describe personal experiences. The objectivity and accuracy of these judgments do not undergo any quality assurance process other than removing obvious outliers. Many sites require some form of authentication to verify the reliability of the source or their right to make a judgment, but institutional clashes occur as data protection laws and rights to privacy confront these websites. A case in point is *spickmich*, literally 'my cheat note'.

The spickmich.de web portal, which allows German school students to evaluate their teachers using the same grading scales as are applied to the students, was sued by a teacher who appeared on this site.[47] The most telling argument according to German law was that as data processing (i.e. the collection, calculation and presentation of data) is the core activity of the site, the site operators must prove that users of the data have a valid and justifiable interest in it. The strict application of German personal data protection laws means that every site user must be identified and every query then related to the user, such that their 'justifiable interest' can, at least in theory, be assessed. This is an enormous obligation for website operations to enter into and the loss of anonymity for users a probable death notice. In business organisations, on the other hand, where anonymity would be the exception rather than the rule, being identified would generally be a disincentive to be critical. However, in June 2009 the German High Court found that the freedom of expression of school students is of higher value than the privacy of teachers. While conservative politicians and journalists talk darkly of the bad old days of denunciation, 56 per cent of Germans agreed with the judgment, with 76 per cent of those between 14 and 29 years being in favour of it. The editorial of the *Frankfurter Allgemeine Zeitung* asks how the (objective) marks a teacher gives a student can be compared to the (subjective) opinion of the students and quotes Ortega y Gasset: 'When the masses act autonomously, they can only do it in one way: they lynch.'[48]

So technologies such as those in the Web 2.0 suite, which gather knowledge (beginning with small but useful increments) from a distributed but often large set of contributors and which allow those contributors to assess (on an often anonymous basis) the validity of that knowledge and make decisions based upon it, are generally powerful, though not infallible, methods of information building and legitimation. Web 2.0 content creation and collaboration tools such as wikis, blogs and social networking software provide functions for social tagging, feedback and review and information rating and voting systems. These are generally built into the standard software products, requiring no further enhancement. The functions can be made available to people within organisations to *build* information and also *evaluate* it. If a *sufficient* number of *diverse* people are *available* and *motivated* to use these features, then the value of the information will be greatly increased and at relatively little cost.

Globalisation

In his bestseller about globalisation, Thomas Friedman describes ten *flatteners* which have interconnected the world and allow instantaneous communication, awareness and sensing without barriers.[49] Most obvious among these is the technology revolution which has introduced universal, mobile and (almost) ubiquitous broadband access overlaid with communications, search and inter-application standards which support immediate, low-cost information sharing. There have been certain events which have spurred on the use of these capabilities: geopolitical changes, the end of the Cold War, the rise of China and the Y2K 'Millennium Bug' challenge, which saw the movement of programming work to India, paving the way initially for massive code remediation and programming and then further IT services outsourcing such as call centre provision and systems programming.

Outsourcing and offshoring via digital communications have enabled massive fragmentation of supply chains to occur in the pursuit of cost savings. This has also introduced new models for collaboration and development which transcend normal pay-for-service stereotypes. In what Friedman calls the triple convergence, web technologies, analytical and managerial know-how and the economic-political liberation of China, India and Russia, we are now confronted with the 'flattened' playing field, open to all and heralding the arrival of true competition for all aspects of work at a global level.

Already much work, both high and low value, has been outsourced and offshored and the flow of work from high to low wage economies will almost certainly continue. For example, the US is expected to send one in four IT jobs offshore by 2010.[50] At least 3.3 million white-collar jobs will shift from the US to India, China and Russia by 2015.[51] Not quite as apocalyptic, the US Department of Labor's Occupational Outlook Handbook, 2008–9 edition, states for computer programmers that there will be a slow decline of 4 per cent in employment from 2006 to 2016:

> ... Because they can transmit their programs digitally, computer programmers can perform their job function from anywhere in the world, allowing companies to employ workers in countries that have lower prevailing wages. Computer programmers are at a much higher risk of having their jobs outsourced abroad than are workers involved in more complex and sophisticated information technology functions, such as software engineering.

Little effort is needed to apply the same criteria to other forms of knowledge work to appreciate the potential scale of offshoring – this even of jobs with very high skill levels and years of training. Radiological diagnosis, call centres, programming, engineering and design and even legal analysis require information inputs and produce information outputs and lend themselves well to outsourcing and offshoring.

However, there are nuances and even outright contradictions in how countries interpret and respond to the demands of the information age, and the US should not be seen as somehow merely a more 'advanced' example of a nation progressing towards a knowledge economy. While the nature of work in G7 countries, for example, is of course transformed through digitisation and networks, the statistics describing structural changes and occupational segmentation vary. While the UK and the US experienced rapid decline in manufacturing between 1970 and 1990 from 38.7 to 22.5 per cent and 25.9 to 17.5 respectively) Japan and Germany reduced theirs only moderately (from 26.0 to 23.6 per cent and 38.6 to 32.2 per cent respectively). And these two countries were the most competitive economies at that time and have the lowest service to industry ratios and the lowest rate of information employment throughout the century. While China has become the world's leading exporter, Germany was until recently the largest by volume and, interestingly, is also the world's major exporter of intra-logistical solutions and technologies. Intra-logistical activity is a major source of costs in manufacturing. This confirms that an organisation or economy can make an efficient shift from manufacturing to manufacturing services (or from 'doing' to 'advising') and that the two can coexist. Value chain fragmentation within a national economy can lead to a competitive advantage on the global stage.

While agriculture diminishes, manufacturing declines and producer services such as health and education grow, and while retail and service jobs increase the ranks of low-skilled, low-paid activities, there does seem to be a hollowing out – an increase at the top and the bottom of the scales, with the relative prosperity of the upper range increasing. So there are two models: the industrial production model (which may grow in the area of manufacturing services rather than actual manufacturing) and the industrialisation of services.[52] As Castells says:

> ... the new information paradigm of work and labor is not a neat model but a messy quilt woven from the historical interaction between technological change, industrial relations policy and conflictive social action.[53]

Put simply, globalisation does not mean that technologies and solutions to working problems will be implemented globally in a uniform way. We only need to look at Cole's comparative international studies of the adoption of small group activities, such as quality circles. He shows that differing national emphases, institutions and infrastructures created quite different rates of diffusion and persistence, with Japan adopting and retaining more successfully than Sweden and Sweden more than the United States.[54]

But the global economic system is of course a massively complicated beast, with multiple significant factors affecting its size, shape and nature. Credit squeezes, oil prices, the rise of China, India and Russia as significant producers and consumers, tariffs, carbon emissions and conflict whether through terrorism or between nations are a few of the imponderables that shape the trajectory of global trading and commerce. For example, the introduction of global carbon trading schemes and emission restrictions will force manufacturers and retailers to become more tightly integrated with their supply chains. In the case of manufacturers, 40–60 per cent of emissions occur upstream in the supply chain (80 per cent for retailers) and reduction in emissions will require greater collaboration between suppliers and manufacturers in resource management, processing, packaging and transport.[55] Greater collaboration (rather than just data exchange) implies potential use of Web 2.0 tools. The global economic crisis also has a massive impact, as political pressures mount to restrict trade and increase protection of local industries – and indeed reduce the rate of adoption of carbon trading schemes.

In a globalised economy, tools which facilitate the establishment of trading relationships and the exchange of information are in demand. There is a natural tension between the requirements for ease of use, ubiquity and speed of establishment (which for example favours e-mail) and control, security and solid information management. Web 2.0 tools are advantageous because they are universal, cheap, flexible and available globally, they are simple to install, learn and use, and are suitable for the iterative and interactive development and exchange of knowledge. Being technologically simple and robust, they are natural candidates for inter-firm communication and collaboration within a globalised world economy.

The information economy

The *knowledge economy*, the *information age*, the *digital economy*: these are expressions which seek to capture the defining characteristics of commercial activity in our time. In simple statistical terms, in industrial countries there has been a clear demographic shift from productive activities involving physical labour to those in non-physical occupations. There is a marked, but not uniform, decline in agriculture and manufacturing and a corresponding growth in services. Those remaining in agriculture and manufacturing have become more skilled and more productive, particularly in the use of technology and labour-saving devices, to the extent where much of the activity could be characterised as 'knowledge work'. The fragmentation of value chains through outsourcing has led to the growth of service companies which supply informational inputs powered by knowledge: marketing concepts, product designs, call centres – the opportunities are endless for the production of informational rather than physical goods. Where a company might once have manufactured something, they now increasingly organise the input services by others to their brand.

In response to this, knowledge management has become one of the signature disciplines in management science since the early 1990s and there has been a substantial focus by technology vendors, consultants and academics upon framing their various products in terms of knowledge and the macro-economic forces which have elevated its status as a key productive asset.

This is a key setting and assumption for Web 2.0 technologies. As a suite of digital tools, they transmit messages from one brain to another. This type of tool is a perfect fit for access to and the generation of knowledge via collaboration, above all in a world that has become increasingly flexible and dynamic. The need to generate information grows undiminished but the networks in which this occurs are more transient and volatile and the processes which are executed are less prescriptive. You may not know who your collaboration partner will be tomorrow, there may be no methodology agreed in advance, and you may not even know what information you will exchange.

Electronic marketplaces or automated inventory management for widgets, gearboxes and paper functions exchange structured data based upon explicitly structured business processes and the pertinent data. But when it is knowledge being developed and exchanged, and not structured data, the precise formats and flows remain unknown in advance. And the speed of partner contact, work ramp up, information exchange and information development must be rapid, implying that the supporting tools must be simple to establish, simple to use, conform to some open standard and be themselves open and simple to integrate into any number of back-end systems. Further, they must permit users of the system to self-organise and establish their own rules of engagement, administration and control. These are the underlying capabilities of Web 2.0 technologies.

Innovation

Innovation, the creation of new products, new services, new business models and improvements to business processes throughout the value chain, is seen by senior management as a key driver for growth and competitiveness. But at the same time, most business leaders are pessimistic about their own ability to achieve the desired levels of innovation.[56] The life of products has reduced in the past 50 years from 20 to five years and now to two.[57] Attalli expects the cycle from 'creation to production and commercialization' to fall for automobiles and household products to six months (from two years currently) and for medicines from seven to four years.[58] Competitive advantage lies in the capacity of organisations to facilitate and mobilise their intangible assets such as employee knowledge, motivation and customer goodwill and turn this into innovative products and services.

Accelerating innovation by opening the requirements gathering and product design processes to inputs, suggestions, ideas and enhancements by customers or partners using Web 2.0 technologies and attitudes is gaining momentum. Atizo (Swiss) and Jovoto (German) are two websites created expressly to allow firms to solicit creative ideas and move them through a business case and prototyping phase. The Atizo community was responsible for the idea of a transparent, safety-check conformant bag for cabin luggage, which was manufactured by the textile firm Blacksocks.com. Mammut took the idea of using deep-freeze bag zippers for mountain sports clothing from the same site.[59] Figure 3.4 shows ideas contributed to a next-generation BMW motorbike and how the tags within the cloud associated with the ideas increase in size according to their usage.

There are many critical success factors for innovation and its diffusion through groups, but there are no recipes to guarantee success. The fundamental challenges are not of a technological nature, but many factors can be influenced by the use of Web 2.0 tools:

- *Leadership* – organisational leaders need to send strong, consistent signals to employees about the importance of innovation. They should design and publicise measurable performance targets for innovation. But conventional methods of management communication are often clinical, formulaic and broadcast. Employees will often see these as yet another management fad or discount them as meaningless exhortations. Blogs and wikis, however, provide excellent opportunities to formulate and project these messages in 'real language', in an interactive form, without them simply being part of organisational spam.

- *Culture* – 94 per cent of managers in one survey said that people and culture are the most important components in stimulating innovation.[60] Trust, risk-taking and norms which value innovation all

Figure 3.4　The Atizo innovation site showing ideas for next-generation BMW motorbikes

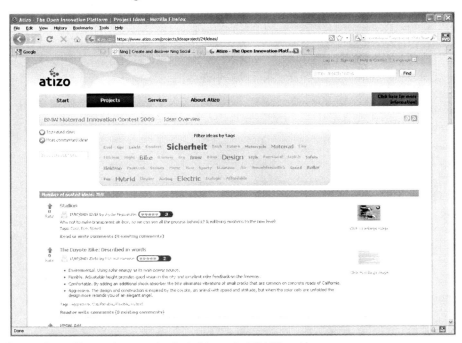

Source: https://www.atizon.com/projects/ideaproject/24/ideas/

need to be created to stimulate innovative behaviour. Leadership and legitimation of the desired behaviours is clearly critical for the development of new norms; Web 2.0 technologies offer the possibility for managers to formulate and repeat these messages and to underpin this with action by participating in innovation forums, discussions, contributions of ideas and so on. When managers take risks, expose themselves to criticism and spend time on an innovation wiki page, then this is clearly not only desirable behaviour, it is legitimate.

- *Networks* – the creation of networks is critical to the development of innovation, more important than individual creativity.[61] There are two key dimensions to organisational networks which support innovation. The first is letting people find each other (or bringing them together) and providing spaces for them to interact. This is directly supported by Web 2.0 tools like wikis and social networking software. The second is to facilitate the use of alternative network paths to develop innovation networks in order to prevent non-supportive nodes, such as negative middle managers, from blocking this process. Web 2.0 tools reduce the impact of such blockages and make it easier to gather innovations and change attitudes in the desired direction.

Fragmentation of business processes

A key characteristic of modern business is the movement of work to the location where it is most cost-effective or where some differentiating competency is present. Design might be done in Italy, engineering in Germany, manufacturing in China and support from India for example. The intellectual and managerial capability to decompose work into its constituent parts, move that work to an appropriate supplier or location, and yet retain coherence and control is one of the major accomplishments of industrial science. It is this that is at the heart of outsourcing and offshoring – not technology or networks. Figure 3.5 shows the fragmentation of the value chain. Although an organisation may outsource a process, it retains the need to manage the informational inputs to and outputs from that process as executed by a subcontractor. There may be a requirement for collaboration and cooperation in this process to transfer knowledge and details of designs and even co-create design solutions.

This decomposition has also highlighted a key aspect of work: that most of it is knowledge work. Fragmentation of work has led to the

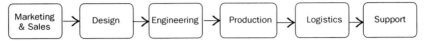

Figure 3.5   The fragmentation of value chains and outsourcing

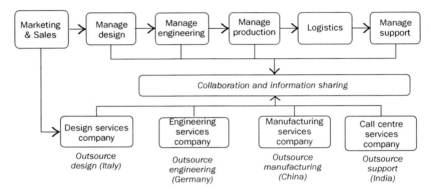

knowledge economy, not because people don't buy fridges or stereos, but because many individual companies provide the necessary services in the production chain before a piece of steel is ever cut or welded. And the inputs and the outputs of this knowledge work are information. While it is easy for organisations to think they are mining companies or manufacturing companies when massive trucks are leaving the pit laden with ore or shiny new cars are rolling out of their factories, the degree of outsourcing in many such companies suggests that they are actually management companies – knowledge management companies.

If we invert the previous figure and, instead of looking from the production chain downward, we look from the service provider outward, we see that each service provider deals with many firms. In Figure 3.6, each service provider has a network of customers (all of whom might build roads or fridges or mines). We see that the business environment indeed consists of interconnected enterprises which function as nodes: some nodes provide services and some integrate services into a value chain. The Internet has reduced most components of the transaction cost: search, bargaining and policing.[62] In the case of information deliverables, the cost of delivery is also reduced. Further, tools which support collaboration between any of these nodes (which

Figure 3.6   Enterprise networks arising from work fragmentation

Enterprise networks

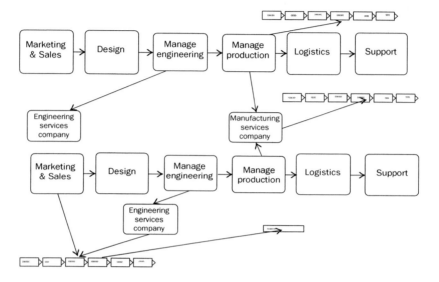

hitherto were separated from each other) will enhance innovation and the rate of idea generation.

So, tools which manage information exchange easily, cheaply and quickly, according to standards, facilitate the flow of work from place to place. The first generation of web applications simply provided a product catalogue and the ability to buy goods, effectively replacing a shop assistant. Then came electronic marketplaces, which allowed customers to place orders and specifications in electronic format at a site for 'reverse auction', and allowed sellers to place commodities for sale in advance of production. ERP products began to provide interfaces which automated the flow of information such as inventory reorder or payments to suppliers: it became a matter of mere configuration of software to automate inter-organisational transactions.

Then these supply chains again began to change – instead of linear supply chains, with bullwhip effects and sudden shortages, large suppliers changed to *hub structures*, where the supply chain vendors could not only see in advance the type of products in the pipeline, they could even participate and co-design products for improved manufacturability and cost-effectiveness. Collaboration, a higher-value interaction than mere supply, has now become a critical component of high-performing supply chains. Collaboration, the exchange of information in conversational mode and at the speed of business, to achieve a common objective or intersection of goals requires non-transactional yet cheap and easy tools – exactly the characteristics of technologies in the Web 2.0 suite.

The average size of US corporation has declined, in one survey from 60 employees in 1960 to 34 in 1990.[63] The fragmentation of corporate value chains and the proliferation of offshoring and outsourcing have led to leaner manufacturing companies and mining companies that no longer produce anything or dig any ore out of the ground: they focus on branding and mineral assets. These companies might more accurately be described as knowledge management companies: they manage expertise and the information required to ensure that others do work for them. However, if a company does not make the institutional transition to seeing itself as a knowledge management company, it will be unlikely to appreciate that tools like Web 2.0 are in fact support for their core business.

The increase in individual contracting

The already mature trend towards shorter-term working relationships is increasing, although the rate and extent vary from country to country. This allows a firm to reduce its costs quickly and without legal or public relations difficulties when orders are reduced or it experiences hardships. Similarly it can ramp up for spikes in demand without committing to longer-term employment relationships. Every country is wrestling to find the appropriate balance between the rights of labour and capital. The Danish model allows firms to fire workers easily, but this is balanced by the high commitment of the state to find work for its citizens and the obligation of citizens to take that work. This seems to be very successful, although it cannot be assumed that the same model would work everywhere. In neighbouring Germany, work relationships are still contractually laid out for the long term, which reduces flexibility and the desire of employers to take on staff.

For some forms of work, individual contracting is not particularly problematic (retail sales assistants, drafting or labouring for example) but in others it is a source of loss of efficiency at the induction phase and subsequently of knowledge leakage and outright loss at separation. While individual subcontractors may bring particular skills into an organisation, they must first absorb much firm-specific knowledge before they can generate their particular outputs: they then take that knowledge with them when they leave. For example, a business systems analyst or solutions designer will often gain a picture of a business area which is original, systematic and insightful: only a small portion of that knowledge might be captured in an explicit report or model. When they leave, the tacit knowledge is taken with them out the door.

The baby boomers notice and generally regret the passing of permanency and loss of belonging, but younger generations know nothing else – indeed, they are more prone to move on, having recognised that employment is based upon transient mutual self-interest. They understand that shorter-term contracts allow firms greater flexibility in adapting resource commitments to economic circumstance: hiring in boom times, firing when the order books dip. They also understand that capital and not compassion is the determining factor.

There are some significant implications for the knowledge of the firm, however. Greater turnover of staff means an increase in the amount of learning and orientation, and smart approaches to induction and productivity acceleration are required. At the end of the working relationship, in-flight, current knowledge walks out the door at short notice, as do the lessons learned by contractors during their tenure.

Web 2.0 tools such as wikis provide excellent 'incidental' records of the information generated during such tenure. If one uses a wiki for project communication, then interactions and decisions are captured centrally around the specific theme, making them easier to find – and rely upon. As part of their contract, specialists can be required to 'blog' their findings and experiences. Social networking capabilities enable communication with departed contractors to be maintained and reopened when their knowledge is needed.

Consumerisation

The pervasive availability and general use of the Internet and its tools has led to those tools being part of a general suite of consumer skills and expectations. Consumerisation refers to the adaptation of those expectations to enterprise environments.[64] At its simplest level, users ask why their organisation doesn't supply a Google search or a Facebook for employees. But if at home, in your lounge, you can rate a book in Amazon, post a question about the best wine to drink with duck ragout and have input to a Microsoft design blog, the question is justified: why can't I do this at work? And that is the tip of the iceberg: why can't I interact with my customers using a Second Life avatar and why can't I chat with the engineers while playing *Warcraft 3*?

The Gartner Group expect consumerisation to be a high-impact trend in driving enterprise product definition and take-up and they say that without recognition by CIOs of the acceptability of consumer-style software in the enterprise, Web 2.0 take-up and exploitation will remain stunted.[65]

Dynamic business models

Analytical capability, combined with rapid changes in technology, has led to a proliferation of ways of organising and structuring work. Whether it is full outsourcing, creative partnering, offshoring or product co-creation with active consumers, modern managers must consistently push the boundaries of possibility in searching for business models which enhance competitive advantage. Technologies which are inherently inflexible, based upon proprietary standards, which require very constrained and controlled data entry or which only allow a narrow corridor of usage do not permit rapid change in business models. Web 2.0 technologies have high degrees of openness and allow local adaptation and situated responsiveness. They are highly malleable forms of technology with substantial local negotiability and open-endedness.

Changes in managerial style

The fluidity and dynamism of the business world places new demands upon managers: orchestration rather than direction, coordination rather than control. In particular, the rapid construction of dispersed teams, many of whom do not report to a single manager, means authoritarian management will not work. Greater consultation, collaboration and adaptiveness are required, leading to new manager profiles, with an emphasis on softer skills and greater visibility of decision logic.

These are attributes served well by the open, conversational tools of Web 2.0. The underlying social processes of knowledge creation, sharing and collaboration are made transparent by tools like wikis and blogs, creating a platform for leaders to engage in this new kind of dialectic with dispersed, qualified knowledge workers and to communicate, legitimate and objectify vision, objectives, means and ends.[66] In such environments, leaders can project these attributes with greater immediacy and interactivity and participate in collaborations which simultaneously project their authority, legitimating certain types of approach, solution and language.

Of course, just because the tools are available does not mean that leaders or middle managers will engage with them or see them as worthwhile. Managers are themselves the objects of key performance indicators and targets. Where Web 2.0 does not directly contribute to these, or only does so such that the benefits will be realised after a manager departs, it is probably unlikely that managers will initiate any such programmes. This style of management is risky and difficult, foreign to many and almost certainly perceived as faddish and unnecessary in many organisations. Further, the privileges of management rest, in many cases, on the maintenance of distance and apartness. As Jeffrey Pfeffer says of companies in the USA, cutting health benefits and salaries, spying on employees, not giving employees a say in decision-making and increasing work pressure is still common management practice, but has the opposite effect to increasing productivity by 'holding and therefore acting on naïve, simplistic, and inaccurate theories of human behaviour and organizational performance'.[67]

Regulation and governance

Since the Enron and WorldCom collapses, greater transparency and oversight has been demanded in the accounting affairs of corporations. Directors are liable for omissions and inaccuracies in reporting and face jail in cases of misrepresentation of the financial health of their organisations – ignorance is no excuse. The Sarbanes-Oxley legislation in the United States, which affects any company listed on its stock exchange, is being replicated in other countries trading with the US. It has made legal discovery a major concern of directors, with e-mail retention now being fundamental to records management. The content of e-mail is accessible to prosecution lawyers without management actually being able to control what goes into e-mail in the first place: how many hostages to fortune are kept in e-mail archives?

Web 2.0 technologies offer a partial solution, in that blogs and wikis are interactions conducted in a public forum. This naturally leads people to be careful about what they say: sales managers would probably not conduct cartel-type behaviour or price fixing on the enterprise wiki. This naturally restricts the recording of sensitive information and conversely gives managers the opportunity to identify and act upon information that may compromise the organisation.

Conclusion

Many of the points discussed in this chapter are encountered in the business and research literature, magazines and journals as being compelling arguments for Web 2.0 in enterprises. In summary, the logic is that the implementation of Web 2.0 tools in the workplace constitutes a successful response to:

- the flood of information and proliferation of e-mails;
- the need to generate greater returns on knowledge as a key production asset;
- the expectations and inclinations of the next generation of workers;
- the loss of deep production knowledge imminent in the retirement of baby boomers;
- the connectivity opportunities offered by network dynamics;
- the need to improve decision-making by the application of many minds;
- the capability to create large sophisticated knowledge products by allowing many small contributions;
- the fragmentation of value chain work to multiple parties;
- the distribution of work across the vast distances;
- the creation and distribution of new knowledge by allowing rapid yet persistent conversations;
- the proliferation of outsourcing of work to contractors and transient staff;
- the consumerisation of software which moulds workers' expectations of corporate software;
- the need for corporations to manage communications for regulatory purposes.

But the devil does indeed lie in the detail. There is a substantial gap between these assertions and the reality of business decision-making. While there is insufficient published research to verify the claims, there is sufficient reason to be sceptical. Above all, as with most social phenomena, enterprises are complex open systems where there are many factors at play, and predictions or 'case studies' of success and appropriateness for Web 2.0 need to be regarded carefully. There are counter- and attenuating arguments which at least indicate that the touted need and the anticipated uptake might not be as dramatic or self-evident as expected:

- The baby boomers are leaving, but not as quickly as you might think.
- To achieve a network effect, there need to be sufficient nodes – this is not the case in many organisations.
- The wisdom of crowds needs a (diverse) crowd – in organisations experts are often alone.
- The net generation uses the new technologies naturally and adroitly, but they adapt to the inertia of the organisation, where sharing and interactivity are not to be taken for granted.
- New managerial styles are needed, but control (and often the protection of privileges) is still the priority of many leaders.
- Flexibility is needed, but over-complexity and product extension lead to losses in efficiency: the line must be drawn somewhere.

Many types of information systems – enterprise resource systems, data warehouses and knowledge management systems for example – are logically excellent solutions to common problems but have substantial failure rates, often more than 50 per cent. We need to understand the underlying social, technological and market logic and the factors which cause failure in order to assist good decisions to be made in the acquisition and implementation of technology solutions. Success with Web 2.0 will not simply happen.

Furthermore, if the logic of networks and the wisdom of crowds are to gain traction, we need to understand how to use Web 2.0 tools in a Web 2.0 way: simply using wikis as glorified file servers or intranet content managers is no great leap forward. Creating private wiki islands where a project team can share their project information is nice, but e-rooms and intranet content management systems do this already. And the information is consigned to invisibility when the project ceases. The power of Web 2.0 comes to bear when the project information is stored in a public place and where those outside the direct team can contribute to or learn from the team's information. And this is the difficult bit to get working.

Logic told us that knee arthroscopies and encainide were the right treatments – but they weren't. Even heart-bypass surgery works but can be delayed without harm and coronary problems instead treated with drugs. Web 2.0 implementation can likewise be delayed or adopted according to a firm-specific logic or other means used to address the underlying problems. We just need to understand these so that good choices and better implementations can be achieved.

Notes

1. Carter (2007: 14).
2. Castells (2001: 67).
3. A 2009 AIIM international survey found that 47 per cent of 18–30s and 31 per cent of over 45s expect to use the same type of networking tools with business colleagues as with friends and family.
4. Sarbanes-Oxley is legislation passed in the United States to enforce greater accountability and auditability of company finances in the wake of the Enron and Worldcom corporate collapses.
5. For example, Kroski (2008), Shuen (2008), Solomon and Schrum (2007).
6. An indication of the confusion is an AIIM 2008 survey, in which 44 per cent of respondents said Enterprise 2.0 (i.e. defined in that survey as the use of Web 2.0 tools in the enterprise) was imperative or of significant importance to their organisation, but 74 per cent had only a vague familiarity with it.
7. Bryan and Joyce (2007).
8. Charman (2006) writes that the average US knowledge worker receives 94 e-mails per day, 34 of them occupational spam.
9. In an interview with CIO Insight, famous blogger Robert Scoble said: 'When I left my old job at NEC, I left behind a gig and a half of e-mail: I couldn't look at it, and they erased it. So my former co-workers couldn't use that knowledge. A collaborative toolset helps to get information out of e-mail into the shared social space. You see productivity benefits. People can see where you're going and make suggestions on who to call there' (*http://www.cioinsight.com/c/a/Foreward/Robert-Scoble-on-Corporate-Blogging/*).
10. For example, see Basso (2008).
11. Postman (1985).
12. Court et al. (2007).
13. Prentice and Sarner (2008).
14. Tapscott (1998).
15. Rigby (2008).
16. See: *http://www.thethinkingstick.com/customization-generation*.
17. Seely Brown (2002).
18. Lecture by Manuel Castells at the International Conference on Information Systems (ICIS), Barcelona, 2003.
19. Court et al. (2007).
20. Bucks Consulting (2007).

21. For example, see 'Rethinking Retirement', *Business Week*, 13 and 20 July 2009.
22. Walker and Bittinger (2009).
23. See Commerzbank (2009) and the comments by the German Federation for Medium-Sized Enterprises (Anonymous, 2009b).
24. The network as a model for mathematical analysis was invented by the Swiss mathematician Euler in his analysis of the problem of the Königsberg Bridges, a puzzle in which one has to cross seven bridges joining four pieces of land only once each in a single round trip. Euler invented graph theory, the precursor of network analysis, to prove that any network (the route around the bridges) which has more than two nodes (the land areas) with an odd number of links (bridges) cannot possibly be negotiated without retracing steps somewhere. A node with an odd number of links must be a starting point or an end point, and there can be only two of these in a network (or route) in which no path is retraced. From this development of graph theory, important insights have been gained about the behaviour of networks consisting of interconnected nodes of pretty much anything – people, animals, atoms, biological cells and computers. For more on network science, see Barabási (2002) and Watts (2003).
25. Milgram (1967).
26. Watts (2004).
27. See Barabási (2002).
28. See Granovetter (1973).
29. Scott (2004: 11) writes that the average size of the US corporation has declined from 60 employees in 1960 to 34 in 1990.
30. Furthermore, there are multiple-sided markets which amplify network effects even further. A multiple or 'n-sided' market is one in which there are many buyers and many sellers: the relationships are many to many. Instead of connecting individual buyers and sellers: these markets connect different sets of partners, where the increase in mass on one side directly improves the profitability or utility to the other side. For example, the Visa Company, as a service, connects a community of providers with a community of purchasers. The utility to the purchasers rises greatly, the more providers there are using the Visa service and vice versa.
31. For example, the Collaboration Project is a resource established by the Obama administration in the USA to foster inter-agency and citizen collaboration. It cites many cases of the use of blogs, wikis, ratings and other Web 2.0 tools to achieve its objectives. (See: *http://www.collaborationproject .org/display/home/Home*: 'The Collaboration Project is an independent forum of leaders committed to leveraging the interactive web and the benefits of collaborative technology to solve government's complex problems. Powered by the National Academy of Public Administration, this "wikified" space is designed to share ideas, examples and insights on the adoption of Web 2.0 technologies in the field of public governance.')
32. *http://www.galaxyzoo.org/*
33. *http://www.patientslikeme.com*
34. *The Economist*, 18–24 April 2009.
35. *http://www.appsfordemocracy.org/*
36. Leadbeater (2009) calls this 'We Think'. He gives a nice historical example of how strict patent enforcement by Boulton and Watt restricted innovation in

pumping engines in English coal mines in the eighteenth century: an alternative engine, designed by Woolf and Trevithick but without patents, rapidly became three times more efficient as a result of collaboration between Cornish mine owners and engineers. Cornwall had the fastest rate of steam-engine innovation and the lowest rate of patents in Britain at the time – and Watt and Boulton didn't sell another engine in Cornwall after 1790. Woolf and Trevithick made their money installing and adapting engines (p. 54). Li and Bernoff (2008) and Tapscott and Williams (2006) are two examples of books describing modern commercial use of this phenomenon.

37. Suriwiecki (2004).
38. Asch (1952).
39. Sunstein (2006: 45).
40. Janis (1982).
41. Senate Select Committee on Intelligence (2004).
42. Columbia Accident Investigation Board (2005).
43. See: *http://en.wikipedia.org/wiki/Illusory_superiority*.
44. Habermas (1996).
45. Suriwiecki (2004).
46. *http://bocowgill.com/GooglePredictionMarketPaper.pdf*
47. Hipp (2009).
48. Zastrow (2009).
49. Friedman (2005).
50. Solomon and Schrum (2007).
51. Pink (2006).
52. Attalli (2009).
53. Castells (2000).
54. Cole (1989).
55. Brickmann and Ungerman (2008).
56. About 65 per cent of the senior executives surveyed by McKinsey were only 'somewhat', 'a little' or 'not at all' confident about the decisions they make in this area.
57. Gray and Larson (2003).
58. Attalli (2009: 119).
59. Stillich (2009: 20).
60. Barsh et al. (2008).
61. Fleming and Marx (2006).
62. Coase (1937).
63. Scott (2004: 11).
64. Smith et al. (2006).
65. Smith (2008a).
66. Bell (2004).
67. Pfeffer (2007: 6).

4

From purpose to space

We have seen that Web 2.0 components can be configured and combined to form knowledge-sharing and collaboration systems within organisations. In this chapter we use the notions of 'spaces' and 'flows' to characterise the different types of usage to which Web 2.0 tools can be put. Where conventional business systems are neatly proscribed by application domains, process definitions, functional specifications and data models, Web 2.0 tools are not. They can be configured and used in many ways and the rules of engagement will vary depending upon the modalities of use. Firstly, this can make it difficult to conceptualise how the tools can be configured, designed and put to effective business use. As wiki guru Stewart Mader says: 'It doesn't just do one thing, and because people are used to thinking of software as having a specific use, it's sometimes harder at first for them to grasp the potential of a Wiki.'[1] Secondly, it makes the framing and development of business cases more difficult and increasingly organisations demand ROI cases to justify any IT project initiative.[2] Business cases for the introduction of application software to improve customer yield by 5 per cent or service turnaround by two days are generally easy to conceptualise. There is rigour, precision, enhanced control and clear payback. But the enhancements to underlying systems of organisational memory, knowledge creation and location, innovation, power and control and social identity are difficult to articulate and enumerate. Web 2.0 can induce a kind of decision-making agoraphobia not present in the closed lanes of enterprise resource planning or financial accounting. The intent of this section is to present ways of describing Web 2.0 technologies so that managers and potential users can conceptualise the different types of purposes to which the tools can be put and match these to their own needs and requirements.

First let us consider the concrete purposes to which Web 2.0 tools can be put. Establishing purpose is the key event in the life of a Web 2.0 tool. The domains of work within which Web 2.0 tools can be usefully applied are almost limitless, as are the ways in which they can be implemented and appropriated: health, road safety, education or environmental protection, while in private industry it might be banking, manufacturing, engineering or construction. Within all these domains there are activity types which can be supported by Web 2.0 tools.

What might be some statements of purpose for which Web 2.0 might fit the bill?

- How can we improve the awareness of safety among young employees?

- How can we improve the distribution and currency of our procedural documentation?

- How can we best take advantage of the experience of our key employees, who are distributed across many locations?

- Given the rate of new hires, how can we accelerate learning and familiarisation?

- How can we learn from previous projects?

- How can our multinational teams collaborate over time zones?

- How can we develop a standard body of construction knowledge?

Purposes like these reflect business objectives or 'points of pain' in performing work. A clear purpose will lead naturally to a value proposition which can be used to underpin a business case and give direction to implementation projects. We now apply the notion of *space* to specify more clearly the various purposes to which Web 2.0 components can be put. *Space* is 'the material support of time-sharing social practices' and is constituted by digital infrastructure, software function and the rules which determine the allowable actions that occur within it.[3] A space is created to achieve the purpose of the productive activity that is to be accommodated within it.

A space is an area in which something happens, where an activity takes place. The space is clearly demarcated by a boundary which accommodates infrastructure, the functions and capabilities of Web 2.0 tools for example, and consists of flows of information and signals between the players.[4] There are spaces where we advise people, where people collaborate or where we tell people exactly what to do. A Web 2.0 tool, like a wiki, might contain many spaces. A space might contain multiple sub-spaces. Each space can be understood as accommodating a kind of game with a more or less clear set of rules and a more or less clear set of players. Engagement with the software capabilities is guided by the game's social institutions which define what is a good move, a bad move, an allowed move or a nonsensical move.[5]

These institutions vary from space to space and game to game. In a 'procedure space', the rules for discussing and authorising ways of working might be very formal, whereas the rules for a 'personal space' might be far more relaxed. Some of these institutions might be explicit and some implicit. Some institutions may function to prohibit or constrain the use of Web 2.0 tools for the conduct of games (the need for secrecy or fear of embarrassment). Some of the institutions are directly concerned with the exercise of power and coercion and may hinder voluntary contribution using Web 2.0 tools, irrespective of how functionally useful they are.

It is like a playing field for a particular game, which is defined by its regulations and some amount of semiotic infrastructure, such as white lines on the grass and some goalposts.[6] The digital space of an empty wiki or blog has editing equipment and storage and tracking capabilities as infrastructure, but the various implementations of wikis and blogs constitute spaces made material in digital form (policies, categories, security restrictions, purpose) in which only certain games can be played. The game defines who the players are: so identified, the managers and users can determine the rules of engagement and institutions that a game in each particular type of space with particular flows will require.

A space is instantiated by *flows* of information through it: meanings and acceptability are given to these flows by the rules of the space as enacted by the players. To use Wikipedia to manage fixtures and communications for your Under 12 soccer club is not a permitted flow within this space, but an article about the history and background of the club is. Web 2.0 spaces generally have boundaries and infrastructure which are malleable and allow flows at different speeds and volumes. Contrast this with another example of an Internet space, that of a business-to-business e-commerce hub using Internet electronic data interchange (EDI): here highly structured data is exchanged between players in rigorously defined interactions. The game of EDI is highly constrained to a narrow corridor of usage.

The notion of spaces helps us to move from the open-ended set of possibilities inherent in Web 2.0 to effective implementation by providing a context, rules and expectations for the implementation of detailed functions. One can easily enumerate useful applications for specific tools, such as e-mail substitution or discussion threads, but a conceptualisation of the specific game is required to lay down the modes of conduct and interaction that go beyond simple policies for use. A space is the context, the flows are the movements of information and both together provide the meaning and purpose to which the tools can be applied. For managers, this may be a more acceptable and constrained method of 'letting go' and helps to articulate to them the specific benefits of using a wiki, blog or company Facebook in a certain way. For users, it provides an orientation for how to design the structure of their information and the necessary flows, without overly constraining them.[7]

The flows within spaces, which are constrained and facilitated by varying *social institutions*, make different contributions to the organisation. One cannot assume that benefits result automatically, as some institutions will inhibit action and behaviour in certain types of space. A collaboration space will be inhibited by fixed ideas about hierarchy and who is allowed to argue with the boss, and a 'Britannica' encyclopaedia space will be inhibited in organisations where knowledge is not valued but will be facilitated where truth is seen as absolute and stable. As shown in Figure 4.1, each space will have its own topology of institutions and norms, a kind of landscape of concepts and behaviour, which makes passage through it straightforward, challenging or doomed.

By conceptualising a space and its flows we can establish ground rules and management strategies for enhancing adoption and shaping expectations.

Figure 4.1   The topology of a 'Britannica' encyclopaedia space

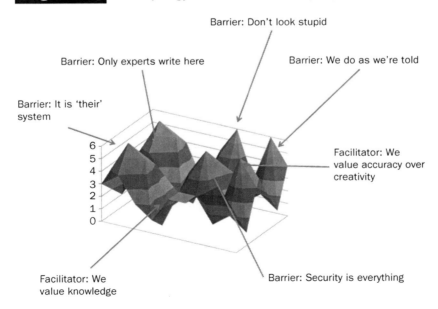

Each space has a particular dynamic and set of outcomes and each space will vary in its interaction with the underlying social institutions, organisational memory, identity building, transactive memory, power and control. The examples of spaces in the following sections have evolved out of praxis and experience, and are usually generated by a situational need to frame the general type of activity that would take place using the Web 2.0 tools. It is up to organisations to clarify their own notion of space, but the following samples are a reasonable beginning and serve to illustrate the idea.

For example, a manager might articulate a problem or purpose to a Web 2.0 administrator thus: 'A lot of our older personnel are retiring over the next two years: how can we use these tools to capture knowledge from these experienced personnel?' Instead of moving straight to functional methods for capturing and uploading videos or blogging, the conversation should turn to the kind of *space* needed; in this case it would be a *departure space*, a place where people go once it is clear that they will be leaving the organisation. What kind of information would be the subject of this *departure space* and what flows would support information capture and usage? What kinds of Web 2.0 functions would work for these flows, and what sorts of resistance or challenges might one encounter? How should one behave vis-à-vis departing personnel? What can one expect *from* them and, in particular, is there an example of a *departure space* from somewhere else in the organisation – or from the Internet?

In summary, the idea of space gives most players an intuitive grasp of what the game is about: we can name collaboration spaces, innovation spaces, advisory spaces or personal spaces and the act of naming the space creates (but does not specify in excruciating detail) a whole landscape of what is allowed and what is not allowed, what is intended and what is relevant. More rules can emerge as the game progresses and players discover too much breakdown is occurring.

Encyclopaedia spaces

An encyclopaedia space is perhaps the best known instance of wiki use, although encyclopaedias meet with mixed success in the corporate world. This space works to facilitate the construction of web pages which reflect the knowledge of a discipline, practice or body of knowledge and is analogous to the paper- or CD-based encyclopaedias like Britannica (now mostly digital) or the German Brockhaus (now exclusively digital), a lexicon or a dictionary. An encyclopaedic page will be a coherent topic, with the title of the page generally reflecting the scope and the content. As a page grows through contributions (it may initially be an empty 'stub' reflecting only a need for a page) it may be divided into more detail, it may be melded with others or it may require a higher level page which provides contextual information.

Although providing a forum for the emergence of knowledge by public contribution, the tone of such a page will tend to be authoritative but not prescriptive. It will tend to reflect best knowledge at a point in time but may not make any exclusive claims. This is the nature of wiki encyclopaedias. In organisations, authors are often experts of which, by definition and resource constraint, there are few. However, their knowledge can be built upon, kept up to date and even corrected by others. There will generally be a high ratio of readers to editors, but this is to be expected and indeed welcomed, as it suggests a high leverage of knowledge by non-experts through greater diffusion and accessibility.

Encyclopaedia spaces serve many business purposes. Above all they increase the leverage of useful knowledge assets, reduce the risk of knowledge loss and:

- externalise organisational memory from tacit to explicit forms;
- legitimate and diffuse distinctive expert knowledge;
- exploit the 'wisdom of crowds';
- increase consistency and standardisation of cognitive systems throughout an organisation.

The pharmaceutical company Pfizer employs thousands of scientists and researchers who continually investigate new drug compounds and discover new treatments. But the distribution of scientists and the volumes of material generated make it difficult to build upon the work of others or avoid repeating work performed elsewhere in the organisation. In a bid to address this, a group of research scientists set up a server running Mediawiki, the open source wiki software which runs Wikipedia. In a low-key but steady process, scientists began to post their work on the wiki for others to make use of, forming a 'Pfizerpedia' of leading-edge chemical and pharmaceutical data (see Figure 4.2).[8] Pfizerpedia now has over 2,500 contributors and over 5,000 content pages. In total, there have been over 11 million page views and approximately 100,000 page edits since it was set up.

Figure 4.2 Pfizerpedia main page – an encyclopaedia space

Source: *pfizerpedia/index.php/Pfizerpedia:About*

Importantly, Pfizerpedia does not replace any document management systems within Pfizer but provides a way to easily link into them while maintaining the access controls to the primary, approved documents. This mode of knowledge sharing behaviour is typical of researchers in many scientific or academic domains, and also serves to establish the credit for who discovered something first.

Not all encyclopaedia spaces are about abstract or 'discipline' knowledge though: an Australian state government agency responsible for finances and budgets needed a better solution for updating and distribution of its procedures. PDF and MS-Word files were too cumbersome and information was difficult to find even when one found the right file on the local networked drive. The IT department mentioned the possibility of using the wiki contained within the free Microsoft Sharepoint product, and so a project was initiated to examine the feasibility of using this. It was very important that the procedures, while they should be available to all users and easy to find and update, should only be updated after review by the relevant manager.

The project was almost cancelled as it didn't seem possible at first to guarantee this. Open update of the policies and procedures was viewed as unacceptable and mentioned by all stakeholders as the first objection to wikis. But a solution was found: the articles can be searched for and read by the whole organisation and anyone can make a proposal for a new article or a change to a procedure description within the wiki, but this first remains in a private wiki area. The proposal is then reviewed by the wiki administrator who checks that the relevant manager has endorsed the content and then moves it into the public wiki area. Now all procedures have been transferred to Sharepoint wiki articles.

This use of wiki software to manage procedures is encyclopaedic in nature. The knowledge in this encyclopaedia is proprietary and prescriptive, so must be controlled; at the same time it needs to be available to all staff within the corporate intranet, easy to find and use (with no or limited training required), and easy to improve organically (particularly without further IT intervention being necessary). The wiki meets all these criteria and the organisation is considering other applications in the future. Whether or not universal update will one day be allowed or adopted will depend upon not only the type of document but more decisively upon the organisation's otherwise fairly conservative and careful culture and people's willingness to put themselves 'out there' for possible embarrassment or critique.

Advisory spaces

It is illusory to think that all knowledge can be codified, or that even any significant proportion of what is known can be written down. Tacit knowledge is not only the overwhelming proportion of what is known, but the application of that knowledge via the human mind to problem situations allows problem contextualisation and the development of specific responses. An encyclopaedia can't look at things another way in an instant, or ask the specific questions needed to clarify your question, match it to similar, previous experiences and develop a unique solution which defines and matches the salient characteristics. This will often happen in conversation, in a complex, interactive series of requests and responses, rather than as a piece of customised wisdom handed down from an expert. The quality of this interaction depends upon many factors, not the least of which might be personal chemistry, clarity of expression, patience, the motivation for an expert to help and their available time. But in order to make a start, you need to find the knower and ask the question. Web 2.0 can provide space for the location of advisors and the enactment of advice.

The most obvious Web 2.0 technology for giving advice is the personal blog: by giving experts the ability to blog their thoughts, thereby creating not only a source of knowledge but also the metadata to search upon to locate the knower, firms give them a persistent medium to advise others. Other staff can also ask questions and seek advice from the expert bloggers who have distinctive knowledge.

But the need for particular advice cannot always be anticipated and experts usually need to be found and asked specific questions. Expertise profiling is the construction of metadata describing the skills and experience of individual members in an organisation. People typically build up personal directories of who knows what and organisations will usually create a series of signs (such as job titles and department names) which guide access to knowledgeable people. However, the larger, more anonymous and dispersed an organisation, the more important networks based upon generally available directories become. The incidence of anonymity, specialisation and refinement of knowledge is likely to be higher, making it more difficult to make knowledge visible.

There are a number of possible approaches to providing expertise profiling, location and inter-personal networking (not the least of which is to arrange for people to meet and talk). First, one can provide a personal profile managed and fully customised by the user, with their preferences, links, group memberships, photo, interests, expertise, past projects and special skills (e.g. languages, specialised training) descriptions and so on. The most suitable and sophisticated tool is social networking software like Facebook, MySpace and LinkedIn. All wiki products have a personal page to which one can add material and contact details. Wiki personal pages do not generally have group formation, friends' lists or 'where I am now' type functions, but do have the advantage of being directly linked to any contributions made by a specific user.

Secondly, there is much metadata kept in wikis, blogs and social networking software.

- There is a trace of who has made a particular change to a particular entry. This can be seen as a proxy for expertise and interest in the page topic. One can work out who has actively edited a particular article and sort these by the number or volume of contributions. This will allow others to find an 'expert'.

- There is tag metadata, which classifies a page as belonging to a certain category (which may be personally or organisationally standardised). Those who edit pages in the same (or related) categories might be characterised as a 'community of practice' and provide a 'go to' group for expertise.

- There is Watchlist and RSS metadata, which records which users wish to be notified when a page changes. Those who watch the same page, or pages belonging to the same category, might be characterised as a kind of 'community of interest'.

Thirdly, there is information about people embedded in many places in organisations. There are commercial products which can 'crawl across' all digital information, collect information about personnel from a variety of sources (HR, project documents, e-mails) and construct knowledge profiles based upon recurring and interconnected concepts. These can then be searched for or navigated through.

This metadata about individuals needs to be findable under a variety of circumstances. An enterprise search engine which has indexed documents, application databases and metadata can be used to locate specific instances of what I am looking for (e.g. I am looking for 'safety engineering' and find a document, a report and a person). Alternatively, because metadata has a far lower volume than object data, it can be visually scanned (as when one looks down a thesaurus or table of contents) or manually navigated, if the concepts are linked with each other. The enactment of advice happens subsequently within the threaded discussion pages of wikis and blog discussion groups or even Twitter.

The business case for advisory spaces is that they will:

- make tacit knowledge part of organisational memory and increase yield on that asset;
- increase the rate of legitimate knowledge transfer via conversation and concept building;
- reduce the time taken to reach solutions to problems;
- promulgate desirable in-group characteristics derived from experienced personnel;
- improve transactive memory.

A mining company conducting geophysical exploration in remote parts of the Australian outback was confronted with the problem of having to make decisions on the spot whether or not to survey and sample large areas of rugged land. A boom in the mining industry had meant that those in the field were relatively inexperienced and needed advice in order to avoid expensive and unnecessary sampling and measurement. Experts were not only scarce but the remoteness of the work meant that to send an expert on expedition put them out of reach of others who needed their advice. The firm implemented a mobile wiki system, in which the field workers could look up information about the area, read up on rules of thumb regarding approaches to and methods of surveying, and so on. If there was no relevant information, the field workers entered questions into wiki forums which triggered experts at the head office to consider and respond through the wiki. These responses were all tagged, classified and stored in wiki articles as part of the advice-giving process and so incurred no additional overhead in the response. However, mission-critical organisational memory was accumulated within the wiki for future use by other staff in other remote locations.

Group spaces

A group space emerges through a need to *share* information within or about a more or less persistent collection of people such as a department or a project. There are a variety of flows in such a space, but it is predominantly an information push application. In such a space one might publish information about what a group does, who is in it and how to contact them, what they are responsible for and how to use their services or access procedures relating to their services or such as records management, audit or quality assurance. It might also be a space to post information about group events, announcements affecting the group and so on.

Prior to Web 2.0, internal intranet websites were often created by groups or divisions to document their services, inform about themselves and declare procedures or rules of interaction and so on. Microsoft Sharepoint or a general purpose web content management system can be used to manage the group space. Web 2.0 tools supply similar services. A set of wiki pages can typically be used for these purposes but has the advantage of being immediately updateable and usually universally accessible within a corporate intranet. One often finds within a group someone responsible for information management and distribution. It might be the group's administrator, for example, or a librarian or research assistant. It could be a project manager or a departmental head.

After initial establishment, the pulse of this information is fairly slow: it generally does not change very quickly but there is a background level of comings and goings, new events and so on. Many intranets have been done in a first flush of enthusiasm for telling the world about a group and their mission, vision and values but have withered on the vine. One reason is the difficulty of upgrading conventional intranets or the need for particular skills or intermediation by technical specialists. A more interesting reason is that the publication of this information does not assist one's own productivity in a way which is measurable or, in other words, is not clearly defined as part of a job specification.

Group spaces will:

- promote cognitive and regulative systems;
- provide a space for easy and flexible information externalisation by or for a specific group;
- enhance weak ties and network effects by identifying knowledge hubs, making it many times easier to locate required knowledge;
- enhance socialisation;
- promote positive in-group characteristics;
- promote the use of prescriptive/normative knowledge.

A global building conglomerate announced a strategic decision to adopt uniform use and principles in their SAP Enterprise Resource Planning system: instead of allowing local modifications and rules, all operational accounting principles would come from head office. They established a global project of technical managers, business managers and executives and a video was released by the chief accounting officer explaining the necessity for the project. From a standing start, a global project had to be structured and simultaneously proselytised. The enterprise wiki (available to all staff globally) was used to quickly establish a space for the group, and the space itself became a vehicle for the formation of the group, its personnel, contact details, roles and structure. A home page was established for the overall project, with key headings such as 'Mission', 'Personnel' and 'Timeline' and so on and the key players were invited to contribute material, questions and improvements. Some information, which was clearly indicated, could be edited by any visitor (all of whom were identified) but key documents and plans were kept in controlled document management systems. Managers directed their staff to the site for information. Several problems were identified in this way early in the project by other stakeholders who were not project members.

Collaboration spaces

A collaboration space is one in which knowledge *is created* as part of the interaction between parties who share a common goal or who have a common interest. In such spaces, the rate of information flow and the need for signals are high. Several people work together in a collaboration space to achieve an intersection of common goals or something to a mutual advantage. The outcome of collaboration in the workplace is usually information or a decision. The participants in collaboration can be within the same organisation or organisational sub-group or from different organisations (possibly multiple different organisations). Collaboration requires flexible, integrated tools for conversing synchronously or asynchronously, sharing information and developing ideas and solutions within flexible but reliable security constraints.

Collaboration infrastructure must be open, inclusive, flexible, simple and self-organising, allowing the rapid formation, integration and dissolution of groups for large and small purposes. These groups must be able to build upon the knowledge of previous similar groups and leave their own contribution to organisational memory. Therefore there is also a requirement for persistence, structure and findability through search and navigation. The information collected will include decision, design or judgment outcomes, decision reasoning, challenges and traceability of participants. These tools have a strong social dimension and must support work at a rate and pulse which mirrors the natural ease of face-to-face conversation. They will also support the construction of a consistent organisational identity and set of values through micro-interactions.

Collaboration spaces will:

- accelerate the development and externalisation of emerging knowledge;
- accelerate objectivation and socialisation of new ideas;
- accelerate innovation and knowledge creation;
- accelerate identity formation according to a favourable in-group prototype;
- capture causal reasoning (i.e. why certain decisions were made) as part of organisational memory;
- increase the quality of outcomes by extending the capability to contribute to a wider group;
- build transactive memory systems.

In spite of pre-emptive and scheduled maintenance on large capital equipment, the maintenance and repair section of a large oil and gas organisation was occasionally confronted with major breakdowns. This equipment is extremely costly and every hour in which the machinery is inoperative means substantial losses. The organisation had a number of maintenance management applications (SAP's Maintenance Manager, for example) which contained structured schedules, actions, machine drawings and so on, but post-event analysis was conducted in a sporadic way and the outcomes not used effectively for learning across the many locations where a particular type of machinery might be used.

The department introduced a process of systematic learning to try and learn from each breakdown and then share this across locations. The analysis of each maintenance event went through a set of standard questions about the event, the machine, the cause and the repair done, and it was decided to replicate this in a wiki. First, a set of linked categories (or tags) was set up in a wiki: a MACHINE has DESIGN PARAMETERS which lead to a MONITORING SCHEDULE. A MACHINE can be affected by a MAINTENANCE EVENT which has a CAUSE and a RESOLUTION. A wiki template was established which generated the pages for each category (linked to each other by hyperlink and placed in matching categories) for any new event. E-mail requests, containing links to the pages, were sent to participants to create collaborative answers to each question in the discussion forum associated with each page. From the discussion contributions, a consensual analysis was then created on each main wiki page. This created well-defined, encapsulated objects within the wiki. Pictures, videos and interviews with personnel involved in the event were uploaded into the matching page. Each page was automatically listed on a menu page and on the category listing page, and could also be found via search.

These pages were then used for training new maintenance engineers and mechanics as well as for seeking information for the possible resolution of future breakdowns.

Learning spaces

A learning space is one in which the primary activity of the user is one of deliberate and sustained information *internalisation*. This is to be distinguished from the activity of information retrieval for a specific and immediate purpose. Within a learning space then, information is provided generally to those requiring both instrumental and contextual knowledge: the why, how, where, when, what. A typical learning space might be for a new starter in a job or a graduate trainee, a position in which a large range of information and context must be absorbed and understood.

Modern digital learning environments such as SAP's Knowledge Warehouse provide structured facilities for the storage and presentation of learning materials. In a time of 'on-demand training', classroom sessions become less viable: the workforce is mobile and transient and the subject matter highly variable, rapidly changing and often job-specific. Job roles are associated with a number of competencies and these are certified by the completion of specified courseware, which, being digital, can be called up at any time, from any location and which can independently manage and record the progress and performance of the student. The job roles are remunerated by course completion. Promotion, or even entry, to a job is determined through the profiles managed in human resource management software.

Online learning environments such as Blackboard or WebCT which are targeted at universities are 'pure play' examples of learning spaces. In these systems it is possible to present materials, form and manage study groups, conduct online tests and assignments, record and present marks and interact with students. Learning Objects Inc is the leading provider in this area and provides the Blackboard educational system with wiki's, blogs and podcasts and the literature on the use of Web 2.0 training is extensive and advanced.

A clear distinction needs to be drawn between structured learning (which reflects a management need for control, measurement and labour management) and unstructured learning which is required to make sense of working environments, become a generally useful contributor and contextualise whatever structured learning materials or processes that are present. As a management imperative, structured learning environments have been established to mandate passage through levels of competency, tie these to remuneration, provide audit trails and ensure management is not exposed to accusations of inadequate oversight (for example for not educating staff in occupational health and safety). However, the unstructured sense-making which is required to accelerate structured learning is often not supported and the effect of this on learning effectiveness is generally not measured or appreciated. Further, the dynamics of modern business make just-in-time, socially based learning a more realistic option than rigorous instructional design.[9]

The knowledge transfer paradigm behind this is one of absorption rather than co-creation, handed down by experts, didactic and Cartesian, not constructionist and social. But while useful and probably necessary, this is partially the *illusion of control* and a useful myth to those who prepare reports using key performance indicators: true learning occurs within communities oriented towards the achievement of certain goals. 'Even in the case of ... tailors, where the relation of apprentice to master is specific and explicit, it is not this relationship, but rather the apprentice's relations to other apprentices and even to other masters that organize opportunities to learn.'[10] Educators realise that students who learn in groups are generally more motivated, better prepared and perform better than students who learn alone. Communities in which this learning occurs have certain characteristics which are not considered in and are perhaps antithetical to the structured approach: communities are social networks which are anti-hierarchical, self-selecting and boundary-spanning. The knowledge shared and created within them is tacit and considered more valuable than the explicit 'knowledge' delivered in mere courses. Any system of learning which ignores such communities is missing the point (which is not to say that communities won't form, only that they are doing so in spite of the learning machinery, not because of it).

Therefore a key potential application of Web 2.0 tools is to support the interactive, co-creating, constructivist view of learning by giving opportunities for peer–peer learning support, as well as intervention by experts and mentors when required to offer advice. Seely Brown goes so far as to call this 'Learning 2.0', borrowing heavily from the tools and metaphors of Web 2.0.[11]

A second key role of wikis and blogs is of course the presentation of content, both specific and contextual: other spaces (such as the encyclopaedia space, the group space, the personal space) provide a (variably) coherent source of background information for the overall firm, the specific department in which new starters find themselves, the task one is expected to do, the tasks with which a task interacts (sales produces orders for the manufacturing group …), methods of managing quality, safety and innovation and so on. Individuals often have personal learning preferences: some prefer to read, others to listen, others to watch. Because Web 2.0 tools can accommodate any form of data (video, audio, text, image), they are able to cater to these preferences in regard to speed, repetition and presentation medium.

A third role of wikis in particular is to link to other sources of information beyond the Web 2.0 suites. It is a simple exercise to create a wiki page which contains background information and links specifically for new starting engineers or scientists or electricians and links to procedures, drawings, maps or data stored in other systems.

Therefore learning spaces will:

- accelerate socialisation and sense-making;
- accelerate internalisation of group identity;
- decrease uncertainty by providing contextualising information and the opportunity for confirmation;
- accelerate learning through peer communication.

One of the challenges of establishing a Web 2.0 space such as a wiki is to reduce the barriers to participation to almost zero. The first barrier is that of knowledge of the tool itself: the capabilities of immediate editing, tagging, RSS, linking pages and the page history and so on. A second barrier is to clarify the purpose of the tool itself: what it is good for, how to use it and how not to use it. This training needs to be available at all times, to all participants in all places.

A division of a company that had implemented a division-wide wiki was confronted with this problem, so the wiki administrator created a learning space for the wiki itself. This 'Tutorial Space' consisted of areas on how to use the wiki editor, how to create pages from a set of templates, how to use categories and how to upload and link files and pages. All these were captured as dynamic screen narrations using the (free) Microsoft Media Encoder product. The second key challenge was to demonstrate what a wiki could be used for. The notion of spaces was used: group, encyclopaedia, learning and collaboration were listed as the possibilities and explained using a narrated PowerPoint presentation which included screen shots. There were also links to operational spaces within the wiki which exemplified the characteristics of the space type. A page was set up for suggestions for improvement, discussions, and frequently asked questions (FAQs), which were subscribed to and managed by the wiki administrator. As the wiki administrator said: 'After this learning space was set up, the Wiki was – almost – on auto pilot.'

Partner spaces

Interaction between organisations has increased as fragmentation of value chains and the reduction of transaction costs open up opportunities for outsourcing or partnering. The spaces within which such interactions take place span a wide spectrum from the highly structured and automated to the discursive and innovative. E-marketplaces, for example, are digital transaction spaces where a firm can reverse-auction an order for nails, gear boxes or paper according to specifications and wait on the most favourable offer to be made. When a relationship is established, the firm's ERP suite will automatically order, reconcile and pay for the items. This ghostly, anonymous, semi-autonomous, data-driven and highly structured process is complemented by Web 2.0 software which stands at the opposite end of the automation spectrum: it is personal, unstructured, spontaneous and emergent. The advantage of such software in building partner spaces is for significantly improved collaboration and communication on significant projects, contract handover and maintenance.

Many business processes are not structured or are, at best, semi-structured. In particular knowledge work is non-routine, non-repetitive and has no clear relationships between the volume of inputs and outputs. There is no easy way to measure either productivity or quality, which has led many to the conclusion that the best way to manage knowledge worker productivity is to enhance motivation and commitment: knowledge work is a volunteer, not command and control, activity. Many companies outsource knowledge work to the degree that it does not represent a core competency or where the expertise elsewhere is better than that found in-house. Depending upon the product, I may decide to do my engineering in Germany and my necktie design in Italy as these represent the best expertise available. Business partnerships will form virtual teams of their best experts who work together to develop a new product or a solution to a project requirement.

The space within which business partners interact can be characterised in many ways: it can have collaborative, group or advisory space functions, but it is governed by institutions which make the flows expected of and by participants different to those of intra-organisational interactions. While flows in partner spaces may be friendly or familiar, they differ in the important aspect of being between different legal entities. The threat within partner spaces is that important distinctions between client and vendor become blurred, behaviour becomes overly familiar, and classified information is shared and leaks out of the organisation. There is a need to maintain ownership of intellectual property, to be wary of making legally binding commitments and to not give away confidential information about profit margins in a contract, internal financial positions or worries about competitors. Therefore participants need to be guided in understanding the nature of the flows of information: that perhaps approval is needed before information is volunteered, instructions given or commitments made. It is nevertheless likely that this panoptical, permanent visibility of exchange serves to restrain foolish remarks more than e-mail.

Partner spaces will:

- accelerate diffusion of proprietary knowledge (especially from client to subcontractor);
- accelerate coherent innovation and collaboration;
- accelerate inter-group socialisation and the development of shared cognition and norms;

- provide a 'public' audit trail of statements and commitments;
- support the development of weak ties and transactive memory into otherwise unknown groups.

Social spaces

A social space is one in which the underlying reason for the use of the space and the infrastructure is social rather than instrumental interaction, where a question asked or a detail given is for a personal reason rather than a business one. It is where the weekend football is discussed, the office party or upcoming holidays are planned and even marital or child-raising issues canvassed. This is not to be confused with business events which are socially pleasant (such as a collegial inventory or design meeting), are the social consequences of business events (such as self-esteem or realisation in a job well done) or are sociological by-products (such as changes in pecking order or work relationships) of business conversations. A social space is delineated for social purposes and represents one of the great fears of management: *excessive personal use of company time and resource.*

The importance of these interactions varies between individuals, organisations, industry types and national cultures: group theory has told us that affective engagement is critical in securing organisational commitment and positive organisational behaviour. So a space which provides a forum for the enactment of a felt and socially appropriate need would seem to be a useful addition to the water cooler. The use of social networking software to conduct such interactions is associated with some generational characteristics as well.

The rate of use of such a space in a work context will vary: it may be in bursts, when particular events occur (either in the private or organisational sphere) which one may wish to discuss intensively when they occur. Or there may be a perpetual level of chatter (Twitter ...), as identity externalisation behaviour starts to move to the digital medium. There is of course a concern that staff waste time on trivia and non-business-related activities; however, staff are embedded in a social context of organisational belonging.

Beyond the firewall there are risks in allowing the use of social networking services (such as Facebook or Second Life). Social groups or individuals may appear to represent the company in an official capacity and do so inappropriately or inadvertently disclose information. On the upside, these are growing forums for corporate self-presentation in a 'cool' and contemporary environment.

One subset of social space is the area of maintaining professional links and networks with peers and colleagues beyond the organisation. One might be a member of the Project Management Institute, a university's scientific forum or the network of Chartered Practising Accountants. Not to be seen purely as instrumental and utilitarian, these social spaces are forums for the enactment of the professional self, one dimension of social identity which is a critical motivating factor in the business world.

Viewed from the perspective of control, professional groups maintain professional standards which enable them to fulfil comparable duties across different organisations. Professions among knowledge workers can be seen to provide self-imposed surveillance of norms of productivity and aspiration. A profession constitutes an *internalised panopticon*, by which members of organisations watch themselves for indications of deviance or under-performance and hold themselves accountable to the values generated and maintained by organisations and professions which have evolved to provide intellectual muscle. These institutions are reinforced within social-professional spaces.

So the utility of social spaces is multi-dimensional:

- the development of personal identity in an organisational context;
- a sense of belonging to the company;
- the development of weak ties and enhanced networks;
- the development of transactive memory systems;
- the development of institutions of social and professional (self-)control.

Departure spaces

Standard attrition rates in organisations can be anything from 5 to 20 per cent, and will be exacerbated by the expected departure of long-serving baby boomers, leading to lost productivity, increased downtime, repeated mistakes and relearned lessons. Some proportion or aspect of tacit knowledge stored in the heads of experienced staff needs to be captured, structured and made readily available to others. This will not only mitigate some of the loss of expertise, but will facilitate greater leverage of the knowledge existing within experienced staff. The use of departure spaces for knowledge capture can be triggered by identifiable events, such as retirement, internal transfer, promotion or resignation.

A departure space is specially constructed to capture wisdom, insight and possibly even a sense of history of the firm. Thought needs to be given to the most effective way to do this, both in the capture and the presentation of the material. Wikis provide ideal departure spaces. Knowledge can be captured and loaded in video and audio format using well-structured interviews and conversations as a means to uncover interesting material: this allows the knower to expand upon a topic, tell a story and illustrate with examples at a low personal cost. They should not need to write or prepare anything – the material might be verbal. In this, the effort for the firm is a little higher than the incidental contribution normally expected of wikis as part of workflow, but the knowledge is deep and worthy of respect: this should be demonstrated.

Blogs are also ideal infrastructure for departure spaces and will suit people who choose to share, who are comfortable with these modes and mechanics of communication and will take the effort to do so. It may be more likely that departing staff (especially long-serving employees) are willing to share their knowledge but will not learn or use a technology which requires them to make a substantial effort. Then the structured, recorded interview technique is preferable.

Departure spaces:

- capture deep, distinctive knowledge in an engaging format;
- can capture and share normative knowledge about the history and principles of the firm (rather than pure instrumental knowledge).

An occupational health and safety consulting company was worried that during the boom years of 2007–8, it was losing too many experienced old-timers. The company was very lean, with little or no redundancy or backup in any of its key positions. An enterprise wiki already existed, so it was decided to use a knowledge capture methodology to interview and transcribe job descriptions, roles and insight about a job into wiki pages. A standard set of questions was developed for any exit interview. The recording of responses was done via video recording, transcribed into text and then loaded to a set of wiki templates specifically set up for job positions. In this way, a history of incumbency was developed, a richer picture of the job was put together than is possible in a formal job description, and the in-flight projects and tasks at the time of handover were described for the new person. In a similar vein, a senior geologist at a large mining company resigned quite suddenly for reasons of ill health. He had been instrumental in surveying, assessing and developing mining plans for a large mine and so was interviewed about the mine history and the mining plans based upon the geology. The reasons for the layout of the mine, the sequence of mining and the particularities of the ore were explained on video and loaded to the enterprise wiki. This was important knowledge which was not captured in any accessible documents. Viewing this video became part of the induction process for young geologists sent to the mine.

Another nice example comes from the electricity sector in Australia, which creates high-value, long-lived physical assets. The manager of the substation design division implemented an online wiki forum and established user accounts and Internet connections for retiring engineers. Through the wiki, the engineers were notified about questions pertaining to older substations. When one substation began to subside, it was a retired engineer who could inform the utility through the wiki that a rubbish dump near the site had probably compressed, causing shifts in the earth. Another one was able to tell the younger engineers that the obscure dimensions were due to the fact that the station was built in a time when yards, not metres, were still being used.

Arrival spaces

While formal, packaged training delivers structured and relevant information, pedagogical theory and research into situated learning recognise the importance of sense-making in enhancing and accelerating learning for new arrivals in organisations. Sense-making is the process of developing a hypothesis or model of elements of which one is aware in the environment in order to render them intelligible. Socialisation is the process of identifying and internalising the prevailing norms and institutions. The knowledge required for making sense of an environment is often most invisible to those already within that environment. Large organisations often have their own acronyms, their own vocabularies, idiosyncratic processes, mission statements and histories, not to mention tacit norms and ways of going about things. In complex environments, such as large organisations, sense-making is achieved through the reduction of ambiguity and uncertainty. The formal learning which is often used as a proxy for induction is slower and less effective if there is high environmental uncertainty or causal ambiguity (the reasons why certain things are done in a certain way).

Sense-making is particularly important for new entrants into an organisation or department. Therefore designers of induction programmes need to locate new learners in a context which reduces uncertainty and ambiguity through providing an informational and social context. This leads new learners to clarity and good decisions. Systems supporting this might provide links to e-learning courses, procedures and process maps, forums for discussion with peers, directories for locating and asking mentors and experts, glossaries and so on.

Web 2.0 technology is ideal for this at several levels. The learning and 'sense-making' space can be built very rapidly and naturally through information integration augmented with specific information for a particular role rather than through the construction of new pages especially for that area. While there may be formal learning management systems and standardised content provision, a wiki page may be ideal as the new learners' starting point, with links to other systems and other knowledge (i.e. wiki) pages which contain existing contextualising information, background articles, FAQs and so on. The directory information (who writes which article) is explicitly tracked in wikis and provides expertise and personnel location systems. Forum management can be set up for questions and answers to experts and other new starters (e.g. wiki talk pages, blog comment pages) and new starters can subscribe to feeds of new courses, events and so on through wiki watchlists and RSS. The ontology of linked categories reveals the very conceptual skeleton of the organisation onto which specific events are grafted.

An arrival space will:

- accelerate sense-making and socialisation;
- increase the consistency of normative and cognitive institutions across organizations;
- accelerate in-group prototype absorption by new hires.

The finance department of a large organisation engaged a web programmer to develop a series of induction pages for new starters in the accounting, finance and marketing branch. The programmer spent several months exploring the available company information, designing and reviewing web pages with users, and then making the pages available to users. The programmer also received a maintenance contract to update the pages as information changed. The wiki administrator at the same organisation was asked by one group engaged in scientific analysis to help design an induction site for the 20 new hires they engaged each year. He happened to look over the shoulder of the young programmer, who gave him the web links to the finance induction site, some of which were general purpose. Within two hours, the wiki administrator had set up the framework for an induction space for young scientists: he had established links to human resource pages for employees, conditions of employment, various forms, links to safety guidelines and procedures and how to get IT support. Links to company-wide material such as the annual reports, business overview, mission and values were included, and some organisational videos were uploaded and made available (they were not available on the intranet). Links to pages specifically for help with scientific matters and contact with experts were also included, as well as an FAQ and 'apprentice forum'. Links were also established to some of the finance pages. No further maintenance or help was required – the users and young starters did it themselves.

Programme spaces

If an activity has the word 'programme' in it, then it is probably a candidate for Web 2.0 style applications. A programme is usually a set of related measures or activities with a long-term aim in contrast to a process which is a set of work routines directed towards a specific and more immediate outcome. In business organisations, programmes often involve regular but not highly structured interactive communication with a wide range of stakeholders. It is likely that several sub-spaces will be utilised within a programme space:

- a group space to propagate key messages, methods and information;
- a learning space to teach those participating in the programme;
- a collaboration space to obtain feedback and exchange ideas with potential participants.

Let us examine some examples of programmes and how a programme space might be shaped to accommodate their needs.

A health programme which encourages employees to cycle to work, exercise regularly or eat a healthy diet will typically provide advice, seminars and classes and organise health events for which registration is important. Access to this information must be universal, though at the same time one should avoid e-mail spamming the entire organisation with event information which is of interest to only 20 per cent. Blogs offer an excellent way to do this. They can be made attractive and interesting, they are under the control of the health programme coordinator and require no particular technical skills to set up. Interested staff can subscribe to the blog, can feed back comments and raise issues or questions. They can register for health events via the blog, their name and contact details being automatically left in a return form via their user ID. One can make simple forms in blogs for demographic information which might determine the level of event in which they participate.

A business excellence programme, or a continuous learning programme, involves learning from experience, the application of methods to generate new insights into experience and the propagation of 'best practices' throughout an organisation. A six sigma programme, for example, might have wiki pages devoted to sharing the notion of measurable improvement, links to procedures and tools, training materials and media files with testimonials, and blogs by organisational experts. On completion of projects (after which people are often dispersed) post-project reviews may be initiated and conducted using a collaborative wiki forum. The results might be posted using a wiki template which generates a tagged page of key lessons learned.

Functionally then, the technology meets a perceived need. It is open and flexible and has the ability to be adapted to these requirements. Almost as important are the non-functional requirements: the technology can be understood, established and managed by someone non-technical. There are no web development tools to be mastered. Further, there is no need to seek services such as site set-up or security administration from the IT department, which incurs costs and takes time. Finally, everyone in the organisation will have immediate access.

Programme spaces:

- directly support externalisation and interaction activities;
- create network effects through providing hubs which will enable stakeholders to self-organise;
- accelerate the development of normative systems (e.g. it is a virtue not to drink alcohol to excess).

A large resource development company ran a number of programmes for employee well-being, health and safety. Communications with staff took place via e-mail containing attachments and links, but in order to avoid 'corporate spamming' the e-mail policy restricted the amount of e-mail they could send. The programme personnel, consisting of health professionals and social scientists, cared deeply about their mission and the organisation's members, and were frustrated at their inability to reach and interact with the staff. When a corporate wiki became available, the staff enthusiastically adopted it as a programme space: from their own health programme home page, they were able to create pages for new events, a photo album of events, and a page for health tips and linking to interesting articles, diets and health activities (hiking areas, bicycle rides and so on). General staff members could place suggestions and questions about health matters or simply find out who to contact privately if they needed to. Staff could subscribe to an announcements page on health matters using their RSS readers.

Personal spaces

A personal space is one which is available to an individual to shape, fill and use according to their need but also their taste. Some of this need may be associated with a job role, for example links to applications or information which is used often by the warehouse attendants or accounts clerks. Some might be taste: reshaping the sequence of applications on the screen, changing the default screen background and so on. A personal space would also allow one to have quick personal links for personal purposes – to allow personal banking, or links to newspapers for example – and perhaps even place personal advertisements – the sale of a bicycle or the availability of birthday cake in the staff room. But to be a personal space, it must also provide the capability for self-disclosure or externalisation of information decided upon by the individual: 'this is the sort of person I am, this is what interests me, and these are my beliefs'.

Such spaces exist most decisively within social networking software, whose very purpose is predicated upon the proposition of the importance of self. Wikis also provide a more modest personal page, which can be completely structured according to one's preferences, with the bonus of being linked to by any wiki page where one has made a contribution.

Personal spaces using Web 2.0 tools overlap partially with corporate portal software in which people are allocated a role that defines a screen interface, providing relevant applications by default, standardising the look and feel of the information environment and accelerating learning and sense-making. These portals generally also have segments which allow a user to customise according to their own job peculiarities or preferences. However, although this is described as personalisation, this is only to the extent that the individual has been 'depersonalised' by the standardisation of their needs into a business role.

There are many managerial and social institutions which complicate the definition and successful adoption of personal spaces. Many managers feel this kind of thing has no place in an organisation and is a trivial diversion, and many workers will feel they have no desire to reveal anything about themselves in an environment that they view as adversarial or quite separate from their personal lives. But as we see on the Internet, and in some firms, the evidence of generational change is substantial, even though this may not translate to an organisational context.

In organisational terms the successful implementation of personal spaces implies:

- the enhancement of a sense of belonging to the firm as a desirable in-group;
- the enhancement of transactive memory and weak ties through personal disclosure;
- personal productivity increase through adapting information maps (links, pointers) to one's own needs regarding organisational memory.

Innovation spaces

Innovation within business describes the generation and institutionalisation of both radical and incremental improvements to products, services and processes. The degree of innovation required in a firm varies from industry to industry, but generally globalisation, technology and new forms of organising have led to relentless hyper-competition and assertive customers who demand personalised yet cheaper products in increasingly short cycle times. To achieve this, both radical and incremental process innovations are important in order to generate and then diffuse improvements. Companies need of course to ascertain the degree and type of innovation they require.

The generation of innovation involves:

- an appropriate mindset, leadership and organisational culture which provides leadership and vision towards innovative thinking and a tolerance of failure;
- the involvement of process users and customers as key sources of innovation;
- the use of specific techniques for idea generation and forums for collaborative idea development;
- increasingly the use of co-creation techniques such as outsourcing and crowd-sourcing.

However, an isolated innovation, while useful, is a lost opportunity. The diffusion of innovation is critical to translating ideas and localised improvements to new products, services and generalised business processes. According to Rogers, the seminal writer on diffusion of innovations, this typically requires five stages: gaining knowledge of the innovation, persuasion of its usefulness, deciding to adopt the innovation, its implementation and confirmation of success.[12] Five factors typically affect the rate of adoption of an innovation: perceived advantage, compatibility with current systems, trialability of the innovation, complexity and the observability of the benefits. Transfer of innovation also depends upon the absorptive capacity of the potential adopter, which is a function of the adopter's prior related knowledge, workload and understanding of the reasons for the innovation.

Innovation is therefore supported in a number of ways by a cross section of Web 2.0 technologies. Wiki collaboration spaces and blogs support idea capture, evaluation, progression and portfolio management (idea management). Wiki partner spaces support co-creation with customers and partners in cross-functional idea exchanges. Wiki collaboration spaces support the collaboration between developers of innovative services (new product/service development). Wiki group spaces support the diffusion of the innovation throughout the organisation by providing low-threshold publishing of the advantages of the innovation to persuade of its usefulness, by publishing implementation methods and expertise, by reducing complexity through information sharing and by sharing stories and audio-video about the success. Wikis and blogs can consolidate and publish measures and statistics of improvement and anecdotal feedback about the innovation. The transactive memory systems within Web 2.0 (blogs and wiki contributions) can be used to locate and involve innovative thinkers.

Therefore innovation spaces:

- accelerate the dialectics of objectifying and diffusing new cognitive systems;
- provide a legitimating forum for new concepts;
- support the generation of emerging knowledge;
- provide opportunities for new, positive, in-group prototypes based upon creativity to develop.

The school of management within a business university decided at a strategic planning session that it needed to improve its research output. Teaching was working well at the time but the level of journal publication was low compared to other universities in the sector. This implied that the teaching was in danger of becoming staid and conventional. One group of academics decided to create a more innovative dynamic by instigating a research cluster in their discipline of human resources. The trouble was that it would result in the same people just looking at each other over the staffroom coffee table: to become innovative demanded new ways of thinking and new relationships. So the group established a Google site, which they opened to the world after initial construction. They began by developing some high-level headings such as 'Publications', 'Ideas' and 'Discussion' and placed their personal information there.

Some of this required them to overcome a natural fear of sharing, because for academics, ideas and insights are their personal competitive advantage. They sent links to the site to their colleagues at other universities who began to contribute their own suggestions and ideas. One sub-group of academics had the idea of writing an article within the innovation space to which others were also able to contribute. The result was a space which led to radically new ways of developing ideas, gained new inputs and ideas and accelerated the innovation trajectory of the human resource discipline within the university.

Workflow spaces

It is possible to use Web 2.0 tools to support routine, predefined workflow, not just ad hoc, unstructured knowledge development and exchange. Technology support for workflow is usually associated with database applications, which use structured data to manage the progress of information through the value chain. For example, a sales order might be captured in a software system with all relevant data such as the customer details, the products ordered, delivery requirements and billing arrangements. The sales order information will be updated as the order moves through different statuses such as being accepted, credit checked, products reserved, products sent, products delivered, products returned or partially delivered, invoicing and payment. This space of work is generally routine and measurable and the data elements precise and clearly defined. There are also work products which manage the movement of unstructured information between knowledge workers. Typically this might include reports, proposals or policies which move from statuses such as in edit, under review, submitted for approval and approved for publication.

Decisions to use Web 2.0 tools for workflow should be taken carefully. Although it is clearly possible to predefine and then implement structured data fields within a wiki or blog, or predefine document statuses and notifications that a document requires attention, this moves the undertaking into the realm of standard applications development and diminishes the degree of personal control and self-organising which is typical of – indeed the defining and attractive element of – Web 2.0. There are risks at several levels. There are technical risks, in that Web 2.0 products which implement technologies to structure data and automate processes are more likely to be immature and have gaps than historically proven solutions such as a database management system or a document management system. There may be user acceptance issues: Web 2.0 systems which are structured and predefined are more like standard applications and may be rejected or not fit the business well enough. There are strategic issues: if a structured workflow is implemented, any strategic move towards agility or self-organising within an organisation or with partners may be thwarted.

One final argument against workflow spaces worth mentioning is that if users are confronted with a predefined workflow system that will constrain independent thinking and innovation, then they will generally perceive the system in that way. All the liberating, interactive and community-oriented capabilities of the software will cease to be salient because the tools will be perceived as incorporating a system of management control rather than one of self-organisation.

Nevertheless, workflow space may be appropriate in some instances. Mediawiki, for example, offers the ability to define data fields within a wiki page using or writing PHP extensions. The Watchlist function will allow a person to ensure notifications are sent to required participants. But most likely a wiki or blog is not the right tool to manage workflow. Take the case of a group responsible for multinational marketing operations and contracts negotiations. With marketing staff in Singapore, Hong Kong, New York and Hamburg, these staff managed contracts, delivery schedules, technical projects to test deliverables and customer relationships using telephones and e-mail. Although they dealt with the same client in different countries, staff in Singapore and Hamburg did not know what each other was doing. The group was too small to justify use of a customer relationship management system, but a better solution was needed than e-mail.

A process analysis was done by a consultant using a wiki as the information-sharing base: the key processes were to record and monitor contracts, to record and monitor contacts with clients, and to follow up and record technical projects which were agreed with the clients to examine the quality of the delivered products. Templates were set up to provide pre-structured empty wiki pages for filling out when a new customer, contract or project was added. Using a wiki as a service from a provider such as Google or Socialtext would solve the key problem of immediate information sharing and universality of access.

From the process perspective, the wiki could supply all functions of information edit, tracking, confidentiality, upload of images and so on. But there was a requirement for what was essentially a data structure: as contracts approached renewal, notifications had to be sent to the participants to remind them to follow up with the client and pursue new contracts. This meant that in some cases, information had to be processed at the field level: the wiki technology (at the time) was unable to do this. And in fact, it was decided not to use the wiki after all: the particular 'reminder' function could not be supported and, in general, it was decided that data was not to be managed within wikis because of the need to apply data management disciplines and oversight within the context of the overall systems architecture.

Customer spaces

The spaces established for direct interaction with organisational customers provide a clear case study of the hazards and uncertainties of Web 2.0. These customer spaces will be messy, difficult to regulate and confusing, so it is very important to establish a clear purpose and rules for the space. Is the purpose to conduct co-design of products or discuss product problems? What are the boundaries of the space and what constitutes the rules of play? How do we send someone off? Do we allow any users or only registered customers to play?

If a truly collaborative and creative ambience is to be set up, maintained and taken seriously a company has to take risks. One cannot anticipate what might be said by customers. So responsiveness and the management of the knowledge transformation processes become critical as do the establishment and monitoring of the institutions which form the landscape within the space. Management attention needs to focus on certain institutions: respect for the customer's ideas and opinion, transparency in responses, fast turnaround and high performance, for example.

The cost of establishing customer spaces may be quite high, but one needs to consider the cost of not adopting them. The relentless appearance of consumer and opinion blogs means that there is an occupation of any company's Web 2.0 territory anyway, with the potential to hijack the agenda – and the brand. A well-managed, responsive Web 2.0 customer space is a start.[13]

Microsoft has enjoyed greater success with customer-facing employee blogs than many other leading technology providers. There is a story of how a customer, Ken Dyck, noticed a spelling mistake in a Windows function. Finding it too difficult to go through the process of formally registering the problem, he placed it on his own blog. A Microsoft engineer picked it up and the issue was taken into the Microsoft review process. From within the firm, Microsoft now has dozens of customer-facing blogs run by its own employees, which can be viewed and commented on by the public (as shown in Figure 4.3).

From a firm that has been notorious for operating behind closed doors, Microsoft has evolved towards the benefits of providing and monitoring blogs to reduce mistrust and increase transparency and satisfaction. As George Pulikkathara, a marketing manager at Microsoft, said: 'If Microsoft does not monitor such issues on blogs and forums they lose

Figure 4.3 **The Microsoft blog portal – a customer space**

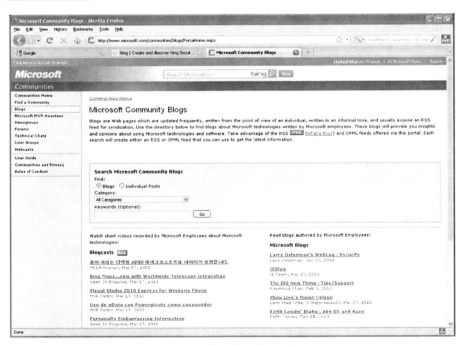

Source: http://www.microsoft.com/communities/blogs/PortalHome.mspx

both the customer and maybe leave some negative PR on the web forever.' Interestingly, this creation of spaces to interact with customers has largely taken place without a unified management strategy in place. There appear to be many schools of thought within the firm, from dread of potential legal consequences to excited anticipation. Pulikkathara also says:

> ... many people at Microsoft recognize that they are in business to serve their customers, and they see that blogs are helping to connect their product teams to customers directly. Effectively blogs are helping Microsoft to redefine their approach to 'customer focus' through one-on-one interaction with customers.

This evolution has changed ways of thinking at the company, making it not only more customer focused, but changing the management insistence on formal lines of communication.

> Not so long ago employees were not encouraged to give out such information, management thinking was that customers should go through the existing channels, plus any value provided by an individual employee should accrue to the company rather than an individual. Blogs are helping employees break out of this large company mentality to help Microsoft become more customer focused.[14]

An excellent example of the establishment of customer space is the way GlaxoSmithKline managed consumer uncertainty about the side effects of its weight-loss drug Alli. It set up the myalli.com community (*http://community.myalli.com/*) which now has over 300,000 members contributing to forums and blogs and which allows the company to provide product information, encourage mutual support and information exchange between customers (such as the formation of weight-loss groups) and above all address concerns in a completely open and transparent way. This has transformed a potential public relations disaster into a thriving marketing campaign.

The elements of space

There are many purposes to which wikis, blogs, social networking and so on can be put. These systems are open, flexible and configurable and therein are concealed great opportunities but also a real problem: how are decision-makers to conceptualise what these tools are good for and ensure they work towards improving outcomes for the firm? In order to frame the toolset we need to first understand the general purpose of the activity and the nature of the interactions which contribute to the purpose. We can then clarify the type of space which is required (is it *collaboration*? is it *publication*? is it *partnering*?) as well as its boundaries. We need to understand the type of knowledge that is to be captured and shared and the flows within the space which contribute to this. The nature of the firm and its various group subcultures will reveal institutions which define the permissible way the flows can move. But unlike structured applications, we need to 'let go' at a far earlier point: we cannot specify in advance what the users will decide is important or what they will choose to say.

Figure 4.4, which demonstrates how these elements hang together, consists of the following elements:

Figure 4.4 The relationship between spaces, flows, information, function and social institutions

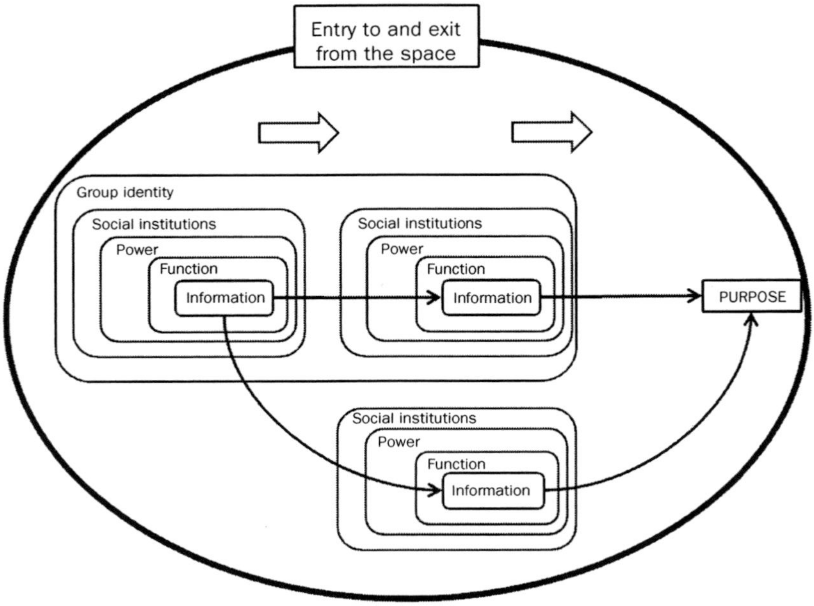

There is a work *purpose* to be fulfilled: this is what is definable by objectives and possibly by measurement.

A certain type of space is appropriate to achieve this type of work purpose. The space is an indicator of the type of game being played and should have clear *boundaries*.

An *entry point* to the space is defined: this is how to join the game and who is allowed to play or watch. This space may include computer-mediated spaces, but also face-to-face meetings and discussions.

Within the space, a consistent *direction of activity* within the space towards the purpose is required and should be observable. These might be articulated in policies and procedures.

Flows are created by the exchange of information using the Web 2.0 tools (among other non-Web 2.0 tools).

With the boundaries of the space, the elements within the space which influence the achievement of the purpose are:

- *information* which is created and changed within the Web 2.0 tools by the use of functional infrastructure;
- *functions* (create a wiki page, a blog entry, a tag) which must be made available to capture, share and change information;
- *social institutions* which guide the entry and update of information – some of these are articulated as usage policies or workflow;
- *power relationships* between participants which constrain action: is use of Web 2.0 mandated, is there social pressure, can one contradict the manager?
- *social identity* which binds participants in the space into groups and which provides a specific set of institutions which guide their use of the functional infrastructure and their creation of information.

Spaces of spaces

Many spaces might be situational and simple: one might only need to establish a single space with a single purpose and a uniform mode of interaction to achieve whatever purpose one has in mind. But a purpose might require multiple different forms of space to achieve its objectives. The Web 2.0 space which emerges to serve this purpose might be complex, have different sub-purposes and activities and so require different forms of sub-space. A space therefore can also consist of other spaces. Each sub-space can be clearly articulated as being served by the components in Figure 4.4: each sub-space might have a different set of flows, functions, information objects, institutions and power relations depending upon the purpose of the sub-space and how it contributes to the purpose of the space of which it is a part.

Take, for example, a large project run by an engineering consulting firm which has an expected duration of a year or more, several engineers assigned to work on it, an audience of interested people (the public and the government) and a set of suppliers. The overall space will be the project space, the purpose of which is to manage information and communications which are needed to complete the project in a timely manner to the satisfaction of the stakeholders. This space is instantiated within company-internal wiki software and consists of a main wiki page containing the project mission and overview and links to the key project sub-spaces: this instantiates the sub-space relationship to the main project space. Tags are established for each sub-space type and pages are tagged with at least the sub-space type. This enables all pages belonging to a space to be identified. The sub-spaces are instantiated in a variety of software products, some of which may not be Web 2.0 tools.

In Figure 4.5 we see how a variety of sub-spaces might be linked within an overall project space.

- A *group space* – here the cornerstone information about the project is kept: the project plan, the key documentation, the procedures, information about the project members, their role in the project, their tasks and assignments and so on. This information is kept within wiki pages.

- A *workflow space* – here the information will be created and itemised which is part of routine engineering and design work. This information must be version-controlled, approved and protected. Only project team members can access or change this. The workflow space is a Lotus Notes area, but the engineering designs are created in CAD packages and stored in a content management system. The workflow space contains information about each design and its status, requests for review and links to the object in the content management system.

Figure 4.5 A project space containing sub-spaces

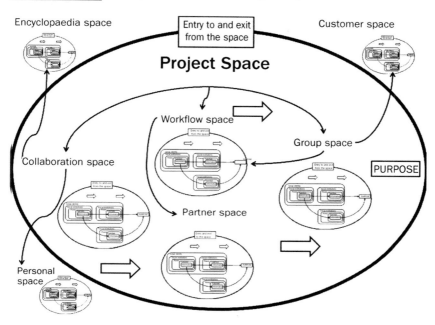

- A *personal space* – this space will probably be outside of the project space. Each project member owns their own personal space, where they manage their personal networks, their personal skills and preference profiles and maybe advertise their mountain bike or the book they are reading. This is managed using WorkBook, the enterprise social networking software.

- A *customer space* – the public are the 'customers' of this project and there is a space for them to ask questions and contribute their concerns and support for the project. This, while open and honest, is managed carefully by the public relations department only. Engineers are not permitted to comment. It is run as a blog on Bloglines, external to the company's system.

- A *partner space* – a space is set up to manage communications with each partner. Only supervisors within the project are allowed to use this, as the communication is restricted to commercial dealings and deliveries. The history of relationships with suppliers is adversarial and hence very formal.

- A *collaboration space* – the engineers within the project need to discuss requirements and design concepts, as well as ask for help regarding materials and structures. This collaboration space is intended for engineers only and is instantiated as a project-specific e-forum.

- An *encyclopaedia space* – the project is a major learning opportunity for the company. As new solutions are created, proposed entries are created in the organisation's encyclopaedia space which are then reviewed and edited by enterprise experts and patrolled by the librarian and for which employees are rewarded for contributing. The encyclopaedia is stored on the corporate enterprise wiki beyond the project space.

While an information system to manage project information communications can be established using a commercial content management system and use 'standard' information and web design principles, the notion of space offered here has some advantages, especially in complex cases. The notion of space involves defining a purpose and the drawing of clear boundaries of flow and participation. The information to be created and used is itemised and the flows which contribute to achieving the purpose of the space can be articulated: it is not just a matter of sitting around at the design meeting asking *what else can we put in here ... where can we put this?*

The identification of information objects and purposeful flows leads to an articulation of the technology functions which create that kind of information and support those kinds of flows. In some cases, the information flows can be managed using wikis, blogs, social networking software, tags and ratings, but in other cases special software might be needed: this can be linked to from within the Web 2.0 technologies. Finally, it allows the expression of the norms and behaviour required and expected of participants in that space, as well as an analysis of whether the social and power institutions will actually support conformational and productive contribution.

Conclusion

One can *almost* paraphrase the cyclist Lance Armstrong at this point: 'Web 2.0 – it's not about the technology.' It is about understanding the information behaviour of people within the workplace. This behaviour is guided by capabilities, intentions and institutions which constitute the infrastructure of specific contexts or spaces. Having established a view of Web 2.0 spaces and flows which encompass work effectiveness, software function, information flow and the institutions which guide information behaviour, in the following two chapters we will drill more deeply and see how to translate this into implementation.

The next chapter takes from the space diagram in Figure 4.4 the constructs of information and functionality to describe a method of designing and establishing spaces which will provide a tool which is *ready at hand* and which will contribute to getting work done. Within a wiki, a blog or a social network site, using text editing, video upload, tagging, templates, RSS and semantic web principles, a system which is 'fit for purpose' can be designed and made available. But this is not enough: the road to technology adoption hell is strewn with tools that are 'fit for purpose'. Somehow people in the workplace must take this tool in hand, as individuals, as workgroups and indeed as entire organisations, and actually start to use the tool in a sustainable way. So we then move to explaining how understanding the other elements in the space (social institutions, power and social identity) can help to manage and steer us towards more successful adoption and use of social software.

Notes

1. Mader (2008: 43).
2. An American Institute of Information Management survey (AIIM – The ECM Association, 2008) found that 70 per cent of businesses required a firm business case for Web 2.0 tools, of whom 77 per cent were unable to find an acceptable level of return.
3. Castells (2000: 441).
4. The notions of spaces and flows are taken from Castells (2000). His focus is on the global component of space and the agglomerations of competencies that evolve to optimise global production. I have adapted this to the local context within firms. For Castells, 'Space is the expression of society ... the material support of time-sharing social practices ... the space of flows is the material organization of time-sharing social practices that work through flows.' For him, there are three layers: 'The first layer, the first material support of the space of flows, is actually constituted by a circuit of electronic exchanges ... The second layer of the space of flows is constituted by its nodes and hubs ... The third important layer of the space refers to the spatial organization of the dominant, managerial elites (rather than classes) that exercise the directional functions around which such space is articulated' (pp. 441ff.). The growing global influence of Web 2.0 tools could very usefully be analysed within this framework.

5. Wittgenstein (1958).
6. Wittgenstein's (1958) notion of the language game is decisive in formulating the space as hosting a kind of game, and I use it because it is so intuitive and easily understood. Although he expressed it cryptically himself, a language game is a set of rule-based communicative interactions which can take place within a form of life. A form of life is 'the system of reference by means of which we interpret an unknown language'. The term 'language game' 'is meant to bring into prominence the fact that the speaking of language is part of an activity, or of a form of life' (p. 23), so a language game defines the allowable moves, what can be said and what nonsense is within the form of life. 'In the practice of the use of language, one party calls out the words, the other acts on them ... I will call these games "language games" ... I shall also call the whole, consisting of language and the actions into which it is woven, the "language game"' (p. 7). A language game constitutes one set of moves one can make, although not all moves in a form of life are to do with language. The meaning of objects is their use in language games: the scope and purpose of the game, that is the *space* within which they are conducted, are therefore what give the equipment, moves and skills of the game their meaning and gives us, as players, the motivation and capability to play. 'We remain unconscious of the prodigious diversity of all the everyday language games because the clothing of our language makes everything alike' (p. 224).
7. In one wiki study, Kosonen and Kianto (2009) explain that a significant hurdle in getting people to use an enterprise wiki was the uncertainty of behaviour: 'However, the culture of openness has its limits and many employees feel uncomfortable about their rights and responsibilities ... It is relatively easy to implement practical guidelines on implementing social software, but it is much more difficult to give guidance and encouragement on how to use it, particularly in the corporate context.' I am hoping that the notion of spaces and flows allows a clearer set of behavioural norms and expectations to be developed, while taking advantage of enterprise-wide availability of information.
8. Available at: *http://www.cipd.co.uk/helpingpeoplelearn/_pfzrpd.htm.*
9. Derven (July 2009).
10. Lave and Wenger (1991: 92).
11. Seely Brown (2002).
12. Rogers (2003).
13. The use of Web 2.0 and the Internet for customer-facing spaces is an area of enormous interest at the moment and exceeds the boundaries of this book. For excellent books in the area see Li and Bernoff (2008), Tapscott and Williams (2006) and Rosen (2009).
14. See: *http://www.backbonemedia.com/blogsurvey/52-Microsoft-case-study.htm* and the article by Efimova and Grudin (2007).

5

From space to function

Having established in the previous chapter the concept of space, we now need to understand how to move from the conceptualisation of the space towards implementing the space's infrastructure such that it is *fit for purpose*. The first three chapters of this book discussed what we need to have considered before we move from space to function. We need to understand:

- the kinds of capabilities which wikis, blogs and social networking possess for processing information and supporting knowledge work;

- the general effects of using these technologies and the establishment of a general level of expectation regarding the advantages and risks of these technologies;

- via the metaphor of space, what kind of activity we are going to be engaged in, so that flows, behaviour and boundaries can be anticipated.

So we now need to move from the idea of the space to a functional system. The following sections should not be seen as a methodology (Chapter 7 on putting it together does this). Rather they should be thought of as establishing a mindset for approaching implementation, that is indeed consistent with the 'softly softly' approach to Web 2.0 that is in fact recommended by many consultants and advisory firms.[1] It provides a framework to help understand where to let go, when to intervene and how to let this happen: how to move from the type of game we are playing and its purpose to the rules of engagement and the type of equipment and infrastructure we will need. We need to:

1. Understand the players and their positions in the overall process of moving from space to function. Who is responsible for design, how should it be managed, how much control is necessary, how much responsible autonomy is possible?

2. Determine the nature of the information to be stored, as information is the vehicle for achieving the purpose of the game (*scoring*). Is it

prescriptive, descriptive, personal or *emerging* knowledge? This will help us decide if Web 2.0 tools are the appropriate tools to manage it. For example, prescriptive knowledge about emergency resuscitation, on which life depends, probably doesn't belong in an open and democratic wiki.

3. Design the specific types of information objects and metadata which will constitute the content of the space: the first component of the game's infrastructure. These will be the objects which constitute wiki pages, blog pages, social networking personal pages, semantic web and social tags, ratings and recommendations and so on.

4. Consider the flows which are required to move the information objects through the space towards achieving the purpose. We then identify the software functionality which will let us process the information in the required way. This is the second component of the game's infrastructure.

Agency and responsibility

Firstly let us look at the question of agency: who should be involved in the movement from space to function, who takes responsibility, who does the work of designing and implementing a Web 2.0 system in the enterprise? Much of the design and take-up of any tool lies in how its usefulness is conceptualised and translated into functional capabilities. The German philosopher Heidegger provides a deep insight into tools and their role in working life, which we shall pursue here.[2]

The value of a tool like a blog or wiki is derived from its role as a piece of functional infrastructure or equipment within a set of activities. The value of such equipment is constituted by its fitness for purpose: it exists in order to perform some function in terms of other related pieces of equipment within that space. Our perception of these tools is at its most immediate in their use, which is paradoxically when we are least aware of them: we are just using them. We simply do things with objects that are ready-at-hand and which, as expected, fulfil their function. We understand the things we do quite naturally and do not carry around explicit instructions to ourselves in our heads. Heidegger employs the example of using a hammer within the set of activities known as carpentry: when we need it, we simply pick the hammer up, grasp and place some nails on wood and use the hammer to drive in the nails. Everything in this process belongs together, it is natural and non-conscious, we are aware of the instruments and the materials, but not in any intellectual or analytical way.[3]

This is how human activity mostly is: experience is immediate and we are one with reality most of the time, we are 'in the world' not just interested bystanders. In an attempt to more genuinely capture our feeling of being alive than preceding centuries of academic analysis, Heidegger's philosophy focuses upon the immediacy of experience and our 'oneness with reality'. Indeed, it is when we analyse and when we seek to articulate being in the world that we induce a kind of blindness, we become oblivious to the obvious. It is not until a work process breaks down in some way because the tools do not suit what we are trying to achieve that we become aware of what the tool is meant to achieve or indeed what sort of tool is needed. We are 'thrown' by an anomaly, a discomfort or something that doesn't work.

In order to be adopted by knowledge workers, tool artefacts, like those of Web 2.0, should be functionally fit for the purposes of the activity that occur within a space. They need to be ready-at-hand, supporting the information flows and game moves that are required in a way that is natural and almost not noticeable: this requires a deep integration of the tools into what we actually do and how we perceive our work. These tools need to be designed and implemented to support activities which are often deeply tacit and themselves performed unconsciously. Remember, knowledge work is non-routine, it does not follow procedures and it is almost impossible to draw a clear connection between effort and value.

Classic systems analysis and design are disciplines generally exercised by others on our behalf. They seek to extract, analyse, decompose and model our activities so that computer functions can be specified, developed and integrated into our working lives, making us more efficient. But this often results in poor outcomes, for all sorts of reasons. In my view, one of the critical differences between standard application software technology and Web 2.0 is the mode in which the transition from space to function can occur. Because Web 2.0 tools are malleable and because they are forgiving, the integration of the tools into working life can emerge. Therefore the first key mode of transition from the open field within a space to a set of functional tools which are ready at hand is *emergence*.

This emergence comes through the iterative application and adaptation of the tools in working life until they cease to break down, where they have reached a state of being ready at hand. Because the tools of Web 2.0 are simple and very often familiar, much of this adaptation and emergence can be decided by the artisan, the knowledge craftsman, the ultimate user of the tool. To be sure, advice is needed and some education will be necessary, in particular in information design. But these tools are used in the home, on the Internet, on personal mobile phones: they are consumer products not intended for specialists. This is the second key mode of moving from space to function with Web 2.0: *autonomy*.

Finally the knowledge craftsman is not working in a Cartesian vacuum: he or she is not in a simple, disinterested cognitive relationship to a piece of knowledge. Craftsmen work with others in a consensually co-created set of meaningful activities: no single craftsman has the privileged blueprint of the right way to do things. The right way to do things is continually reinforced and reinvented by the group and its leaders. So any creation of a set of tools to support this 'right way of doing things' will be done by the group. This is the third key mode of moving from space to function with Web 2.0: it is *collective* and *self-organising*.

The time point at which these characteristics come into effect in Web 2.0 projects will vary widely: some implementations will have their hands held until the last drops of self-determination have been squeezed out by the care and love of a paternal systems analyst. Others might wander aimlessly on the open field, breaking every law of good information management in an orgy of user-driven creativity. And yet others sit still and quiet, fixed to the spot by negligence-induced agoraphobia. In my view, the best default position for the taking of responsibility for design and implementation, the move from space to function, is one of emergence, autonomy and collective action for the users of the space.[4]

This is not to say that advice, training, support and governance are not critical or cannot be called upon when required. Quite the contrary, adequate assistance in how to use the tools and how to apply them to business needs is critical. But the mode of delivering these should be open-ended rather than closed, peer-to-peer rather than instructional, exploratory rather than fully formed, on demand rather than according to a schedule. The building blocks, not completed structures, should be supplied to potential users. Web 2.0 is a *platform*, not a completed structure.

Many potential users of Web 2.0 spaces will need information on how they can use the software, what functions exist, what the pitfalls are and how to ensure the information in the space remains current and useful. It may take a passionate 'champion' within the organisation to promulgate and raise awareness of the tools. And it may well be that a consultant or business analyst observes that their particular business process or area of activity is a perfect candidate for Web 2.0 application and offers help and design guidance. But nonetheless, the factors that drive good design and successful adoption are often not on the functionality radar. Design, particularly of solutions to fuzzy and non-routine knowledge-based interactions, must often emerge in the interaction with the tool, not as the result of an analytical exercise. And adoption of the outcomes of this design may depend upon the very act of being responsible for it rather than it being a particularly good design. Apart from 'ownership' of the outcome, there are other attributes of the social environment which co-evolve with the design activity: leadership and the participation of leaders, direct measurable contribution to business outcomes, trust and the evolution of other social institutions which drive collaborative behaviour.

There is another, more mundane argument for these principles. Even with the best of intentions, IT departments and specialists are simply another complicating factor: wherever it becomes necessary to involve them, there will be delays and miscommunication and a de facto sacrifice of some autonomy and self-determination. In my view, entry by potential users into the Web 2.0 space should be able to be immediate: everything that is necessary to commence active use should, in principle, be present and available.

Finally, the degree of responsible autonomy depends upon the technical capability of the 'designer-user'. Given the current penetration of technology in business, the home and in education, this capability is heightened from two ends: from one end, the tools of the Web 2.0 suite are a consumer item – robust, simple and used at home – so the degree of particular capability required is fairly undemanding. From the other side, the knowledge workforce is filled with people who are IT savvy, who already write complicated spreadsheets, who might have set up an MS-Access database on their laptop, who use Facebook, Wikipedia and comment on online newspapers. Wikis, blogs and social networking present little intellectual or technical difficulty for these people. So the initial challenge comes mainly in the area of information design and information management: being able to conceptualise the information to be produced in a way which will lead to effective, appropriate use of the tools and information which is useful, maintainable, accurate and up to date. How do we achieve this with Web 2.0 tools?

A taxonomy of knowledge in organisations

The knowledge in organisations consists of the mental schemas, mental models, explanatory frameworks and facts which enable us to order the world, predict consequences, take action and learn from the past. This can be classified in a number of ways. The most commonly used classification of knowledge is Michael Polanyi's distinction between explicit and tacit knowledge. Polanyi (1891–1976) was a chemist and philosopher who, although a passionate believer in the superior value of objective positivist science, observed that scientific insight actually emerged in non-logical ways. Background 'tacit' knowledge, belief, gut feeling and commitment were clearly critical in the creation of ideas but had to be distinguished from the validation or test of any resulting scientific theories, which had to be clear, articulated and 'stand on their own feet' as it were. Explicit knowledge is written down or captured in some form, so that it can be easily understood, transferred and shared. Tacit knowledge, however, resides in the mind and describes knowledge which is hard or impossible to express and which reflects expertise, experience and know-how.

All organisations already use technologies to manage information and knowledge exchange and the communication flows which create and share it when it is of commercial or productive utility. In framing Web 2.0 to an organisation, it is critical to be able to explain clearly where it fits within an existing suite of tools and the circumstances in which Web 2.0 may provide a more appropriate instrument. For these purposes we take a fourfold knowledge taxonomy which is differentiated on the basis of what makes sense to information management within organisations. It is not intended to be philosophically watertight but is a heuristic and explanatory taxonomy.[5] The four types of knowledge cover what are called:

- *proprietary prescriptive* – definitive and normative knowledge within a firm;

- *proprietary descriptive* – a particular way of understanding or doing things within the firm;

- *emergent* – knowledge that is within group interactions and which emerges from those interactions;

- *distinctive* – deep expertise, insight and experience.

Knowledge can of course change its type as circumstances change. Distinctive knowledge can be passed verbally from a mentor to members of a group, who discuss it in an online forum as emergent knowledge, apply it and make it part of their approach to work, and upgrade it to proprietary knowledge by placing it in a site wiki. Subsequently the knowledge becomes recognised as 'best practice' and is integrated into the procedures, thereby becoming prescriptive knowledge. Figure 5.1 summarises the knowledge types in this taxonomy and gives examples of types of tools which are appropriate for managing each type.

Figure 5.1 Taxonomy of knowledge types in organisational memory

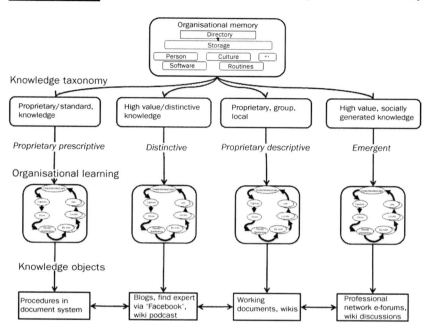

Just because knowledge might be universally accessible on a wiki or a blog (instead of in a paper report or in a corridor) does not automatically make it prescriptive, any more than shouting at a meeting means your point of view becomes law or that it will be taken seriously. Rather it means that the processes of developing and sharing proprietary or prescriptive knowledge are taking place in Web 2.0 tools rather than e-mails or conversations, with the added bonus of being widely available and open to scrutiny. Precisely this openness and scrutiny will of course dissuade some people from using the systems.

Proprietary prescriptive knowledge

Proprietary prescriptive knowledge is definitive and normative. It lays down how staff must perform their tasks, how they must act to achieve their assigned goals, perhaps even how they must treat each other. This knowledge is highly explicit, controlled and generally contained in procedures, manuals, strategies, mission and value statements, organisational role descriptions and so forth. It can also be tacit in the form of unambiguous behavioural norms and values: laughing might be unforgivably frivolous here, a tie unacceptably uptight there. But it is usually explicit and must be externalised and available to all relevant staff at all times, and be unequivocal and definitive in its form of expression. Knowledge is already strongly shared and understood when it reaches this strength of institutionalisation. This knowledge is usually authorised and legitimated through a formal process of consultation or management fiat, approved, signed-off and published so that universal, concurrent access to an authorised version is guaranteed. This knowledge is close to being reified, a concept used often by Marx to describe ideas which, although of human creation, appear to have an existence that is unassailable and non-discussable, independent of criticism: his favourite example was God.

The requirement to develop and manage versions of procedures, gain expert input, receive management authorisation and train users means this is a slower-moving and conservative type of knowledge. There is a need for all employees to understand and follow universal, normative, controlled procedures, not the least argument for which is to mandate safe behaviour and the avoidance of hazards under a duty of care. Therefore document management systems, workflow management systems and formal publication tools such as the intranet are the ideal tools to manage this kind of corporate memory in most large organisations. If wikis and blogs were to be used as publishing vehicles for this information, one would have to restrict the ability to change such prescriptive information to authorised people in order to retain control over content.

The managerial imperative for control and optimisation makes many leaders suspicious of wikis and blogs. Immediate publication by an individual bypasses the normal controls and erroneous information available on a wiki can appear authoritative and prescriptive. This may have serious consequences, not only for productivity but for human life, for example if it is incorrect information about how to dismantle large machinery or construct scaffolding for multi-storey building construction. The question is not only one of control of versions of the 'truth'; in some industries it is one of unambiguously distinguishing normative instruction from other sorts of information. While scepticism and judgment is applied regularly by users in the Internet sphere, this is not necessarily replicated in organisations.

Proprietary descriptive knowledge

Proprietary descriptive knowledge is about how tasks are usually done, can be done or might be done, providing a description of operations and heuristics (or rules of thumb) that have been accumulated within groups over time: 'it's the way we do things here'. Proprietary descriptive knowledge is 'proprietary' in that it represents the organisation's own way of doing things (although similar problems, regulations and environments often lead to similar solutions in other firms of course). It is created as individuals or groups work on projects, operations or allocated tasks and socialise each other into this way. This knowledge is generally stored in people's heads as tacit expertise and know-how, but it can be shared by being written into reports, meeting minutes, e-mails, additions to procedures, notebooks and so on. Generally it is externalised in conversation, through the socialisation of new hires, through meetings or planning events, and so on. This is knowledge of business value, but it is often restricted to specific groups which have a specific responsibility or which are physically separated and develop individual solutions to a common problem over time.

Proprietary descriptive knowledge often remains tacit and manifest in group behaviour but represents the most common type of actionable knowledge found in firms. It can be shared via e-mails, intranet websites and document management systems or contained in archives, but wikis are an ideal tool for managing and sharing this kind of knowledge. Wikis have low barriers to entry, they are easy to use and multiple users have the ability to change content from multiple sites at any time. In some senses it is precisely because they are usually not authorised or signed off that wiki entries are most appropriate for this knowledge. The social and organisational effort in mandating and certifying information is very high and the rate slow; wikis support a pulse and tempo which match everyday work and the contents often describe 'the best way we have of doing things at the moment'.

Wikis, as tools which allow collaboration and synthesis of knowledge under page names and conceptual categories, are ideal tools for the development, location and use of proprietary knowledge. However, there are important issues to consider with the legitimacy of knowledge in organisational wikis and the impact of errors and misinformation.

Distinctive knowledge

Distinctive knowledge is deep knowledge coming from many years of experience and is usually stored in a person's mind only. This knowledge is rare and valuable, but its value is difficult to ascertain and there is no relation between the volume of the knowledge and its value at a certain time. These people are often known as 'the guru' and are valued for their insight. Distinctive knowledge is generally accumulated over a long period of time, either through internalisation and socialisation in a sphere of activity (or within all parts of an organisation over a long period) or through careful in-depth study and research. It is overwhelmingly kept in the heads of individuals; the knowledge is often voluminous and highly tacit, not obvious often to the holder of the knowledge; it is difficult to capture, perhaps even impossible, but will often be accessed when these individuals are questioned to provide solutions or insights, triggering a specific response which can be extremely valuable. This knowledge has not been externalised or objectified to the extent that it is common or assumed by a significant number of others.

Distinctive knowledge is usually shared by the guru via conversation, told in stories or simply by being observed on the job for the way they attack problems and tasks. It is seldom stored, but if it is, it is as organisational case histories and stories. Some of it might be captured as video-recorded oral debriefs, narrated as lectures or by using the experts as trainers. Web 2.0 enters the scene by providing firstly a forum for externalisation: a blog is the ideal vehicle for expressing distinctive knowledge but of course is limited by many personal and social institutions like modesty or shyness or lack of time to become familiar with the technology. The oral debriefs and stories or lectures can be captured, stored, classified and published as learning objects embedded within wiki pages, constituting a kind of organisational 'podcast' or even a corporate 'YouTube'. If transcribed, the recording can be inserted into wiki articles as text which can be upgraded and changed by others in the future. Blogs provide a vehicle for an expert to express and develop an idea which they personally consider important.

Emerging knowledge

Emerging knowledge becomes manifest when articulated and socially constructed by groups. This knowledge is not necessarily in one head but emerges through the combination of knowledge held by different people. At any point in time in an organisation, knowledge is in flux towards becoming proprietary and at the same time is being acted upon. It is an outcome of a social process: several members contribute and through interaction create a way of understanding or doing things, find a solution to a business problem or make things clearer to themselves. Emerging knowledge represents potential rather than discrete information or facts. When three people engage in a discussion of facts A, B and C to create new ideas D and E, the knowledge is a complex, responsive, interactive process rather than an entity.[6] The knowledge is objectivised and legitimated locally when participants agree, but does not have wider ranging authority than their own consensus. The knowledge is developed further into organisational knowledge by being promulgated and accessed through the managerial ability to create forums and opportunities for bringing the right protagonists with diverse knowledge into a single discussion space.

This emerging, often interim and 'becoming' knowledge is created and stored in the minds and conversations of formal and professional networks, tea rooms, pubs and communities of practice. With the crowd-sourcing possibilities of the Internet, it can even take place on specialised websites. Conversations at event reviews, meetings, corridors and break-outs continually create new knowledge while reinforcing the old as they combine in new ways and for new purposes. Electronic forums, e-mail, video and teleconferencing have been key technologies for supporting these interactions between people who are displaced in time and space.

Technologies such as instant chat, video-conferencing or phone are generally transient and unstructured: as the Roman poet Catullus said, it is as written on the air or swift water. E-mail is fragmented and personal. Electronic forums can capture the exchanges but are typically issue-based and prompted by a specific question within an overall community title. Forum technology is generally issue-focused and lacks ways of organising and synthesising the subsequent conversation under a discipline or knowledge category. This also leads to fragmentation and so these tools do not represent a good option for turning emergent knowledge into coherent, proprietary knowledge.

Web 2.0 technologies provide strong solutions to these drawbacks. Blogs and wikis, and at an even faster rate Twitter, are very interactive and conversational. Wikis can link threaded discussions directly to a knowledge page or classify knowledge in conversations according to known categories. Each wiki page has a talk page, which can be in threaded discussion format, which links the conversational contributions to a specific knowledge object (i.e. proprietary knowledge item). The emergence of knowledge is coherent and stored, and the reasoning behind certain solutions can be seen by future users.

Flow and function

Identifying flows

Within the boundaries of a certain space we can enumerate the flows of information that are required to achieve the purpose of the overall activity. In a process of progressive elaboration, we need to specify the activities performed in a particular space. For example, an encyclopaedia space will probably have a set of flows that is fairly constrained and standard: encyclopaedia articles in any organisation or context will have similar flows and layouts, although of course decisions need to be made whether the flows are more like Wikipedia than Britannica. Some spaces may have very few activities: for example, an advisory space via a blog might just be considered a vehicle for publication by a group (similar to an intranet home page) or opining (as performed by an expert blogger), in which case very little analysis is required. But usually even the simplest activity will require some process analysis and the identification of key events. So some kind of group planning session will usually be needed to develop a picture of what activities the wiki, blog or social networking site will need to support. Let's look at a case study of a change implementation team in a large engineering organisation.

A project team is responsible for implementing document and records management standards in a large organisation through the use of a sophisticated document management system (DMS). They are moving through each department, developing DMS folder structures, training people in how to use its functions for storing and versioning controlled documents, answering questions and providing support. Most communication is via e-mail, telephone, training sessions and face-to-face meetings. Progress is slow and cumbersome and they have to repeat themselves for each group. So they decide to move to the wiki for information distribution and interaction. Within a two-hour group meeting, they model these flows on a whiteboard and come up with the following list:

- Publish the standards and obligations of records management.
- Publish the overall schedule, when each group will be committed to become involved.
- List and link to the standard contact details of the support team members.
- For each user group:
    - publish the draft folder structure and invite comment by the user groups;
    - publish the final folder structure for each user group.

- Publish frequently asked questions about the folder structure and invite any further questions.
- Link to the document management system software user guide.
- Resolve questions on software functions.
- Capture the training on video/screen capture and upload here for those unable to attend class sessions.

The project identifies a number of different spaces – advisory, project and collaboration, for example – which will engage different groups of people with different rules and standards. The information contained in the spaces is a mix of prescriptive, descriptive, distinctive and emerging knowledge, and each is handled differently. Prescriptive information is kept on the Internet content management system, the personnel address list of the organisation or within the new document management system, but is linked to directly from the wiki. Descriptive knowledge, such as project-specific dates or hints and tips, is entered directly into wiki pages by the support team. Emerging knowledge is developed and stored via the comments and user forum pages associated with each wiki page. Distinctive knowledge is not stored initially in the wiki – it is kept in the heads of people such as the software experts – but these 'gurus' can be easily found and activated by their subscriptions: users place questions on the 'questions' page which triggers them to provide a response. These responses are given by the experts on the FAQ page: the users are directed to the link on the FAQ page which directly answers their question.

This is a sophisticated communication and collaboration environment but in reality *it took less time to implement than the planning meeting*. The wiki pages were set up with immediate effect, links to the information (much of which already existed but was dispersed throughout the organisation) entered, and other information, previously sent in e-mail attachments, was uploaded. The team filled in the gaps. In future, any phone call or e-mail queries are referred first to these wiki pages. The amount of time needed to explain verbally dropped dramatically, the number of reported errors dropped as people learned to use the systems more quickly, and the reworking of folder structures reduced substantially as more people can comment on them and identify problems prior to implementation.

It was particularly helpful that the wiki is an enterprise system – that is, all staff automatically have full read/write access. All members of the implementation team can update the information for users, and any user can read or comment on the information. All administration is independent of the technical department. All support team members are notified of changes to a wiki page, including new comments, which take place in a threaded forum format associated with each information page.

Identifying functions

After moving from space to a more detailed consideration of the flows within the space, we need to look at which software technology will actually support the flows: the knowledge transformation processes which are the basis for all knowledge work. How will information be created, how will it be shared, how will it be classified, how will the right people be involved in a conversation or discussion, how will people be told something has changed, how will it be legitimated, how will we know it is true? Unfortunately, it is not possible to enumerate here a list of blog, wiki or social networking functions. First, these are extremely numerous and products vary widely in their implementation! Secondly, products are constantly evolving and improving. Finally, products and tools are converging and integrating functions from other 'tool types'. Therefore you will need to refer to the relevant documentation for the product you are considering using.

There is of course a limited set of functions within the technology: how can this set meet every such possible demand? It seems to me to be important at this stage to be able to articulate the requirements for knowledge exchange in simple language which is associated with the specific information. Table 5.1 is an example of the correspondence between the flow and the wiki function, and the knowledge type and the controls, for some of the flows in the above case study.

But not all functions are immediately or intuitively available to users. Here is an example. A department within a large construction company decided to use the corporate wiki, running the Mediawiki software, to distribute information to its members instead of e-mail. This has many advantages: the information is present at once and can be easily updated and even discussed or amended by group members. This information consisted of information about new procedures, meetings and conferences. A notification of new information could easily be placed by the group administrator on the group's RSS feed, which was a special type of page within Mediawiki. In order to be notified, every member of the group had to subscribe to the group's RSS feed, but this subscription had to be initiated by the receiver. How could this be guaranteed? A simple fix was needed: as it happened, a Mediawiki extension called 'Who Is

Table 5.1   From flow to function, knowledge type to location

Information flow	Function	Knowledge type	Storage location
Publish standards	http link from within wiki page	Prescriptive knowledge	Kept in controlled DMS
Publish schedule	Wiki page edit	Proprietary descriptive	Wiki page
List contact details	http link from wiki page Manager form	List is proprietary descriptive Contact details are prescriptive	Wiki page Enterprise address list (Outlook)
User group draft folder structure	Wiki page edit Wiki comment page Watch comment page RSS read of changes	Page is proprietary descriptive Comments are emerging knowledge	Wiki page Wiki comments page Wiki Watchlist
Frequently asked questions	Wiki page edit Wiki comment page Watch comment page RSS read of changes	Page is proprietary descriptive New questions are emerging knowledge Questions sent to team RSS	Wiki page Wiki comments page Wiki Watchlist
Training	Video uploaded to wiki page	Page is proprietary descriptive Training video is prescriptive	Wiki page Non-changeable video file
Locate all project pages	Tags	Proprietary descriptive	Wiki category page

Watching' was found which allowed one person to add other people to a Watchlist for a page, thereby ensuring they were notified when something changed in that page (see Figure 5.2). This was found in Mediawiki's extension list by a member of the IT team and illustrates that although autonomy and self-determination might be crucial for adoption, the technical expertise and advice should never be too far away.

| Figure 5.2 | The Mediawiki extensions list showing 'Who Is Watching' extension |

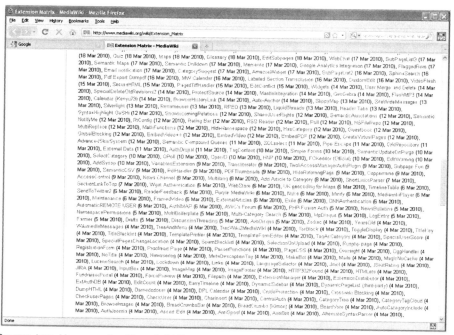

Source: http://www.mediawiki.org/wiki/Extension_Matrix

Information design

Having understood the flows and the knowledge type which will be stored or linked to from within the Web 2.0 tool, we need to define more precisely the information objects and their layout. Information design within Web 2.0 is about establishing a framework so that information will grow in an orderly way, making it simpler for workers to create, update, locate and use. Generally, a group of knowledge workers who need to collaborate or create information will have a language or vocabulary which defines their sphere of activity and provides the conceptual backbone for knowledge to grow within and upon. At certain times (which may or may not be routine or regular) or at points within a process or activity, information is needed or should be added to the space. It is therefore generally necessary at the beginning to decide upon the key information objects around which information will cluster. Some objects might be information products, the outputs of collaboration, such as a monthly progress report, a proposal in response to a request for tenders or a document which analyses a reduction in sales in a certain area. Some objects are persistent information objects which will grow over time: information about complex work machines, business process descriptions, particular customers and so on. Some of these objects will be updated as part of a business process, for example a customer contacts page. Others will not be part of a business process and are updated when new knowledge or experience is accumulated, for example an article about a particular enzyme or geological formation. This is the great advantage of wikis and blogs in particular: they can be about anything.

Another important part of information design is the creation of a set of normative tags, the semantic web, which is the conceptual skeleton of the system of thought within the space. These need to be agreed within the group running the space. They may or may not be linked to each other, but it must be possible to at least tag any of the basic information objects with the appropriate standard term. So, for example, the previous case might have defined the standard tags shown in Table 5.2: DMS Project, DMS Training, DMS Help, DMS User Group Page.

These might be linked together into the category tree shown in Figure 5.3. Someone examining a DMS Help page can navigate via the conceptual category tree of tags contained in the page to the DMS Project Page and of course then, via the tree, to any other page in the project.

Table 5.2 Flows and tags

Information flow	Tag
Publish standards	DMS Help
Publish schedule	DMS Project
List contact details	DMS Project
User group draft folder structure	DMS User Group Page
Frequently asked questions	DMS Help
Training	DMS Training
Locate all project pages	DMS Project

Figure 5.3 A project category tree (semantic web)

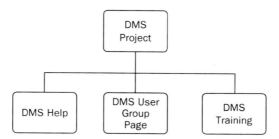

So information design is a very important part of the implementation of a Web 2.0 space. It is critical to consider the types of information object, the level of detail required, the conceptual classification (or tag) for each information object and the relationships between these classifications.

Conclusion

The point of this chapter has been to give an idea of the sorts of decisions that need to be made in moving from the conceptualisation of purpose and space to a set of rules and functions which will allow information to be processed and flow in a way that achieves the purposes of the space but within boundaries and limits. Wittgenstein's 'game' metaphor is particularly useful in this endeavour: what constitutes the boundary of the space, the goalposts, the ball and the passing sequences? What is a good passage of play and what is not? What is a move at all in the game and what is not? And the games in Web 2.0 spaces can be adapted by the players as circumstances change.

Of course there are many methods for systems analysis and information design which may serve the same purpose as the idea of space and the game played within it. But it seems to me that with social software the objective must be not only to provide software function which is familiar and easy to use, but also methods and frameworks for design and implementation which are already partially embedded in the understanding of the participants. I hope *space*, *flow* and the paraphernalia of the *game* might provide some of that liberation.

Notes

1. For example, Gartner, McKinsey, Forrester.
2. This conceptualisation of tools is taken from Heidegger (1962: 96ff.).
3. This is well put by Michael Polanyi: 'When we use a hammer to drive a nail, we attend to both nail and hammer, but in a different way. [...] The difference may be stated by saying that the latter (i.e. hammers) are not like the nail, objects of our attention, but instruments of it. They are not watched in themselves; we watch something else while keeping intensely aware of them. I have a subsidiary awareness of the feeling in the palm of my hand which is merged into my focal awareness of my driving the nail' (Polanyi, 1973: 55).
4. This is not as scary as it sounds. Many studies have shown the measurable productivity benefits to be gained from full, democratic participation in work process design, e.g. Coch and French's (1948) classic study of clothing manufacture.
5. This taxonomy is adapted from Bryan and Joyce (2007).
6. See Stacey (2001) for a systematic treatment of the emergence of knowledge and the dynamics of such behaviour in organisations.

6

From function to use

The notions of spaces, flows and games are heuristic objects which help make a transition from general assertions about how useful wikis and blogs are to specific functional capabilities which can make a contribution to business. Spaces and flows do this by providing an explanatory vehicle to managers which helps them conceptualise how a particular group can conduct a certain type of activity more effectively using Web 2.0 technologies. But projects which introduce new technologies, irrespective of their usability and usefulness, usually fail to meet expectations. Failure statistics from many sources underpin a general litany of disappointment and methodologies to ameliorate poor performance and critical success factors are legion – *and yet projects continue to disappoint*. However, change and improvement in certain dimensions of performance are critical to business survival – and technology is at the core of many such changes.

If we continue to approach such projects in the same way, the same kinds of problems will lead to disillusionment. Therefore I'm suggesting here that we look at this particular species of technology using a different theoretical lens. In Plato's words, perhaps there can be no end to the 'troubles' of failed and 'challenging' projects, until managers become philosophers and philosophers become managers. In other words, ways of framing the implementation of Web 2.0 tools are required that are richer and more insightful than day-to-day operational logic and to this end, there is 'nothing as practical as a good theory'.

This approach is depicted in Figure 6.1, which shows how business systems succeed only insofar as they are supported by social systems of organisational memory, knowledge building, identity formation, the use of transactive 'knowledge' directories and so on. These alternative perspectives are important because they describe the interpersonal and informational systems which drive the effective adoption of knowledge-based tools such as those contained in Web 2.0. In the diagram, we see that it is business systems and work routines that deliver outcomes which

Figure 6.1   The social systems supporting Web 2.0 tool use

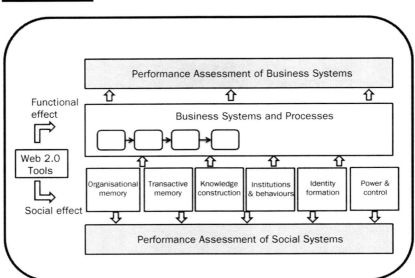

are assessed for high or low performance: the number of goods produced per worker, the rate of rework or the responsiveness to customer problems. But without an organisational memory which can be built and reused by staff, and without staff who identify in some way with the work that is done, those performance criteria will either decline or not be sustainable at high levels. Corporate knowledge building, the formation of identity and the exercise of power constitute other, less visible, systems within the overall ecology of the workplace. These systems must also be maintained at a high level of performance.

At the same time, being largely social and institutional, these are the elements which are difficult to change and which only change relatively slowly and under certain conditions. The creation or changing of social habits and ideas requires a kind of reprogramming of what is shared rather than what is personal: a long, fragile and complex process. This is one of the reasons that technology often disappoints in the short term but exceeds expectations in the longer term: operational benefits begin to become visible when underlying social systems have co-evolved with the technology and other changes in the environment.

Space and flow constitute the point of departure in trying to make Web 2.0 work: a space, once defined, articulates an institutional topology which users and managers will navigate to achieve organisational, group and individual objectives. So beyond the notion of space, we need mechanisms to understand what is happening within the space and how to optimise the flows between the players. This chapter therefore describes some appropriate social-theoretical perspectives which can be used to understand the challenges of implementing Web 2.0 facilities in social terms and how to make them work in business organisations.

We are taking the view here that Web 2.0 is knowledge technology: it supports the creation, sharing, storing and classification of information. But in contrast to current methods of knowledge creation such as e-mail, teleconferences, conversation and face-to-face meetings, it is hoped that strategically implemented Web 2.0 will make information exchange persistent, structured, asynchronous and available to the entire organisation as part of a series of natural flows and interactions between intelligent people. This results in *organisational memory*, the shared, more-or-less coherent, firm-wide knowledge of how to get things done. It is axiomatic that the quality and accessibility of this corporate knowledge are key determinants of organisational performance and competitive advantage. So this chapter deals with the application of Web 2.0 in the context of corporate knowledge.

We start by asking what exactly is organisational memory and how we can describe the types of knowledge it 'contains', as the type of knowledge which is involved will determine the most appropriate storage technologies to be used to manage it. Then we move to how this knowledge is created, shared, found and used using theories of *social constructivism* and *transactive memory systems*: to be fully effective, Web 2.0 function must support the social processes employed by people in everyday interactions to build and share knowledge and must provide capabilities for maintaining, finding, classifying and retrieving knowledge.

If theories of knowledge tell us why and how the Web 2.0 tools build organisational memory and support knowledge-building processes, we then need to understand how to motivate people to adopt these technologies. We use *institutional theory* to understand what norms drive people to contribute to organisational memory: ways of organising work, personal networks and supporting technologies already exist in organisations for creating and sharing information, so why would anyone migrate to methods which benefit the organisation but not necessarily the individual? In order to understand how to move people to change habits, overcome institutional inertia and understand the impact of these tools on power relationships and managerial control, we draw on *critical theory*. We conclude by using *identity theory* to understand what concepts of self and group prototypes might drive people to participate in organisational memory processes using these tools. In the following chapter we combine these perspectives with spaces and flows to arrive at a method for assessing, designing and implementing Web 2.0 in business organisations.

Organisational memory: storing knowledge

Organisational memory is a pivotal notion in the use of Web 2.0 in the enterprise and provides a key metaphor for conceptualising its usefulness. Organisations are social groups which absorb and develop systems of knowledge to the extent that this knowledge serves their purposes. They can be understood as information processing systems within which collective interpretations exist and emerge. Organisations, so perceived, have a particular *memory*, which is the knowledge of how to do things, how to approach problems and issues, how to treat each other, who to obey and who to command, who is the expert and so on. The instrumental, or operational, view of organisational memory is that it is that knowledge which can be brought to bear on present business activities. It is hoped of course that this will lead to higher levels of organisational performance because 'lessons learned' and solid experience will be retrieved and applied, but this is not necessarily the case. Some memories may inhibit higher performance: reluctant attitudes to new ways of doing things because of previous pain, for example, or a lack of concepts to frame innovations (the 'not invented here syndrome', 'core rigidities', 'defensive reasoning routines' to name few from the academic literature). There is another view of organisational memory which says it is the collective system of sense-making, the knowledge which gives structure and meaning to events and allows shared interpretation to emerge within organisations: it is the system of shared understandings which constitutes organisational effectiveness and cohesion, insofar as the organisation is effective or cohesive of course.[1]

Learning takes place when individuals in the organisation experience a problematic situation or task and resolve it on behalf of the organisation. It becomes *organisational learning* when that resolution changes the way members of the organisation frame and approach that situation in future, either through being told or shown the new way or through it being captured in some documentation, procedure or schema. It is an activity in which processes such as situation interpretation, innovation, information capture, information storage, and search and retrieval move knowledge from a person's isolated memory to make it accessible to others in the collective.[2]

The performance of business activities may have organisational learning as a by-product, when people learn and become accessible as experts for example, or it can be supported by explicit management techniques such as reflection in action or post-project review. Learning might be a straightforward incremental improvement or adaptation (single-loop learning), or it may involve changes to fundamental principles and sense-making perceptions (double-loop learning).[3] These knowledge processes can be facilitated through personnel being given capabilities (technology, training, time and space) and motivation (recognition, self-fulfilment, rewards) to contribute knowledge to the organisation as a whole.

Figure 6.2 shows how the organisational learning processes fill and use organisational memory. After a problem is solved, a new method developed or a new standard established through learning on the job or innovation, new knowledge is *created*. This is then *captured* in some form (perhaps only in a person's head). It may then be *stored* in some repository (which is more appropriate) or simply noted in an organisational directory that a certain person is now an expert on that particular problem. The knowledge will be *classified* in some way so that

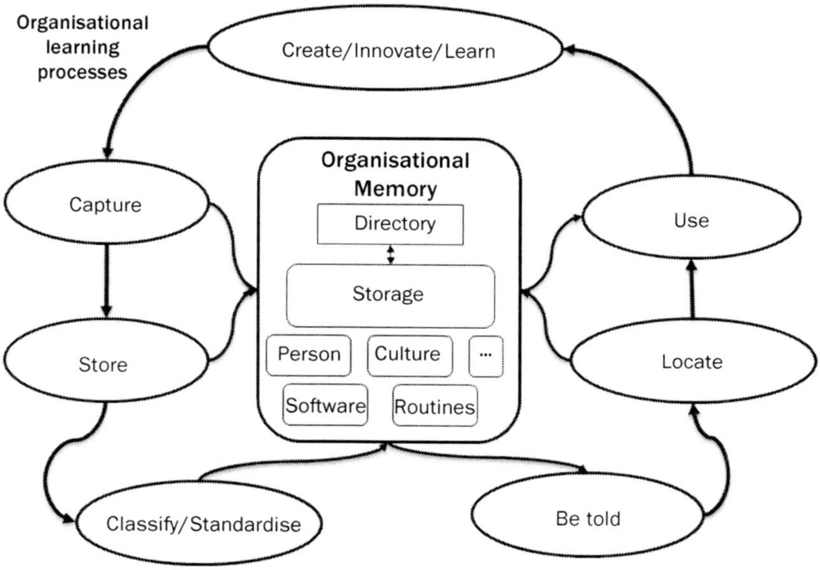

Figure 6.2 Organisational memory and organisational learning procedures

it can be located using standard organisational concepts or words, and is made visible to those who need it by them *being told* about it or being *located* at the time it might be needed via search. This knowledge can then be *used* and, sometimes, adapted and *placed back* into organisational memory. These learning processes can be described in many ways, but the model in Figure 6.2 serves as a simple approximation of how organisational learning might take place.

Organisational memory, the store of organisational knowledge, is said to reside in several different types of physical repository.[4] Each repository has particular characteristics and advantages and can play different roles in the production process and therefore contribute in different ways over time to improving the competitive position and effectiveness of the firm. For example, a database is a good organisational memory repository to serve highly structured, routine processes, a person's head is a good repository for stories of experiences in complex situations, and an intranet is a good repository for organisational documents which need to be shared across distance and time zones. Typical repositories used to store organisational memory are the heads of individual experts and managers, technology and software systems, procedures and routines, organisational culture and behavioural norms and the design and layout of the workplace, such as buildings and signs, and job roles and organisational structure diagrams.

Positive correlations have been found between strong organisational memory and organisational performance,[5] organisational learning,[6] improvisation[7] and speed of decision-making.[8] Quite simply and intuitively, an organisation which can make available to others what one person or group has discovered or resolved will not repeat the mistakes of the past – at least not as much. This 'learning curve' is widely accepted as a key factor in efficiency gain, not just from cumulative production experience, but 'from the application of expertise culled from sources other than experience in producing the affected product'.[9] Organisational memory can improve productivity by improving routine work, developing better control over production, logistics and service delivery, and identifying the best skills for a job.[10]

Organisational memory is an emergent property of organisations and can be consistent and coherent or fragmented and contradictory. Generally, management will seek to standardise and develop practices to achieve the former state, so organisational memory is a kind of permanent 'work in progress'. It is the appearance of routine over time that distinguishes the organisation from other social collectives. It forms a sequence of cognitive, normative and regulative patterns in which members partake. It is cognitive, in that it is the way the world is *perceived and ordered*; it is normative, in that it provides the standards and values that reflect this is how things *should* be done; it is regulative, in that it describes the *routines and practices* which the firm has evolved in order to get things done. These are often formulated in a private organisational language and in proprietary sequences of activities and recognisable patterns of behaviour. Organisational memory is what makes those patterns special and distinctive, and worth utilising in contrast to other collectives.

Organisations offer the opportunity to participate in the memory. This participation is mediated through capabilities to draw down from and to contribute to the common stock of knowledge. We talk to our colleagues, we use standard procedures stored in document management systems, we update the databases of ERP systems, and we ask the experts and managers for advice. Structurally, the memory can be fragmented, for example when there are many different ways of doing things and we get different answers depending upon who we ask. Or it can be monolithic, when there is great regularity, control and consistency. The capabilities for maintaining and using organisational memory can be informal or formal.

Web 2.0 offers enhanced capabilities to manage and develop organisational memory. These technologies provide easily searchable storage capabilities which are available to the entire organisation and functions which support contribution and application. They support the movement of memory which would otherwise remain isolated and local, from personal minds and small groups to entire organisations.

Figure 6.3 shows where various Web 2.0 technologies might connect into the processes of organisational learning which supply and utilise organisational memory. In the figure we see that all the organisational learning processes of capturing, creating, classifying and so on have some technology support through a Web 2.0 tool of some kind. Some of these tools, like wikis and blogs, might also be repositories as they actually store information, videos and images, but it is their software function which provides an entry point to contribute to or use the memory. Because of this, the system of organisational learning is continuous and uninterrupted. But we need to understand the storage repositories in which the knowledge is kept and the directories which enable us to find that knowledge. So in the next section we proceed to look at the directories which let us order and find the relevant piece of memory when we need it and the processes by which those directories are maintained and used.

Figure 6.3 Knowledge processes and Web 2.0 tools

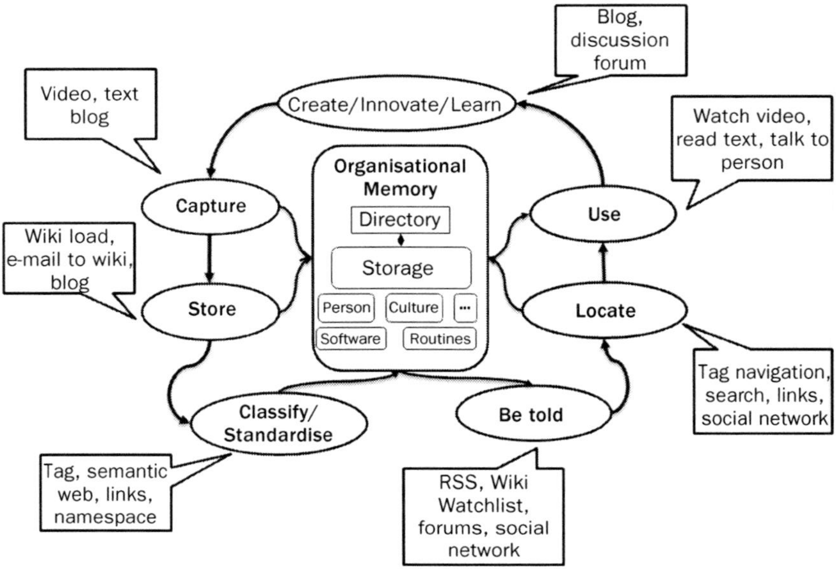

Transactive memory systems: finding and retrieving knowledge

Now we move our attention to understanding the signposts which guide members of firms to the content they need to get work done. It's all very well to have lots of organisational memory, but how will you find it when you need it? Any system of signposts needs structure and maintenance and must be accessible across the organisation. A psychological theory which deals directly with the concept of 'knowledge signposts' (or directories) and which is highly applicable to understanding how to manage the directories of organisational memory is Daniel M. Wegner's theory of Transactive Memory.[11]

While originating in research into studies of dyads and small groups, the concept of Transactive Memory Systems (TMS) has been extended to describe knowledge storage and retrieval in organisations. TMS describe the processes which are employed to maintain and use directories of knowledge within groups. Through knowledge specialisation, members of a group develop specific responsibilities for expertise. When knowledge enters the group it is *allocated* to the responsible member. In the process, it is encoded by group members into their personal *directory* structures that *this* expert has *that* piece of knowledge, and they subsequently *retrieve* that piece of knowledge from the expert responsible for that general area when they need it.

In small groups, like families or couples, responsibility for cooking or repairs might be divided up between husband and wife (respectively): they specialise and information gets allocated to the responsible person (new recipes, a window not closing, a new kind of putty). When a child cooks, they ask the mother for 'that new recipe' or where the pots are kept. The members of the group get to know who knows what and manage things accordingly. In larger commercial organisations, similar processes occur, although they might be more complicated and the media upon which transactive directories are stored might be a loosely linked network of personal brains, paper, organisation structures and roles, and electronic databases. These media are *maintained* and *used* via a variety of modalities: chatting, updating personal pages or going to meetings for example. The key point here is that a well-developed TMS turns personal or local memory into organisational memory by making it findable, available and retrievable. And this is done without having to capture the actual content in some explicit, shareable medium or technology such as a database or 'lessons learned' report.

TMS describes *social cognition* which is driven by information about the characteristics of group knowledge and the associated processes of maintaining and using that *metadata* to retrieve and store knowledge. It separates the knowledge which group members have about a particular area from knowledge that groups members have about each other. It describes how a group exchanges information about the specific expertise of each member, thereby facilitating access to expertise when it is needed. A TMS is characterised by specialisation of expertise, which develops as members of the group differentiate themselves from each other through capability or particular interest. The respective specialists need to be credible in order for the directory to be of any use and the processes which then lead to the knowledge in the group actually being used need to operate in a coordinated fashion.

TMS can be seen as a key component of 'group mind' and explains how a group can appear to have a collective consciousness without needing to fall back on telepathy or metaphysics to explain the apparent single-mindedness.[12] The purposeful and coordinated nature of groups and the patterns and regularities in task execution convey the impression that there is a single organism at work. The information-based TMS approach goes some way to explaining the coordination and consistency in group function while remaining solidly materialist. Metadata about group knowledge is collected in group processes (where information is exchanged) and this data is maintained in the personal minds and artefacts of group members. The social nature of these processes means that there will be a general consistency in the content of directories ('We all know that Fred is the expert on project management'), while leaving room for personal preferences ('I find Fred difficult to deal with so I won't ask him for advice').

The research shows that a well-developed TMS can decisively improve group capability. In one experiment, a TMS developed through group training improved group performance far more than individual training with team-building exercises – good news for those who hate group hugs and just want to do a good job.[13] There is a strong positive correlation between strength of TMS and knowledge-worker team performance.[14] Group performance is believed to reflect the ability of a group with a well functioning TMS to store and recall more knowledge than any individual,[15] to use the knowledge of others better,[16] to match problems with the person most likely to resolve them,[17] to coordinate activities more effectively because of better anticipation of the capabilities of others and appropriate allocation of roles and tasks,[18] to make better decisions through the recognition and evaluation of the expertise contributed by group members,[19] and to reduce cognitive load when others act as external memory stores and allow greater specialisation.[20] TMS is a theory of group activity which focuses upon *cognition* and the transfer of information rather than culture, communication or motivation.

Transactive directories are maintained automatically or as a by-product of online activity in Web 2.0 and are searchable and navigable electronically. One can hyperlink from an author to a personal contact page or vice versa. Wiki entries are searchable based upon the knowledge they contain or can be found by navigating conceptual (or 'category') hierarchies. Each editorial change to a Wiki page is linked to a specific, identifiable editor. That editor may have a personal page describing their contact details, role, preferences and interests, and prior experience. The page may show links to other 'friends' with similar interests and knowledge.[21] So the directory maintenance functions and the information retrieval functions are well supported. Wiki and blog pages can be made RSS capable or 'watched' for changes, so that individuals or groups can subscribe and be notified of new knowledge entering the system. This of course is direct support of the allocation process of TMS.

Transactive memory systems are strongly supported by Web 2.0 technologies through their directory and link capabilities and the fact that a wide range of information is being digitised and made searchable. Figure 6.4 shows the interaction between the TMS processes and various Web 2.0 capabilities and how the key transactive processes of (1) building and maintaining a directory of group knowledge, (2) distributing new knowledge to the responsible repository and then (3) retrieving the knowledge when it is required by using the directory can be supported by Web 2.0 tools.

It's useful to divide transactive directories of organisational memory into two parts: a part which tells you where things *should be* and a part that tells you were something *actually is*. The first is the normative part and the second is an instance part. The *normative part* is prescriptive metadata, the formal model (or 'ontology') of the organisation describing what counts as knowledge. You would find these official signposts in glossaries, thesauri, keywords, procedures, role statements and departmental responsibilities and also in the language that some groups have developed to manage their work. Of course those groups will have brought such words into the organisation as part of their professional training as well: accounting or engineering concepts for example. This is a model of how management and experts wish the organisation to be. It facilitates a coherent understanding of the organisation as a whole: it is its semantic web.

Figure 6.4   Transactive memory systems and Web 2.0 tools

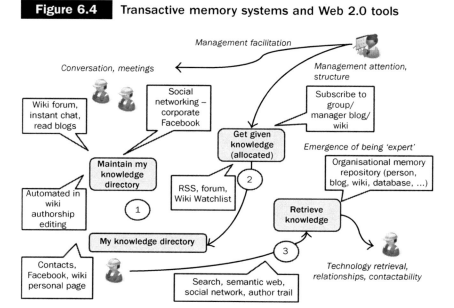

The *instance part* is specific knowledge gained as work is done, is particular, sometimes chaotic, and is not necessarily categorised or even registered using standard organisational nomenclature. So where the normative part of an organisational transactive directory will tell you what a project is and where (you ought to able) to find project knowledge, the instance part will tell you where to find the information you need about 'Project 4711' (which was managed by Fred who is now working in the Human Resource Department). Without systems which support the development of normative and instance transactive directory entries, the power of the information and knowledge embedded in your Web 2.0 tools is unlikely to gain full traction and organisational memory will remain hidden.

Figure 6.5 shows the transactive paths that may be followed in organisations through the use of formal and instance transactive metadata. We see that:

1. The concepts and facts that describe cognitive and routine systems are grouped into domains, so a set of concepts like machine, maintenance schedule, tools and repair can be seen as being in the 'Maintenance' domain.

Figure 6.5　Transactive memory in organisations

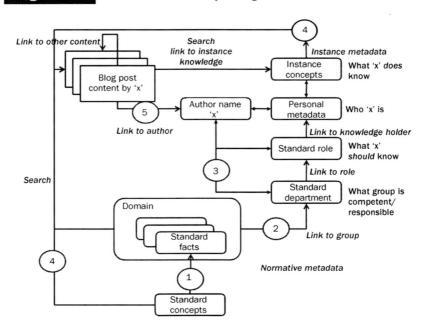

2. These domains are the responsibility of departments and roles, so the maintenance department is the place to go for information about the maintenance schedule.

3. These standard departments and roles can be used as links to find knowledge holders. Within the maintenance department there is a group responsible for scheduling and they have a manager, Fred, who can be approached for information or further 'directing'.

4. The use of a standard concept, like 'maintenance schedule', to search through networked drives or the document management system, or simply by asking, leads us to specific content about maintenance schedules for machine ABC or factory XYZ.

5. The creation of instance content, for example who has engaged in specific maintenance activities or who developed a specific maintenance schedule, creates metadata pointing to the author, repository or other relevant knowledge repositories, whether it is a wiki, a blog or a person.

Transactive memory has many positive implications for organisations other than the obvious informational and cognitive ones. Further to the research in small groups, a well-structured, maintained and supported TMS will function to reduce *social uncertainty* in organisations. It will do this prior to and during situations characterised by change or disruption. An effective TMS will give confidence and capability to staff in an organisation to achieve the level of certainty they require when they require it.

In summary, TMS is not only a descriptive theory explaining group cognition; it also points a path towards performance enhancement. The storage and maintenance of metadata about group expertise is an effective method of managing specialisation and division of labour, storage and retrieval, and task allocation. Further, TMS processes are social activities which can build useful connections between people, increasing group coherence and integration.

Social constructivism: building knowledge

Having looked at the key types knowledge that exist in organisations and the directories that point to them, it makes sense at this stage to outline how this knowledge is created, accepted, shared and reinforced because this sets the scene for what kinds of technology tools can support what we call 'knowledge transformation processes' in organisations. The knowledge transformation processes around receiving orders (proprietary prescriptive, normative) is quite different to a sales offensive (proprietary descriptive) or solving problems with deep-sea drilling equipment (emergent) or assessing why a power substation built thirty years ago is subsiding (distinctive, original expert) and result in a different set of knowledge outcomes.

The theoretical base we use to understand knowledge is called *social constructivism*, or the 'sociology of knowledge'. It characterises knowledge as the sets of beliefs or mental models people use to interpret actions and events in the world. This way of looking at knowledge contrasts with *empiricism*, a philosophy of knowledge which tells us the way we see the world is pretty much how it actually is. Social constructivism tells us we build knowledge as ways of understanding the world, and that these ways of understanding are a subset of how the world could be understood. When we consider the wide diversity of world views, this seems a very sensible idea, if a little more complicated. A shaman's knowledge of the spirit world allows him to interpret naturally occurring phenomena as portents or signs. Moral knowledge allows us to assess behaviour as right or wrong, criminal, unethical or fair. Knowledge of invoice processing allows a programmer to generate automatic reminder letters. Social constructivism does not judge whether or not there are actually such things as 'spirits' or 'right and wrong' or even 'invoices'. 'What is 'real' to a Tibetan monk may not be 'real' to an American businessman (or even a Trappist for that matter).

This reality is constructed by individuals within social groups over periods of time, whether Pathan tribesmen or Wall Street bankers, mostly in conversation and through social rituals, which are ways of bridging the gaps between the personal consciousnesses of different individuals. Language, artefacts and symbolic behaviour are the shared, physical embodiment of a group's collective, permanent solutions to its ongoing problems. These solutions persist in groups as interpretive structures which are continually articulated, enacted and thereby re-created in processes of social behaviour.

The process model in Figure 6.6 seeks to capture the core elements of social constructivism. The terms in the boxes in the model are those used by seminal writers on social constructivism, Peter Berger and Thomas Luckmann, while those outside each box are our translation into more everyday expressions.[22] We explain these in more detail below.

What an individual knows is (1) personal knowledge, consisting of 'typificatory schemes', which are the frameworks used to interpret and

Figure 6.6	The knowledge transformation processes in social constructivism

Source: Jackson and Klobas (2008).

make sense of the actions of other people and the physical world (writers like Peter Senge and Chris Argyris call these 'mental models' or 'theories in use') and recipe knowledge, which is 'know-how', or 'knowledge limited to pragmatic competence in routine performance'. This personal knowledge is constructed through a number of processes. One can absorb knowledge in a process of (2) internalisation, which describes the absorption of knowledge by a recipient. Or one can (3) create new knowledge by combining existing knowledge in one's own head or through habituation (the development of knowledge into useful routines through repetition of work or tasks) and transformations (radically changing subjective reality and creating new ideas). The new knowledge one absorbs or creates can be (4) externalised, which is the expression of knowledge in a symbolic form such as speech, artefacts or gestures into the physical world, such that others can perceive and internalise it. Once externalised, (5) objectivation is the creation of shared, social constructs that represent a group rather than an individual understanding of the world. This objective knowledge is 'stored' in physical symbols such as language, behaviour or artefacts which are endowed with social significance and which can be shared. Objectified or shared concepts are then subject to (7) legitimation, a process whereby knowledge is authorised by people or groups who have power and meanings are validated and accepted as 'correct' or 'standard' by others. They become 'institutions'. Finally, over time, (8) reification acts upon legitimated concepts to make them unquestionable and self-evident. Reification is 'the apprehension of human phenomena ... as if they were things.' It is a process in which concepts (such as witchcraft, incest taboos or loan approval) harden in the minds of the group and attain an existence, apparently independent of human beings, which can no longer be challenged.

There are processes which combine together to form recognisable suites: (9) *socialisation* is the 'comprehensive and consistent induction of an individual into the objective world of a society or a sector of it'. It is the internalisation of role-specific language and knowledge that comprise the objectified knowledge of a group. This process shapes the individual's behaviour and interpretation of organisational meaning. Internalisation of objectified social structures and externalising oneself into that (and being corrected and guided in the case of wrong moves) involves newcomers directly in the knowledge transformation processes of a group. Individual identity is formed as people recognise and adopt roles and behaviours. (6) *Institutionalisation* is the process over time of establishing predefined 'patterns of action' which cause certain actors in certain roles to behave in certain ways, thereby setting up systems of control and behaviour vis-à-vis an objectified and shared typification or concept. Institutions 'consist of cognitive, normative and regulative structures that provide stability and meaning to social behavior. Institutions are transported by various carriers – cultures, structures, and routines – and they operate at multiple levels of jurisdiction.'[23] Institutions are shared between actors; they are not personal preferences or ideas. People are habituated into *roles*, which define the relevance of an institution to one's own or other people's behaviour. Roles are linked to typificatory schemes which define acceptable modes of interaction and which define the degree of 'sharedness', objectivity and authority of knowledge.

We maintain social reality and co-create knowledge with others in the most basic of all human interactions, face-to-face conversation. Conversations occur within a space (work, pub, family) within which we adopt and act out our allocated or adopted roles. We not only exchange information flows on multiple channels (facial expression, gestures) but do so with great rapidity. Intended and unintended distortions can occur regularly in communicative interaction and are caused by differences in social background and status, uncertainty and fear, purposeful manipulation, personality biases. In face-to-face conversation we are not just exchanging information with our partners in conversation, we are creating, forming and legitimating views of the world. We are not allowed to stray, we are constantly being corrected and correcting others, bringing each other to the belief that these are the things that exist (love, duty, trees and politicians) and this is the way they are. It's a little like sketching – we do not draw by moving our hand to the perfect form of what we observe, but by correcting deviations in our hand as we move the pencil to the paper.[24]

Web 2.0 tools are social software, supporting conversations which are time-delayed, open and public and without physical presence. The processes in the model and the associated conversational signals are moved to new media. They take a number of forms, and these usually dictate the characteristics of the resulting knowledge outcome, for example:

- A legitimating process that includes the CEO will usually result in a carefully controlled and polished final artefact whereas approving a new tolerance benchmark on a machine might be done by a mechanic with a blue sticker.

- Announcements to an entire department will be externalised via an announcement on the corporate intranet but externalisation to a small maintenance team will be done verbally in a team meeting.

- Externalising a best practice method might be done by an expert on a blog but externalising that practice as a procedure will be done by the quality manager.

Understanding the knowledge transformation processes provides a toolbox for asking important questions about the most appropriate type of technology support, security and scope of access: How is this knowledge created – who should participate? How and to whom can it be externalised? Is this knowledge objectified (i.e. commonly understood) or is it a work in progress? What level of legitimation does it require to be expressed? How will these things translate to a wiki or a blog? In particular, we can express these transformations in terms of the game played within the space we have defined: Who are the players and what are the roles they adopt? How are we to socialise players into their roles? What constitutes an act of legitimation or objectivation?

The modern business environment, with higher turnover, physical dispersal of staff and outsourcing changes these knowledge transformation processes, often making them more difficult. E-mail is the currently preferred method of overcoming time and space asymmetries in business, but open

Web 2.0 tools like wikis provide a persistent, public and more integrated means of executing social processes around knowledge development and exchange. Knowledge transformation processes are moved to a medium not requiring physical presence. It certainly is one that is far more public and permanent than conversation, but it is nonetheless *emerging knowledge*. Procedures, mission statements, reports and other fully *legitimated* documents do not appear from nowhere – they are the result of conversations which mirror the constructivist processes of *externalisation*, *internalisation, legitimation, objectivation* and so on. These conversations can now take place in a forum using Web 2.0 tools which overcomes the difficulties of dispersal, coordination, lack of persistence and structure.

Institutional theory: influencing organisational behaviour

In the previous section we saw how certain processes led to the formation of new concepts ('objectivations'), norms and institutions, in terms of which the world is perceived, according to which social patterns emerge and through which normative pressure is exerted on the behaviour of organisational members. This normative pressure is often identified as 'culture': implementation problems and the lack of take-up of new methods, tools or innovations are often explained in organisations with a shrug of the shoulders and the appeal to 'oh well, it's the organisational culture'. But this culture, while appearing monolithic, is the result of perpetual co-creation by participants via micro-interactions within social situations. These are the processes of knowledge transformation and reality construction we identified in the previous section. The change to a new method of working, such as that inherent in Web 2.0, requires changes in routines and behaviour and how people see the world. There will be a move from an e-mail to a wiki, from the corridor discussion to a wiki threaded discussion, from a heated outburst at a meeting to an incendiary blog, from a management initiated discussion to a grassroots argument.

Successful change implementation is the transfer of a desired routine or pattern of behaviour into an environment such that the new pattern becomes sustained and perceptible. Social routines and patterns are *institutional structures* which have an existence independent of the behaviour of any particular individual: managing change from an existing (presumably lower-performing) routine aims to not just change a particular individual, but to change sufficient individuals within a target set such that their amended behaviour pattern becomes salient and constitutes a desired pattern. In this way the pattern becomes the norm, a new or adapted institution. New members coming into the target set are socialised into this institution and the target set can withstand turnover or loss of a certain number of individuals before the pattern disintegrates. Where there is incongruence between existing behavioural structures and patterns, and new tools and technologies, the outcome will generally be low or ineffective adoption.[25]

In the previous section we saw how institutions emerge in the face-to-face interaction between people in conversations and rituals within a space. Institutional theory, building on approaches like that of Berger and Luckmann,[26] argues that organisations are to be understood through their regulative, normative and cognitive institutions which define how the world is perceived and how one is expected to behave and respond to symbolic expressions of facts defined in terms of institutions.[27]

- The *cognitive system* reflects the development and codification of dimensions of meaning and the constructs within an organisation which are material to production and service delivery.

- The *regulative system* embodies the rules of routine action, procedure and response to facts or configurations of objects

- The *normative system* is that of values and norms, of acting upon a state of affairs as the right thing to do, or attacking a task in a certain way because it is the right way to do it.

The institutional approach has generally taken a 'substantialist' view, where social structures are regarded as having a strong ontological status, being *really out there* in some sense. Duty, morning coffee, invoices and promotion are clearly socially constructed and yet so massive in their impact on everyday life at the firm that they are given the status of existing in some sense. An emerging institutional approach influenced by Giddens is to view institutions as structures which build and are built by individuals in processes of co-construction.[28] This places more emphasis upon the process of conception of institutions and the dynamics of institution creation and enactment. The professions, engineering, law and medicine, for example, are social groups which create and patrol institutions relating to the performance of work in that profession.[29]

Weber in his classic work *The Protestant Ethic and the Spirit of Capitalism* describes the results of increasing set piece-work rates for harvesters of grain in Germany in the early twentieth century in order to accelerate the harvest.[30] At harvest time, the employer has a strong interest in increasing the intensity of work due to the impact of bad weather. But increasing the set piece rate from 1 mark per acre mowed to 1.25 marks very often led to less being harvested rather than more, as harvesters chose to work less and continue to earn what they had previously earned per day. In the absence of other needs to satisfy, a man 'by nature' will simply chose to live as he is accustomed. Weber calls this 'traditionalism'. Other institutions such as *acquisitiveness, prestige in wealth* and the *shame of poverty* developed to provide the incentives to increase work intensity.

This analysis resonates with much current experience in the introduction of Web 2.0. The use of Web 2.0 requires new modes of working, which may either conflict with existing institutions or require new ones to form. Why should someone switch from e-mail to wiki-mediated communication or submit their knowledge to the free-for-all marketplace of a wiki article? To get knowledge workers to use Web 2.0 tools in their workflow may require that the structure of the work is made to fit the capabilities of the tool – this means workers need to understand and engage with the features of the tools. This is a process which may take some time. The focus of change management has often been on rewards and incentives, but knowledge work is tightly bound up with internal motivation and commitment. To get knowledge workers to contribute to Web 2.0 memory, there needs to be some kind of institutional drivers, for example the existence of a behavioural norm that it is a desirable thing to improve one's own productivity and that of the organisation as a whole for their own sake.

At the very least there should be no *traditionalist* institutions which actively militate against the adoption of new technology. To use Weber's example, consider the likely consequences of increasing efficiency in harvesting: an increase in work intensity, a possible reduction in hiring and the bitterness of colleagues who are revealed to be less zealous. Coercion and material rewards such as those offered to the harvester don't work because of the *inertia* of traditionalism. This suggests that institutional changes are needed to provide a set of constructs which support the adoption of new modes of working to overcome the inertia of traditionalism in the modern workplace.

Institutions and Web 2.0 technology

Let's first consider institutional facilitators and inhibitors to the adoption of Web 2.0 to accomplish knowledge transformation processes. Figure 6.7 shows how institutional theory helps us understand the relative chances of success in firms.

Figure 6.7 Institutional theory and contributing to Web 2.0 tools

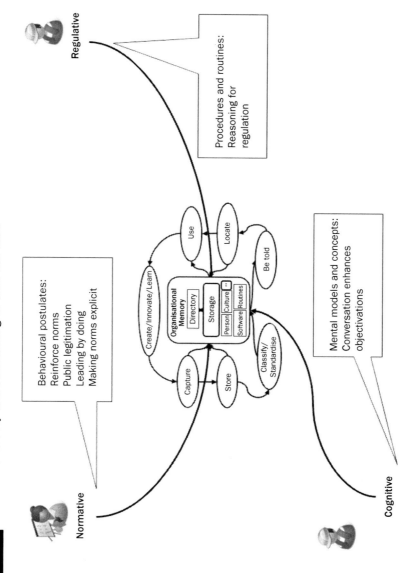

Figure 6.7 looks at the relationship between pattern change and reward. Any tool which supports existing routines or which conforms to existing norms will generally be far easier to introduce than one which requires the simultaneous amendment of cognitive, regulative and normative systems. It will be judged to be 'ready at hand' because the expectation of what constitutes usefulness is formulated in terms of established operational or social structures. The early generations of transaction processing systems did this, automating existing processes ('bituminising the goat tracks' as Michael Hammer said), replacing paper with electronic records, but not providing great increases in productivity. Recognising the limitations of this form of implementation, firms which subsequently attempted 'business process re-engineering' achieved less than exalted results, with most such projects failing or achieving limited success. Exploding and reconstructing social life-in-progress is an extremely complicated process, but one that is necessary in some form if the fundamental opportunities within computer tools are to be realised.

The decision matrix in Figure 6.8 illustrates the key criteria for proceeding with a change such as Web 2.0.

- If the institutional change required to implement and embed a tool is low but the benefits are high, then the decision is almost a no-brainer – just do it.

- If the institutional change required is low but the return is low, then although not urgent, it may still be worthwhile because it replaces an expensive or ageing tool or may position the group to move to other more useful tools in the future.

Figure 6.8   Decision quadrant – Web 2.0 adoption

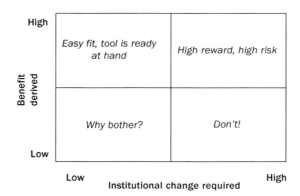

- If the institutional change is significant and the benefits to be realised are low, then there would seem to be little point in implementing a new tool.

- If the institutional changes required are substantial but the potential rewards are high, then the effort may be worth it. But the risks need to be recognised and the firm's capability to change must be realistically assessed.

The *institutional systems* of multiple stakeholders will play a key role in whether or not a system is successfully implemented and adopted. How can we make such prevailing norms explicit and discussable, holding up a mirror to the various organisations, posing the question: 'With this institution in place in this organisation, is it ever likely that wikis and blogs will work?'

Most rapid and successful adoption of technology seems to be when the change to *regulative systems* required is low, particularly when there is a high immediate payback. This includes changes to work processes, but also the appropriation of new structures involved in using tools (such as ease of learning or ease of use). For example, using a wiki to store, discuss and distribute video training instead of e-mails or having to conduct training in classrooms is worthwhile and very simple and I have observed very rapid take-up in this area. But the necessity for a slight structural adaptation can cause a quick breakdown in adoption rates. For example, changing user behaviour so that experts write informational responses to questions in a wiki instead of an e-mail seems simple. It has the benefit of allowing others to find answers in the wiki in the future, without the intermediation of the expert. But this change is often too public and indeed of no particular use to the individuals whose behaviour one is trying to change. A similar obstacle lies in moving from file-centric document creation using Microsoft Word to wiki use. MS Office and even Sharepoint users have generally developed a file-centric mentality where content management processes and the very idea of 'completion' are bound to the individual file. It is very unnerving for such people that changes are immediate and can be done by anyone: the institutions of *completion* and *responsibility*, previously critical to job definition and even satisfaction, become fuzzy and unclear (*perpetual beta*). This is particularly so in the absence of social institutions which orientate personnel towards improvements which benefit the organisation as a whole.

But there is a more fundamental cognitive institution associated with the adoption and use of Web 2.0 tools, and that is the institutionalised self-concept of the firm itself expressed by the question: 'What kind of firm are we?' The self-concept of a firm is a primary, direction-giving institution: it is what is enacted and legitimated by leadership and which pervades decision-making at all levels. Web 2.0 survey data tells us that knowledge-oriented firms not only take up and use these tools at a higher level of sophistication than others, but also that they generally do not bother with a business case: the business case is self-evident and these tools are an assumed cost of doing business. If a firm conceives of itself as a manufacturing company or a mining company, then knowledge will be seen as an input cost for executing manufacturing or mining tasks. Instruments to manage knowledge will tend to be evaluated in terms of their cost-benefit ability to improve those tasks.

Normative structures and habituations can be very effective roadblocks to effective adoption of tools. We need to understand that these roadblocks include structures held not by only the potential users, but also by the potential managers and technologists associated with the changes. Managers in a safety constrained environment or one in which security is important may be concerned about the free flow of non-approved information in a Web 2.0 world. Technologists trying to maintain integrated tool sets will be concerned about the flow of data and conflicting repositories. Outsourcing vendors will be concerned about the availability of cheap tools requiring little or no vendor support, thus threatening revenue streams. These are patterns of thinking, structures which are created with social groups of managers, professionals, vendors and system architects who have purposes and roles and who have developed patterns of thinking, norms and institutions to serve those purposes.

Every social group is defined by the behavioural patterns which represent a limited selection from the totality of potential behaviours, both personal and collective. The selection of these patterns as rules and sanctions is not arbitrary: once a group has been in existence, the selection of rules and the boundaries of acceptable behaviour are made in accordance with a set of dominant and discernible (though not necessarily explicit or codified) values. The group is defined by a set of behavioural patterns and relationships which characterise that group.

In terms of planning Web 2.0 implementations, the guiding norms need to be identified and articulated in a way which allows an empirically based, logical and compelling decision to be made regarding implementation: should one proceed, is the ground fertile enough, and what might need to change in order to make an implementation successful? For this we look to the work of E.A. Hoebel, a cultural anthropologist who studied the development of law among tribal peoples.[31] In his work among the Eskimo, Hoebel applied the concept of 'postulates', which are deeply held views and assumptions about the nature of the world. These postulates lead to certain behaviour. For example, the Eskimo postulate 'life is hard and the margin of safety is small' has the corollary 'unproductive members of society cannot be supported' and leads to the consequent actions relating to assisted suicide or even abandonment of elders on snow drifts. Although extremely traumatic for the participants, this is performed as a necessary behaviour. In incredibly moving terms, Hoebel describes how a young Eskimo assisted his father's death (at his father's insistence), because the father could no longer contribute. This was devastating for the youth but constituted 'acceptable' – indeed 'necessary' – behaviour.

Postulates, taken alone or in combination, logically justify or set the ground rules for certain types of action. Hoebel is interested in particular in how these postulates interact with the legal system, but for our purposes, the postulate system serves as a method for articulating the deeply held beliefs which lead to the adoption or non-adoption of a technology type. Technology tools may support the cognitive dimensions of work by allowing definition and expression of the organisation constructs. They may facilitate and even improve the routines associated within the regulative framework of an organisation by supporting workflow. But if the normative constructs, which we can express as postulates, deny the use of the tools as an acceptable means of work, then they will not be used.

What might postulates look like which prevent the adoption of Web 2.0 tools to support knowledge work and the creation of organisational memory? In one long-term study of e-forum implementation we found a number of these.[32] It is important to note that these postulates are not only associated with motivations to contribute to Web 2.0 tools – there are also dominant norms concerning the use and reuse of the knowledge and the nature of knowledge itself:

- The project code is king and time is scarce.
- Our work is too individual and personal to be reused effectively.
- Knowledge resides in people, not systems.
- We do not boast about our knowledge.
- We do not *reuse* knowledge – we are creative.
- Our work and client environment is too simple to need knowledge management tools.
- My first priority is myself and my next job.

Such postulates lead logically to the corollary 'we minimise time spent on tools which are useful to the organisation but are of no use to ourselves or our projects' and the subsequent non-adoption of tools such as enterprise wikis or blogs which contribute to organisational rather than personal or project memory.

The impact of Web 2.0 technologies on institutions

Perceived through the lens of the institutional theory of organisations, the successful implementation and adoption of wikis and blogs may influence the normative, cognitive and regulative systems within organisations and vice versa. Reflection on the capabilities of Web 2.0 knowledge tools along with practical experience and case studies suggests the following likely outcomes.

The *normative system* is probably amplified through the scope and openness of wiki engagement. There is a reinforcement of behavioural norms through watching how others behave (indeed if they use the tools at all, it is an indicator of something), watching how leaders engage with subordinates and the messages they give and embody (for example to make a joke, to spell incorrectly, to admit to being wrong, to dare to put themselves up for criticism) and the occasional making explicit of norms. The successful implementation of the Sun Corporation wiki is at least in part due to the well-known hands-on leadership of their CEO Jonathan Schwartz. Interestingly there is a set of norms which seems to be universally articulated on nearly all wikis, which is to be considerate and polite to others (the rules of behaviour on the wiki). This is a norm not always found in face-to-face situations – many companies (and there are of course differences between national cultures) have a more robust mode of interaction.

The *cognitive system* will be enhanced. The reason for this is the ready salience of instrumental organisational knowledge in support of a coherent and consistent set of concepts and 'facts'. People throughout the organisation will learn standard concepts and process information in a more coherent and consistent way. A simple example is the publication of an organisational glossary in a wiki, and the ability to link directly to its definitions as required from other wiki pages. While anyone can place anything in a wiki, the publication of beliefs on 'the right way to attack truck maintenance' should lead to greater consistency because of the ability for a dialectic of knowledge transformation to develop around a published idea. The result will be a shared synthesis or one of the parties accepting correction. There at least seems to be a greater possibility of synthesis and uniformity developing than if groups remain physically separated; in isolation, ideas remain entrenched and alternate approaches are not visible. Because of the public forum, *objectivation* will be supported, leading to the development of more or less uniform concepts.

The *regulative system* will be enhanced. A regulative system, being patterns of work behaviour, is usually partially explicit and partially tacit. An example of a fully explicit regulative system would be a database system with automated actions ('If a tenant has not paid rent within two weeks of the due date, create, print and send a reminder letter'). On the other hand, an example of a highly tacit regulative system might be schmoozing big-name clients at Christmas. But most regulative systems within organisations will be a combination of procedures and defined processes augmented by tacit knowledge to fill in the gaps (or indeed to ignore the procedures as senseless). The most significant regulative processes are often articulated in computer applications such as order entry, work order management, inventory management or complaints, which again are augmented by the tacit knowledge of experienced users. Placing the 'tacit knowledge' explaining the reasoning behind procedures in a wiki or blog can be a very useful way of embedding the desired behaviour as well as reducing the complexity within the procedures themselves.

Critical theory: the role of power

We come now to the role of power in the implementation and adoption of Web 2.0 and the subsequent effect of Web 2.0 tool use on power relationships. If we are convinced that these tools are of potential benefit to organisations, how can we influence people to take the time to learn and use them? We need to understand a little about the nature of power and influence and how these tools might be perceived by knowledge workers and managers. A knowledge worker may baulk at the thought of giving away their hard-earned professional insights, a manager may fear the erosion of their authority through democratic collaboration, and neither might have much interest in changing the status quo. Indeed the Gartner Group states that even many sceptical IT departments push back against Web 2.0, fearing loss of control, security issues and user empowerment.[33]

It is often claimed in the popular press, industry literature and research, that Web 2.0 provides a more democratic and accessible forum for commercial, political and intellectual expression and the formation of grassroots communities. The low barriers to entry and the simplicity of the infrastructure combined with immediate publication to a universe of potential readers has the capability to disrupt money and information flows, smoothing out information asymmetries and reducing the competitive advantages of accumulated and expensive productive capital and established broadcast networks. When we transpose this to the use of Web 2.0 tools within specific enterprise contexts, it seems clear that disruptive capability is inherent in the immediate publication of 'non-approved' material within a wiki, the broadcast of personal opinions via blogs and the self-organising formation of groups through social networks. If we want to understand how power and control will be influenced by the introduction of new interactive technologies though, we need to understand the nature of power and how control is established in the first place. This of course will also help us to understand how to take influence to promote the use of these tools.

So why do people do what is required of them in the workplace? Traditional forms of management have emphasised command and control using procedures, measurement and standardisation. *Direct* control is the management of a resource towards achieving a goal, in the case of companies towards commercial ends. Systems of control introduce targets, rules, routines and measurements, and monitor conformance to rules and the production of desired outputs. Procedures, quality management, hierarchy, rules, budget, task allocation and discipline are direct forms of behaviour control, where the measurement variables can be directly related to the task. There are also *indirect* forms of control, such as job descriptions, positive organisational norms, performance appraisals, career development, compensation, training and flexible work arrangements which try to optimise secondary variables in the belief that these steer performance in the required direction.[34] Indirect and direct controls are the unilateral exercise of power by those who command resources.

Bauman and May analyse power from the sociological perspective.[35] The first method of exercising power is *coercion*: within the workplace, the knowledge worker (irrespective of how smart, powerful or important they may be in other contexts) is forced to work through rules and commands. Their ability to choose is restricted and they lose their personal 'enabling capacity'. As a result, conformance must be constantly monitored and controlled. The second method is the strategy of *enlisting* the desires of others towards one's own ends: the knowledge workers are given the means to achieve what they desire, but what they desire is achieved by following the rules and wishes of management.[36]

In the case of Web 2.0 technologies, it is possible to use forms of direct control (or *coercion*) to enforce use of Web 2.0 technologies. For example, it can be made part of a duty statement to update a wiki with a daily report or use a blog to record events that have occurred during a work shift at a mine for the following shift supervisor to read. In the area of librarianship, for example, Deitering and Bridgewater found that wiki updates only seemed to occur when the update was part of a job instruction, and this was confirmed by Ravas, whose analysis of wiki statistics at the University of Houston found that by far the greatest frequency of wiki edits occurred in the 'evening and weekend duty log' and the 'evening gate count stats'.[37] It was a required part of the student-staff duties to update these pages. But while able to harness and direct work, these forms of organisation are often adversarial and appear to be inadequate in increasingly unstable, non-routine and complex environments where productivity is difficult to measure and compliance is given rather than taken.

A more persistent and reliable form of control than direct control is to *enlist* the knowledge workers through the *institutionalisation* of the self, such that they align themselves directly with the interests of the firm. If knowledge is socially constructed by people in groups over time to overcome the persistent challenges to survival or comfort posed by the environment, it is legitimate to ask: why do certain constructions come into being, assert themselves and become the institutional fabric of our group? The Protestant work ethic and the 'secondary' virtue of punctuality are two useful examples of such norms that legitimate and enhance work performance in the service of capital. The notion of the secondary virtue was used by Oscar Lafontaine to demonstrate how German bureaucrats could fulfil their Teutonic duty to punctuality by making the trains for Auschwitz run on time.

Peter Drucker says that *knowledge work* is a *volunteer* activity, not subject to command and control, with the consequence that 'the primary means of managerial control of knowledge work is the regulation of the employees' self rather than work flows or tasks.'[38] In other words, to get the most out of knowledge workers, the exploitation and control must come from within.

Institutional control describes the use of social technologies to direct the subjectivity of individuals. What happens in my head – my ideas, thoughts and judgments – is my subjectivity, my private realm, but it is guided in certain specific directions by notions manifest in language and inculcated in me by socialisation. Emotive and evaluative responses to objects of perception are where the objective structure of shared social order reaches into the mind. The institutions which constrain dialogue and guide responses are developed in conversations which are repeated and objectified, consensually and continually co-created between individuals and in groups. To one social order, 'unions' are a plague, to another the only hope of salvation in a cruel world. Authority figures and certain symbols legitimate these conversations and imbue the institutions with normative, cognitive and regulative force: *this is the way the world is, this is how you must act, and it is good to do so.*

As the repetitive use of social software approaches conversational intensity, so the micro-interactions which constitute institutionalisation are able to be computer mediated. Those small, everyday instances where forms of control and judgment become manifest in the ordering frameworks we impose on the world (and which constitute our world) are perpetuated and evolve in every utterance or symbolic expression we give from ourselves.

It is of more than incidental value to consider the genealogies of those technologies of the self which keep the worker attentive and dedicated to their task. In *Governing the Soul*, Rose describes in detail the genesis of the modern self in industrial psychology, how the emergent self became defined and then retrofitted into the people as the dedicated professional, the expert worker, the company man.[39] In *In the Age of the Smart Machine*, Shoshana Zuboff describes the origins of punctuality and work culture at the time of industrialisation, when on virgin fields it was necessary to not only create the physical factories and means of production, but also the social institutions to get them up and keep them running – institutions to replace the logic of seasonal agricultural workers who would want to work one day and spend the next two drinking the proceeds.[40] The institutions that the resulting poverty was bad and that God loves the rich (who of course accumulate their wealth by hard work and thrift) are examples of ethics in the service of capital.

The creation of disciplines, of notions of excellence, of total quality management served by platoons of dedicated professionals, has created an extraordinary alignment between the realisation of self and the realisation of the goals of capital.[41] 'The government of work now passes through the psychological striving of each and every one of us for what we want.'[42] This replaces the notion of work as a constraint, an imposition, with a view of work as a means towards fulfilment. This is decisive in its influence in the workplace, not just as a set of ideas but as a set of practices concerned with how work and reward systems should be designed, namely '... to create conditions such that the members of the organization can achieve their own goals best by directing their efforts towards the success of the enterprise'.[43]

And it is in this sense that Foucault writes of the panopticon, an all-seeing means of perpetual observation first envisaged for prisons by the English utilitarian and political radical Jeremy Bentham in Enlightenment England.[44] While many facets of the techniques of disciplinary power were already in evidence in the workshops of the Industrial Revolution, Bentham introduced the idea that persistent surveillance (the all-seeing eye of the 'panopticon') could become a central managerial function in the control of prisons:

> It is obvious that, in all these instances, the more constantly the persons to be inspected are under the eyes of the persons who should inspect them, the more perfectly will the purpose X of the establishment have been attained.[45]

Foucault uses this as a metaphor transposed into the inner eye of modern industrial and professional man: self-imposed surveillance is an 'internalised panopticon', where members watch themselves for indications of deviance and hold themselves accountable to the values generated and maintained by the church, the team, the country and the organisation. As a consequence, 'He who is subjected to a field of visibility, and who knows it, assumes responsibility for the constraints of power; ... he becomes the principle of his own subjection.'[46]

So given this more finely-grained perspective on power and control, we are interested in two things. Firstly, given that the knowledge work is a 'volunteer activity', what *power* does it take to achieve successful adoption of Web 2.0 tools such that they serve the interests of the firm? Secondly, how does the new medium and mode of dialectic with these tools influence the prevailing institutions of power and the development of new institutions? Writing about managerial control and the use of Web 2.0, the influential and insightful Internet thinker David Weinberger writes of the need for managers to 'let go':

> Enterprise 2.0 is not out of control. Rather, it is in control just enough, for Enterprise 2.0 recognizes that while control manages risk, control also carries its own risks.[47]

This is true of course: the modern workplace demands flexibility, availability and self-organisation which require the locus of decision-making to be distributed and devolved. But we must look beyond direct control.

The adoption of Web 2.0 moves control to a different apparatus. It is the evolution of technologies and interlocking concepts which form self-monitoring and mutual monitoring functions. Paradoxically, the 'freedom' of Web 2.0 technologies might only be truly used when the subjection of the individual is complete. Successful adoption implies the higher order of power to which the worker willingly subjects him or herself through the internalisation and acceptance of norms which lead to self-actualisation through high performance in the workplace: in the service of capital on behalf of the firm. Without the exercise of this power, Web 2.0 will be as lifeless as the communities of practice which withered in previous incarnations of knowledge management.

Web 2.0, through the capability of immediate and edited publication, while appearing to be letting go, might also be seen as tightening the noose in several other ways (see Figure 6.9).

- If network density increases as the number of possible contacts a person has in a social network approaches the number of nodes, then that person becomes answerable to a greater number of people and therefore a wider span of norms regarding what is acceptable and discussable.

- Self-organisation, as opposed to managerial instruction, may lead to a tighter exercise of control by close-standing peers whom one is unwilling to contradict or question and where the withdrawal of consent is more obvious.

- The individual contributor, or non-contributor, becomes more transparent in the quality and quantity of (non-)contribution to wikis, blogs and tagging.

When we observe power and influence at the level of the group, then more specific factors become apparent – factors which should be noted by those who wish to implement Web 2.0 technologies. Conformance to organisational norms and rules of behaviour can be illuminated by psychological research into the adoption of group norms. The research of Sherif into the formation and influence of group norms and subsequently of Asch into conformance showed that people will subject themselves to group thinking, even when they know that thinking to be wrong. Sherif's experiments showed differences between individuals' judgments of the movement of tiny lights when done alone or in a group (the autokinetic effect).[48] In a group, a 'norm developed' which was a convergence of the individual judgments. The group norm persists in the individuals, even when they revert to being asked individually for their judgments of the light movement.

Figure 6.9 Power and control and Web 2.0 adoption

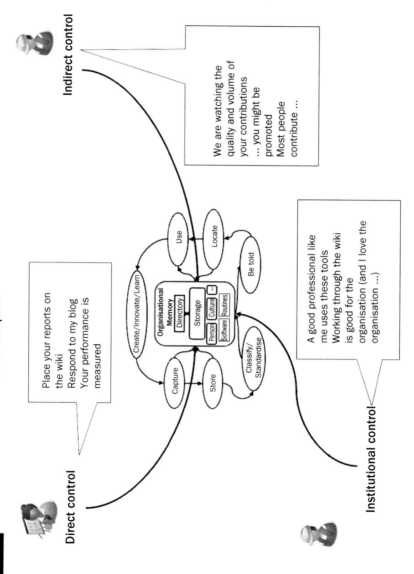

Asch's experiments involved a pre-organised group and one unknowing subject who were asked to choose which of three lines was the same length as a standard line.[49] After selecting the correct line a few times, the pre-organised 'conspirators' began to choose the wrong one, leading to some discomfort in the unknowing subject. One third of all estimates (which were incorrect) were conformed to by the subject and 72 per cent of all subjects conformed at least once to a decision they observed to be false. On the other hand, it takes only a small amount of dissent (one other 'planted subject' for example) to shake off that self-imposed conformance and say what one believes to be correct. It is indeed likely that group norms and conformance will be reinforced by the open articulation of principles on organisation-wide Web 2.0 systems; it is also possible that any published dissent (if it is ever expressed) will make others aware that 'they are not alone'.

When trying to influence people within a group to adopt a new pattern of work such as using Web 2.0 tools, the role of the group 'leader' becomes extremely important. There has been much research in cognitive and group psychology using experiments, action research and case study analysis of situations of power and influence.[50] Let's look at this from two perspectives: that of the leader trying to implement a change, and the person or people who need to adopt the change.

To effect a change, a group leader or change initiator must firstly have resources of power (money, intelligence, the ability to promote or physical presence) and these must be valued by the group. The leader must be motivated to assert power – the gains must be worthwhile, the losses bearable and the outcome likely to be achieved. It must be the generally accepted role of the person to initiate change: the wielder of power should be fulfilling a role which is expected of them. The gains and costs for the subjects of the change should be within the scope of the leader to deliver. The most effective mode of exerting power is through persuasion, not coercion: coercion will lead to the withdrawal of consent and the need for constant performance monitoring. In other words, a manager of a work group who is worth following, who can reward and convince the team and who is motivated to use the Web 2.0 tools is more likely to wield influence effectively in the implementation of Web 2.0. In contrast, managers who are themselves not measured with regard to the improvements that Web 2.0 can bring to work systems (and so may be unlikely to see it as their role to effect such a change) or who cannot articulate them will be unlikely to succeed.

The people in the group who might be influenced to change will also do so under certain conditions. They must desire the rewards that are on offer (*reward power*) or fear the consequences of disobedience (*coercive power*): this might take the form of an appeal to one's values. Or they may want to be like the admired person who is leading the charge (*referent power*) or just accept that that person has the right to command them (*legitimate power*). Finally, it may be that it is clear to the group members that the leader is right: that the leader has special knowledge which makes their influence desirable (*expert power*).[51] Given the complexity of the power relations in effecting behavioural change, it is scarcely surprising that it is so often resisted or ignored.

Social identity theory: guiding individual behaviour

Understanding and articulating *organisational* institutions, their power over social behaviour and the processes that create and sustain them provide a useful mechanism for framing and planning change to Web 2.0. As we saw in the last paragraphs of the preceding section though, one further level of detail is necessary. The modern workplace provides a major platform for the development and enactment of who we are – our identity and self-concept. Social identity is recognised as playing a major role in influencing the degree to which people demonstrate organisationally appropriate behaviour. We are interested next in understanding the conditions under which people will act and adopt behaviours which value the group's well-being as a good in itself. Not the least important reason for this is that the adoption of Web 2.0 technologies is in the interest of the firm, not the individual. Social identity, by operating at the level of the self-perception of individuals, gives us a level of granularity for observing and predicting behaviours of people in specific groups. This predictive model is more specific than that of the norms and patterns perceptible as the whole of organisational culture, so we look now to *social identity theory*.

Self-identity is the feeling of the 'self', the foundational continuity that makes us 'us'. Social identity is constructed by the lens we cast inwards to classify and judge our own being. While each of us is clearly many things inhabiting the same shell – parents, teachers, rugby players, engineers and rock musicians – within this there is a persistent self which adopts these roles to a greater or lesser conscious degree. Our social identity is taken mostly from the various groups in which we participate: this is also called the *collective self*, and generally our social motivation in this context of interdependence is to strive for collective welfare and agreeable relationships. The *in-group prototype* describes and prescribes the attributes which are appropriate to signify group membership in specific contexts. Our *relational self* defines us in terms of our dyadic relation to individual others. But we also define our self in terms of our unique traits and in this frame of *personal self*, motivations are generally egocentric and directed towards self-benefit. Indeed, the greater the strength of this personal self-identity, the lower the commitment of group members to group identity and its behavioural patterns.[52]

Group membership is characterised by three dimensions: the *cognitive*, the *evaluative* and the *affective*. We *understand* the criteria and boundaries of the in-group prototypes, we *judge* whether the group is attractive and gives status, and we *feel* an emotional bond with the group. The criteria around a particular identity allow a person to categorise themselves and create a subjective belief structure which drives behaviour. Belonging to a group is a strong determinant of how we perceive and act towards other people, institutions and objects.

The socio-cognitive processes around self-identity have two major drivers: the motivation to increase self-esteem and the need to reduce uncertainty around what I am and what I feel. Let us consider some aspects of how identity development influences effectiveness in business organisations:

- Cooperative behaviour, that is the disposition to act in ways that are beneficial to the organisation and refrain from actions which harm the organisation, will be augmented in groups which enhance self-identity through being high-status. There is also a correlation with the group's size – small groups, or groups that feel small, will tend to be more cohesive.

- People's affective commitment with a group, where their social identity has a strong emotional component, appears to be a crucial factor in determining whether group members behave in accordance with their group membership.

- The development of identity through effective socialisation (with the associated acceleration of productivity) gains in importance when one considers the trend towards hiring temporary workers.

The exercise of power is intimately connected with self-construal and self-identity.[53] A highly salient personal self is more likely to display competitive and assertive behaviour, where collectivist identity will lead to cooperative behaviour in accordance with group norms and values.

Both the strength of social identity and the group's norms are within the sphere of influence of organisational managers and leaders – if they know how. Experience and research show, however, that the relational self (and therefore willingness to cooperate) is enhanced by soft influencers, yet managers persist in using hard tactics.

Web 2.0 is technology which provides communication and collaboration facilities which contribute directly to the stock of *organisational memory*. It is in the interests of the *firm* that people adopt the more public and accessible Web 2.0 solutions. How do we mobilise people to adopt technology which leads to better outcomes for the group? We need to understand what motivates people to engage in any behaviour which is a good outcome for the group. For example, if the in-group prototype, or self-concept, for an entire firm is one of hard-hatted construction or steel making that disdains discussion, innovation or openness, then the desirable in-group attributes will militate directly against the adoption of Web 2.0 tools at the firm level.

From a Web 2.0 perspective we should also attend to the capability of these social software tools to facilitate positive in-group prototypes and provide access to participation in such groups. Figure 6.10 shows how we might use the social identity construct to predict the likely adoption of Web 2.0, the behaviour within the Web 2.0 nexus and how the use of Web 2.0 might influence social identity.

So why do certain groups of people adopt the wiki and start writing and not others? Who will start to use social networking software in your firm? Will it be the young, scientifically oriented males? Broad demographic features are insufficient: demographic analyses show that 30 per cent of 40-year-old web users have a MySpace or Facebook profile and around 20 per cent are in LinkedIn, the professional networking site – so we cannot restrict ourselves to a specific generation. Social identity theory provides insight upon which we can build expectations of who will use the systems and how. Self-categorisation occurs through the application of an in-group prototype: this prototype includes certain behavioural expectations, some of which are instrumental (for example to generate certain outcomes such as reports or accounts) and some are affective or modal (aloofness versus familiarity, self-promotion versus modesty). Observations of successful and unsuccessful wiki implementations (or of disparities between groups within the same organisation) suggest that a necessary (but not sufficient) condition of adoption is a group identity profile which aligns with blog and wiki functionality. The sorts of characteristics we would expect would be dispositions to:

Figure 6.10 Social identity and Web 2.0 adoption

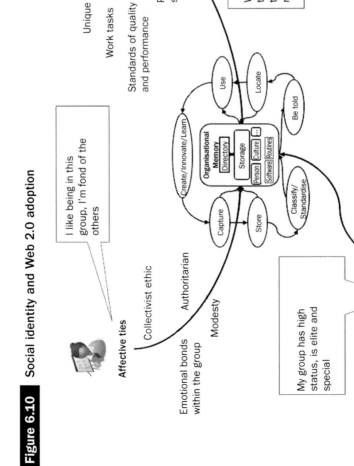

- participate in non-directive, evolving behaviour;
- accept group norms;
- produce imperfect 'works in progress'.

For example, take managers as a group with social identity and a standard in-group prototype. The very leadership behaviour required to transform a group to use Web 2.0 software to enhance knowledge growth might contradict managerial in-group prototypes which require a manager to be aloof, authoritative and above critique – not very Web 2.0, in other words.

Conclusion

So why have we taken this excursion through a bevy of social theories which reveal some of the mechanics of social behaviour and knowledge construction? I drive a car and don't need to understand machinery, so why do I need to understand the combustion engine of knowledge? Well, my answer is simply this: if you think your car will break down, it's a good idea to check it before you decide to head off on a long journey. And by the way, you should also have a pretty good knowledge of the inside of cars – just in case. These perspectives provide explanations at a social level: they are something managers and users can understand and do something about. Similarly, if researchers are seeking to find the factors which influence effectiveness or uptake and the impact of these technologies, then these theories seem to me to be a good place to start.

Web 2.0 has enormous potential for use in organisations. It is very simple software, with enormous flexibility. While it must be fit for purpose, and while there are certain functional and information design features which need to be considered and executed well, we need to understand what it is that contributes towards individuals and groups actually investigating, adapting, adopting and using the software. As Figure 6.11 shows, there are a number of theoretical perspectives that help us to do this.

Notes

1. Some key readings on organisational memory theory include Ackerman and Halverson (2000), Anand et al. (1998), Krippendorf (1975), Leonard-Barton (1995), Stein (1995) and Walsh and Ungson (1991).

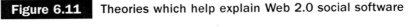

Figure 6.11   Theories which help explain Web 2.0 social software

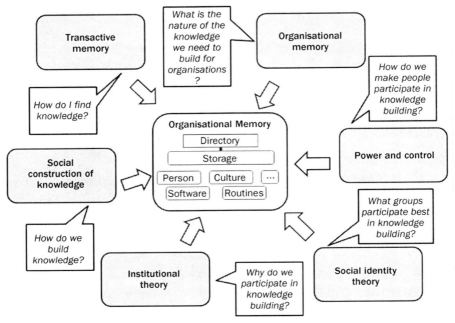

2. Some key readings on organisational learning are Argote (1999), Argyris (1999), Argyris and Schön (1996), Huber (1991) and Nonaka and Takeuchi (1995).

3. While used in organisational learning theory by Argyris and Schön, the concepts of single- and double-loop learning are taken from the work of Ashby (1956) in cybernetics. Argyris and Schön express it like this: 'Single-loop learning is like a thermostat that learns when it is too hot or too cold and turns the heat on or off. The thermostat can perform this task because it can receive information (the temperature of the room) and take corrective action. Double-loop learning occurs when error is detected and corrected in ways that involve the modification of an organization's underlying norms, policies and objectives' (Argyris and Schön, 1978).

4. Boisot (1998), Davenport and Prusak (1998), Leonard-Barton (1995), Walsh and Ungson (1991).

5. Zhang et al. (2004).

6. Cross and Baird (2000).

7. Moorman and Miner (1998).

8. Haseman et al. (2005).

9. Sinclair et al. (2000: 31).

10. Argote (1999), Stein and Zwass (1995).

11. The key resources for TMS are Wegner (1995), Wegner et al. (1991), Wegner et al. (1985).

12. For a detailed description of social cognition see Hutchins (1995).
13. Moreland et al. (1998), Moreland and Myaskovsky (2000).
14. Lewis (2004).
15. Hollingshead and Brandon (2003).
16. Moreland et al. (1998), Stasser et al. (1995).
17. Moreland and Levine (1992).
18. Wittenbaum et al. (1998).
19. Stasser et al. (1995).
20. Hollingshead and Brandon (2003), Wegner (1987).
21. Müller (2008) found that communities and their cooperation can be derived from wiki entries. The Mediawiki database is also structured to allow a view of people interested in the same topics or who contribute to similar themes.
22. Berger and Luckmann (1967).
23. Scott (1995: 33).
24. A fascinating realisation of this is the MEART project, a cooperation project between artists, anatomists and computer scientists in Australia and the USA. A camera photographs the faces of people who enter an art exhibition in Australia. The photo is digitised and an 8 × 8 encoded greyscale raster sent through the Internet to Georgia in the USA. Here the signals are passed through an electrode array around which rat neurons have been cultured. The adapted signals are then sent back to a robotic hand in Australia which draws on a piece of paper. This drawing is compared by software to the original photo and the difference encoded into the raster and sent again to Georgia and so on. The robotic hand is 'corrected' by the remote 'brain' – an interesting metaphor for global e-commerce perhaps? (*http://www.fishandchips.uwa.edu.au/*)
25. There are several ways of articulating this, but generally people will have the ability to absorb, adopt and adapt a toolset like Web 2.0 in terms of the sense-making social structures available to them. Social constructivism tells us that humans use tools according to how they are seen through the lens of structures which define shared and personal dimensions of social reality. Individuals make sense of a tool and its functions through frames they have developed through a lifetime of personal, social and organisational interactions.
26. Berger and Luckmann (1967).
27. Key readings for the institutional approach to understanding organisational behaviour are Scott (1995) and Scott and Christensen (1995).
28. Giddens (1984b).
29. DiMaggio and Powell (1983).
30. Weber (1930).
31. Hoebel (1972).
32. Klobas and Jackson (2007).
33. Phifer et al. (2007).
34. For example, see Braverman (1974), Thompson (1989).
35. Bauman and May (2001: 62–7).
36. Power is a tremendously important concept in social and behavioural analysis, but often underestimated in research into and implementation of information technology systems. As Giddens says: 'The study of power cannot be regarded as a second-order consideration in the social sciences ... There is no more elemental concept than that of power ... Power is one of several primary

concepts of social science, all clustered around the relations of action and structure. Power is the means of getting things done' (Giddens, 1984a: 283).

37. Deitering and Bridgewater (2007), Ravas (2007).
38. McKinlay (2005: 245).
39. Rose (1991).
40. Zuboff (1988).
41. Boje and Winsor (1993).
42. Rose (1991: 118).
43. McGregor (1985: 328).
44. Foucault (1991).
45. Bentham (1995), Letter 1.
46. Foucault (1991).
47. Weinberger (2008: 73).
48. Sherif (1935).
49. Asch (1952).
50. See Cartwright and Zander (1968).
51. This taxonomy of social power is taken from French Jr and Raven (1968).
52. Whetten and Godfrey (1998) and Leary and Tangney (2003).
53. See Wisse and van Knippenberg (2009).

7

Putting it together

If a theory explains something, then it can be applied to stop it from going wrong. In this section, I employ a kind of 'muscular philosophy' to characterise a strategy of using the constructivist and critical theories we have discussed previously to design implementation methodologies to make Web 2.0 work. These perspectives would normally be thought to be too 'academic' and unwieldy for practical purposes, but if technology projects continue to disappoint, then perhaps, as Plato suggests, we need to find alternative ways of looking at things. So this section is a step-by-step approach for assessing and preparing the ground for the planting of the Web 2.0 seed.

Where previously much of technology implementation has been about the technology, training and precise fit to business purpose, the familiarity, ease of use and open-endedness of Web 2.0 tools shifts almost the entire emphasis of implementation to conceptual and motivational activity. And this is about understanding and restructuring social institutions – we are not just moving the furniture. Even though it is possible to write or adapt customer-built programs and interfaces for Web 2.0, the bulk of the business benefit will come from the use of basic functions; technology, on the whole, is not the key issue and should not be allowed to set the agenda. It is no surprise that McKinsey found a strong correlation between successful Web 2.0 projects and *business* initiation and implementation of those projects.[1]

It is also critical to recall one of the key attributes of Web 2.0 here: the *perpetual beta*. Unlike the chimerical aspiration of conventional systems development to deliver a complete package of functions, the idea of continual development and delivery is built into Web 2.0. Traditionally there has been a focus in information systems projects on requirements gathering, software development or acquisition and then implementation as a set of activities directed towards embedding the computer functions into business processes. The focus has been on short-term measures to stimulate 'adoption': training, motivation, rewards, user support and so on. But the knowledge work activities which are the usual candidates for Web 2.0 tools are (usually) far less structured and routine than order entry or inventory management so are (often) less well understood and more difficult to specify in advance. And Web 2.0 is far more forgiving than ERP or CRM. As new possibilities for use emerge, as people learn about the software features, as underlying cognitive, regulative and normative institutional structures catch up with the technological possibilities, so those possibilities can be taken up because their readiness at hand can be appreciated.

As usual, the reason to implement technology should be driven by some form of business requirement which reflects a new business function or a need to overcome a problem of some sort. However, requirements can also be driven by strategy: operations may be smooth and efficient, but relentless competition and innovation may force management to introduce changes such as outsourcing, business process redesign or workforce distribution. Outsourcing the design function will increase the need for rapid, rich interaction with partners; business process redesign may require greater information sharing with a larger number of participants in a hub rather than linear configuration; workforce distribution will mean that corporate knowledge may need to be available to (and from) staff in remote locations. Web 2.0 provides solutions to these kinds of changes.

You may notice that in the methodology below there is no step for 'Tool Selection and Installation'. This reflects my own experience and belief that these tools should be part of the standard operating environment of an enterprise, much like e-mail, word processing and a virus checker. There should be no need for any particular business unit to go through the budgetary and product selection processes: the software should be made available to all, and training and advice on how to use it placed within the software (such as wikis and blogs) itself. The step from recognition of need by any part of the business to the capability to use should be able to be taken with immediate effect. This decision to use can then be taken by management or triggered by a situational need by a project, a group or an individual. The alternative is that business units or groups will select their own wikis, blogs or tagging methods, leading to fragmentation and further islands of information and knowledge. Under some circumstances, this may be their only way of making progress, but it is preferable not to do so. The point of Web 2.0 is the sharing of knowledge as part of workflow, often with the unanticipated future use of that organisational memory by others beyond the immediate business unit. This places a demand on senior management and technology managers to take a strategic and architected view of Web 2.0 for their company.

So once the business purpose is understood and Web 2.0 tools are recognised to be the appropriate type of knowledge tool then the steps to be taken by the business unit are:

1. Define the space and its purpose.

2. Develop the business case for the space and make a decision to proceed.

3. Define the knowledge types which will exist in the space.

4. Define the knowledge transformation processes for the knowledge types in each space.

5. Define the transactive memory processes to ensure knowledge can be easily found.

6. Analyse the social groups who maybe involved for adoption readiness and develop adoption strategies.

7. Identify the inhibiting and facilitating social institutions for each space and develop adoption strategies.

8. Understand power relationships and how to facilitate adoption.

Define the space

Spaces and flows are the defining characteristic of Web 2.0 use for organisations. Web 2.0 tools are the Swiss army knife of knowledge management technologies – but the impulse for specialisation in enterprises generally leads them to buy cleavers, chisels or scalpels, tools which fit a specific task and achieve a unique purpose. Defining the space in Web 2.0 means establishing the purpose of the space and then the nature of the game to be played within it in order to guide subsequent design and implementation decisions and give an overall coherence to the information to be created and used. What kind of thing are we building here – is it for collaboration, to become an encyclopaedia or to communicate with partners? Where are the boundaries and when can a manager or participant says 'stop, enough, this doesn't belong here!'?

Deciding upon the type of space will lead to clearer decisions regarding the purpose and application of Web 2.0 tools and clarify subsequent decisions like access rights, knowledge type, rates of update, information distribution, administration, appropriate behaviour and the meaningfulness of statistics. It will also give a clearer idea of the social institutions (facilitators and inhibitors) one is likely to encounter.

A key decision regards the scope of access to the space. Should a wiki be corporate, enterprise-wide and available to everyone, or restricted to a group? If it is corporate, should every user be allowed to edit, change and upload content or should that be the domain of moderators, nominated editors or privileged experts? Every organisation needs to examine its objectives and assess its mindset, organisational maturity and capabilities when making this decision. Many organisations prefer to keep things local for reasons of comfort or control. But I vividly recall a meeting I conducted as a KM facilitator in a government organisation charged with natural resource management. The director of scientific research announced to the meeting that he was not interested in participating: 'We have no knowledge management problems'. This was greeted with horror by the administrators, policy-makers and field staff present who found it impossible to get information, reports and advice – about scientific issues. The consequences of restricting access and contribution rights to the group level must be very carefully considered. Restricting wiki, blog or tagging access to a sub-group is not true 'Web 2.0' and will lead to:

- a reduction in the exploitation of *organisational memory* through the exclusion of potentially interested parties and particularly unanticipated potentially interested parties;
- an increased likelihood of *organisational memory loss* when the group or project disbands and the content is simply archived or not accessible;
- a decrease in the potency of *weak ties* and the *transactive memory system* of the organisation as the authors and groups interested in the information are hidden;
- alternative *sense-making* and *knowledge transformation processes* which produce deviating concepts and ideas which are not strongly integrated with other organisational knowledge;
- perpetuating alternative *power structures* and competing *institutions*;
- *social identity construction* which is self-referential, elitist or hostile.

Therefore it is far preferable to create organisation-wide wikis and blogs. If absolutely necessary, one might restrict writing to certain pages or areas and allow comments and discussion by other organisation members who are not in the particular group. This may restrict knowledge creation but at least aids sharing and externalisation. A closed wiki or blog with a restricted readership is at most 'Web 1.1' – a limping, mewling effort of no particular interest.

Define the business case for the space

The business purpose of the Web 2.0 system must be clearly understood and a business case at an appropriate level of sophistication must be made. The attention deficit in most modern organisations means that a presentation about oxygen will only get someone's attention when they're drowning. Immediate usefulness is probably the single most important factor in spontaneous, non-coerced adoption of technology solutions – although this is neither a sufficient nor a necessary condition. But it does create that sense of Heidegger's *breakdown*, where existing tools no longer appear *ready at hand*. It is even better when the pressing informational problem can be addressed with little or no latency to becoming productive, as is the case with universally available, easy-to-use wikis or blogs.

Nonetheless, an AIIM survey concluded that 40 per cent of respondents required a definitive business case for Enterprise 2.0 and 30 per cent an indicative one.[2] Of these, 77 per cent were unable to find an acceptable level of return. Of the remaining 23 per cent, 45 per cent anticipated a return after two to three years. These results are surprising, given the cheapness of the software, the low cost of infrastructure and the negligible need for technical support. Further, 54 per cent of respondents stated that their organisations did not measure the success of Enterprise 2.0 the same way they did themselves, suggesting that there is a wide discrepancy between tangible cost-benefit analysis and the perceptions of working staff that the technology is immediately useful.

Another significant correlation in the AIIM survey is that organisations not requiring a business case (that is, seeing the technology as just a cost of doing business) were generally classed as knowledge-oriented. These organisations are twice as likely to be actively using Web 2.0 technologies, leveraging their knowledge assets to greater effect and advancing themselves to higher levels of performance. On the other hand, a similar German survey of 156 senior managers in 'knowledge-intensive' companies with more than 100 employees found several key reasons for them not introducing these tools into their companies: 62 per cent cited unclear business benefits, 48 per cent cited 'lack of openness of employees' and 30 per cent cited 'lack of openness of management'. Only 2–6 per cent currently use these tools in a company-wide context while 29 per cent agree completely and 21 per cent agree mostly that 'Web 2.0 applications will be part of the company business in a few years'.[3]

Defining the *ex ante* (before implementation) value proposition of technology is often difficult and rates of disappointment *ex post* (after implementation) are often scarcely inspiring. Yet although the short-term results are often disappointing (or inadequate to justify investment), the longer-term effects are often considerable. The short-term challenge in justifying the investment cost in Web 2.0 comes largely, with the notable exception of marketing and customer interaction, from its lack of immediate linkage to a specific business process. There is no shortening of cycle time or reduction in headcount. So what is the value proposition?

The overarching value of these tools to an enterprise is that of organisational memory: every interaction through these tools builds and structures corporate knowledge for reuse, building upon and improving. But this is often too vague for investment decision-makers. The notions of space and flow provide a framework for the articulation of this higher level value proposition as a specific business project. *Space* forces proponents of a project to articulate a system boundary, a purpose and the participants. These translate into a business context, a business objective and the business beneficiary. *Flows* within the space are the informational actions of the knowledge worker, group or organisation in which improvement can be gained and in terms of which the contribution of the flow to a business objective can be understood and measured.

There are many ways to define a business case, but the received wisdom is to ensure that the system 'pays its freight'. This should not be difficult for software that is generally free or very low cost and which requires little technical or administrative support and almost no training costs. The key is to identify specific spaces for specific activities: the distribution of information by an internal *programme space*, the capture of expert knowledge for an *encyclopaedia space* and the generation of process improvements through a *collaboration space* for example. Table 7.1 enumerates three examples. These examples of tangible and intangible benefits can be enhanced with concrete numbers for return on investment calculations if required.

Table 7.1   Developing a business case

Space	Flow	Tangible benefits	Intangible benefits
Encyclopaedia space	Information comes in (pre-recorded) from experts and is read by new hires, transferees, etc. Information is created and extended by interested parties and semi-experts	Fast lookup of information Provision of background information Assists unified view of organisation	Reduction in uncertainty Increase in general knowledge

Table 7.1   Developing a business case (*cont'd*)

Space	Flow	Tangible benefits	Intangible benefits
Collaboration space	Problem or opportunity arises and people form a collaborative space Information flows are fast, high-pulse Asynchronous, remote contributions Automatically informed of changes	Easy inclusion of right people Rapid issue resolution Involvement of best people leads to better decisions	Better outcomes Simpler information management
Group space	Information is published by administrators, subscribed to and read by group members Group members publish information useful to other group members	Reduced project start-up time Reduced project/ group information management costs Accelerated provision of information Provides points of access for other groups	Single version of the truth Diffusion of good ideas to other groups

Define the knowledge types for the space

After having established the effectiveness and viability of the use of tools to support spaces, we move to the detail of the knowledge content to be kept there and how to design the information. The taxonomy for knowledge objects is fourfold: *prescriptive, descriptive, distinctive* and *emerging*. While these categories are a useful starting point for deciding which types of knowledge to place or develop in Web 2.0 tools, there may be some variations in how organisations decide to deal with them. Organisations will vary in their need for certainty, speed, innovation focus, audit trails and so on. They will also vary in the starting point of their current infrastructure and strategic plans for technology acquisition: some will have content management systems, others will use shared network drives. So the type of knowledge to be created within a particular Web 2.0 space will be a decision contingent upon these factors.

- Prescriptive knowledge – how do we wish to create, manage and protect the information that people *should* conform to?

- Descriptive knowledge – how do we wish to create, manage and protect the everyday information which describes the *generally accepted way* of (or reasons for) approaching tasks at the moment?

- Distinctive knowledge – how do we wish to create, manage and protect the *deep knowledge* that is held by our experts?

- Emerging knowledge – how do we wish to conduct those *conversations and interactions* which lead to new knowledge or which develop our understanding of our work?

Deciding the type of knowledge is only a first step in the information design process, however. After establishing the general knowledge taxonomy and who will engage with that knowledge, it is necessary to create the part of the space infrastructure which deals with actual information objects and their structure. For example, an encyclopaedia space will contain proprietary descriptive knowledge which will be stored in 'knowledge pages'. These knowledge pages should have a consistent structure and layout where it is clear what type of content is expected. If all the pages in a wiki for example have an ad hoc structure, then it will be hard to ascertain the levels of quality and content which are expected. On the other hand, a page layout which demands that information be entered into specific fields with prescribed possible values may be too constraining and alienate users. Those who are creating knowledge pages need to be presented with a standard 'template' of some kind, with an appropriate level of structure to assist with orientation and give a clear indication of what the 'desired' information object will look like.

We might define three levels of template discipline within blog or wiki pages. Each level of template increases the degree of conformance required of users and decreases the level of autonomy users will enjoy in defining the shape of information:

- *No template.* This will cover completely free-form pages where the author can create a page design according to their desires. At most there might be a consistent look and feel using standard fonts and corporate colours and logos. This kind of freedom will work well within personal, social or collaborative spaces where knowledge should emerge within a more or less spontaneous process.

- *Loose template.* This template might create a page layout with suggested headings and descriptions of the kind of input and authoring style required. The template might insert a number of services, such as links to key pages or to a main page, a standard tag of the category to which the page type will belong, and perhaps even standard macros written by IT specialists.

- *Tight template.* This template will create more structured and prescriptive layouts with data fields, pull-down menus of permitted values, possible validity checking of inputs and so on.

Table 7.2 might help in generalising some answers to questions of rules of participation and the structure of knowledge in this step.

Table 7.2 Matching knowledge types to spaces

Space type	Knowledge type	Participation rules	Structural rules
Encyclopaedia spaces	Proprietary descriptive knowledge	Anyone can contribute	Loose template, headings only
	Distinctive knowledge	Only experts contribute	Loose template, headings only
Advisory spaces	Distinctive knowledge	Only experts contribute	No template
		All can ask	
Group spaces	Prescriptive knowledge	Administrators contribute	Loose template, headings only
		All can read	
Collaboration spaces	Emerging knowledge	A group can contribute	No template
		All can read	
Learning spaces	Proprietary descriptive knowledge	Administrators and experts contribute	Tight template
	Prescriptive knowledge	All can ask	Tight template
		Only experts contribute	Loose template
	Emerging knowledge	Students contribute	
Partner spaces	Proprietary descriptive knowledge	Only experts contribute	Tight template
	Prescriptive knowledge	All can read	Tight template
		Only experts contribute	
Social spaces	Personal knowledge	All can read	No template
		All can ask	

Table 7.2 Matching knowledge types to spaces (*cont'd*)

Space type	Knowledge type	Participation rules	Structural rules
Departure spaces	Proprietary descriptive knowledge	Only experts contribute All can read	Loose template, headings only
	Prescriptive knowledge	Only experts contribute All can read	Loose template, headings only
Arrival spaces	Proprietary descriptive knowledge	Only experts contribute	Loose template, headings only
	Prescriptive knowledge	Administrators and experts contribute All can ask	Tight template
Programme spaces	Proprietary descriptive knowledge	Only experts contribute	Tight template
	Emerging knowledge	All can ask	Loose template, headings only
Personal spaces	Personal knowledge	Self can contribute All can ask	No template
Innovation spaces	Emerging knowledge	A group can contribute All can read	No template
Procedural spaces	Prescriptive knowledge	Only experts contribute	Tight template

Define the flows within the space

The knowledge transformation processes which *externalise* and *internalise* knowledge as symbolic behaviour and speech take place in wikis and blogs as reading and writing. Concept creation (*objectivation*) and innovation (*knowledge creation*) are products of this interaction. Authorisation (*legitimation*) of new ideas, concepts and ways of doing things can also occur in the technology when the appropriate managers are involved or group consensus is reached. And the *institutionalisation* and *socialisation* of staff into the knowledge of the firm also occur here. If we take more straightforward expressions as rough correlates of the academic names, Table 7.3 emerges.

Having understood the types of knowledge transformation we can then proceed to identify and design the types of flows involved (see Table 7.4). These are not decisions made once during project initiation: they should be considered whenever new flows or information types are to be added.

Table 7.3 Defining the knowledge transformation processes within spaces

Space type	Knowledge type	Participation rules	Knowledge process
Encyclopaedia spaces	Proprietary descriptive knowledge	Anyone can contribute	Sharing Legitimation by group
	Distinctive knowledge	Only experts contribute	Legitimation by expert
Advisory spaces	Distinctive knowledge	Only experts contribute All can ask	Sharing Socialisation Legitimation by expert
Group spaces	Prescriptive knowledge	Administrators contribute All can read	Sharing Socialisation Legitimation by manager
Collaboration spaces	Emerging knowledge	A group can contribute All can read	Sharing Objectivation Legitimation by group
Learning spaces	Proprietary descriptive knowledge	Administrators and experts contribute All can ask	Sharing Socialisation Legitimation by group
	Prescriptive knowledge	Only experts contribute	Sharing Socialisation Legitimation by expert
Partner spaces	Proprietary descriptive Kowledge	Only experts contribute All can read	Sharing Socialisation Legitimation by expert, manager
	Prescriptive knowledge	Only experts contribute	Sharing Socialisation Legitimation by expert
Social spaces	Personal knowledge	All can read All can ask	Sharing Legitimation by individual

Table 7.3 Defining the knowledge transformation processes within spaces (*cont'd*)

Space type	Knowledge type	Participation rules	Knowledge process
Departure spaces	Proprietary descriptive knowledge	Only experts contribute All can read	Sharing Legitimation by expert
	Prescriptive knowledge	Only experts contribute All can read	Sharing Legitimation by expert
Arrival spaces	Proprietary descriptive knowledge	Only experts contribute	Sharing Socialisation Legitimation by expert
	Prescriptive knowledge	Administrators and experts contribute All can ask	Sharing Socialisation Legitimation by expert
Programme spaces	Proprietary descriptive knowledge	Only experts contribute	Sharing Legitimation by expert, manager
	Emerging knowledge	All can ask	Sharing Objectivation Legitimation by expert
Personal spaces	Personal knowledge	Self can contribute All can ask	Sharing Legitimation by individual
Innovation spaces	Emerging knowledge	A group can contribute All can read	Sharing Objectivation Legitimation by group
Procedural spaces	Prescriptive knowledge	Only experts contribute	Sharing Socialisation Legitimation by expert

Table 7.4   Identify flows and functions, knowledge type and storage

Information flow	Tool function	Knowledge type	Storage location
Publish standards	Http link from within wiki page	Prescriptive knowledge	Kept in controlled DMS
Publish schedule	Wiki page edit	Proprietary descriptive	Wiki page
List contact details	Http link from wiki page Manager form	List is proprietary descriptive Contact details are prescriptive	Wiki page Enterprise address list (Outlook)
User group draft folder structure	Wiki page edit Wiki comment page Watch comment page RSS read of changes	Page is proprietary descriptive Comments are emerging knowledge	Wiki page Wiki comments page Wiki watchlist
Frequently asked questions	Wiki page edit Wiki comment page Watch comment page RSS read of changes	Page is proprietary descriptive New questions are emerging knowledge Questions sent to team RSS	Wiki page Wiki comments page Wiki watchlist
Training	Video uploaded to wiki page	Page is proprietary descriptive Training video is prescriptive	Wiki page Non-changeable video file

Define the transactive memory arising from the flows

Transactive memory is a key method in couples, groups and organisations of finding what you need to know, when you need to know it. Without current, informative transactive directories and the effective transactive processes to maintain and use these directories supported by technology, the strength of weak ties, network effects and knowledge retrieval from organisational memory will be far less effective in organisations. For the various spaces in your Web 2.0 tools, you will need to ensure that key metadata about knowledge and information in the organisation, such as creator, holder, interested party, knowledge repository, locations and other attributes, are recorded, understood, linked and made searchable by the Web 2.0 system. This will generally be the role of wiki administrators supported by technical staff.

Generally the identity of participants is recorded automatically and usually this can be linked to a personal page or contact details in a corporate address list. The mode of searching and using the transactive memory metadata must be simple, be well publicised and become an acceptable means of taking up contact with knowledgeable colleagues or finding the right documentation or database. Anonymity and distance make casual, conversational transactive directory maintenance difficult in large organisations, so to make a functioning transactive memory from Web 2.0 tools requires first:

- a glossary of concepts which provides consistent terms and meanings across the organisation: for example, *In the world, there are machines, raw materials, workers, tools*;

- a description of the relationships between concepts describing 'facts' about the organisational world: for example, *A machine needs raw materials, a worker uses tools, and tools can be drills, hammers or pliers*;

- a description of the collections of facts which constitute domains of knowledge or key business processes: for example, *Production is about how to set up machines, re-tool and use tools*;

- a set of role and group definitions that defines which departments and repositories are responsible for domains and business processes: for example, *The Operations and Production Planning Department is responsible for production, and their machinists should know about drills and how to mount them on a work machine. Inventory management is about how to order, store and move goods.*

This provides a *normative, meaning-based* map of organisational memory, which shows where you *should* be able to find an appropriate repository of organisational memory by following directory entries (or searching for) words, domains, departments and roles. But this does not account for *instance* knowledge, which is specific knowledge about an event, area or project possessed by a particular person, database or group; for example, a particular machinist has done maintenance often on (the troublesome) machine 4711 and knows it well, or was a drilling specialist in Indonesia in 1998 on Project Pisces.

Instance knowledge will be found by specifically searching for a term (by search engine or asking around the closest-matching role knowledge for pointers), tracking down the instance repository and then approaching the repository linked to the instance (for example, who was the author of a report or the project manager at the time).

This normative part of transactive memory is the *ontological backbone* of a company and the instance part is what accrues as people within organisations learn. Without an ontological backbone which fulfils the role of a transactive map, the power of the information and knowledge embedded in your Web 2.0 tools is unlikely to gain full traction.

The normative part of transactive maps needs to be established through standard glossaries, thesauri and ontologies which define the key concepts of organisational language. These concepts should be combined to provide adequate descriptions of domains of competency which are linked to organisational charts, descriptions of the role of departments and descriptions of job roles within the departments. Information repositories, be they databases, people or documents, need to be locatable via classification schemes, search engines or tagging. Information needs to be linked to other information in order to provide context and trails to follow. The Apollo 11 Project should be able to use standard tags like 'Spaceship' or 'Lunar Module' to mark-up its web pages, documents and data.

The instance part of transactive maps needs to be established by giving users or administrators the opportunity to create and apply social tags describing the events, projects or undertakings they feel are necessary to classify information. The Apollo 11 Project should be able to create linked tags for its own instance information, when standard tags are insufficient or when they are simply breaking new ground. People need to be able to have a home page describing their own 'instance' knowledge using 'instance' keywords ('I was a member of the Apollo 11 programming team ...'). Résumés should be available online and be searchable to track down specific instances of knowledge.

Understand and address the institutions which influence adoption

One of the fascinating aspects of Web 2.0 is the disjunction between the cheapness, easiness and usefulness of the tools and the elephantine efforts companies can make at implementing it. Whether it's corporate procedures, the not-invented-here-syndrome, IT methodologies for testing and implementation using gold-plated consultants or glacial approval processes, it is clear that it is the institutional structures of business, not the tools, which define the initial playing field and the rules. Two surveys, from the Aberdeen Group and McKinsey, relate the intentions to use Web 2.0 tools to the performance of the organisation, and highlight the importance of this point of departure. Although these examples are from external-facing use of Web 2.0 (and we are focusing on the use of Web 2.0 for supporting knowledge work), they serve to illustrate how the institutional launching pad influences the trajectory of use.

The Aberdeen Group survey first establishes the relative strength of the marketing function of the organisation using five dimensions: process, organisation, technology, knowledge management and performance management.[4] It then finds that, although all companies seek to use Web 2.0 tools to increase brand awareness, there are significant differences in how they apply them. Best-in-class performers seek to use Web 2.0 technologies to interact with customers and collect their observations regarding brand and marketing to develop new products. The average and laggard performers seek simply to 'improve the online experience', which is simplistic Web 1.0 thinking dressed in Web 2.0 capability. The survey concludes:

> Best in class companies realize that metrics such as customer satisfaction cannot easily be increased simply by providing Web 2.0 portals on a company website; there must be an internal process where the insights exchanged in these forums are used to grow the business.

The McKinsey survey divides its respondents into those who are satisfied with Web 2.0 and those that are dissatisfied.[5] Satisfied respondents confirm:

- higher levels of change in communications with customers and suppliers (26 per cent of satisfied to 12 per cent of dissatisfied), talent hiring (27 per cent to 13 per cent);
- the creation of new roles (33 per cent to 9 per cent);
- movement to a flatter hierarchy (33 per cent to 13 per cent).

Of the companies that were dissatisfied, 46 per cent say it has not changed the way the companies operate. Only 8 per cent of satisfied companies say the same thing.

Clearly, the application of the tools varies according to the capability of the tool users to *conceptualise* improvements and *implement* them. Every organisation has inertia. This inertia is a vector property with force and direction. The results of these surveys suggest that Web 2.0 is a tool which will amplify inertia. It allows well functioning organisations to move to a significantly higher level of performance: product co-creation, organisational restructuring and new job roles are generative structures which enhance performance. So this technology will increase the capabilities of the already capable – but to move into this realm of capability, tools are not the answer. Giving average organisations Web 2.0 tools is as little the answer as giving a power saw and router to an apprentice for a month. A good tool must be ready at hand, but the hand must also be ready.

How might one assess the capability of a firm's institutions to catalyse new approaches? Looking at history is a good start: if similar tools have been tried in the past, and if communities of practice have stuttered, if formal networks languished and bulletin boards lament 'is anyone there?', then Web 2.0 tools probably won't work either. As Peter Senge says, a lag in achieving success will generally lead to the abandonment of a project: this has nothing to do with the underlying capability of the tools. Therefore it may be better to make a realistic assessment of a company's ability to change its practices to make a success of the use of new tools. If the company's capabilities and institutions are not conducive to adoption, then the norms which will influence adoption should be worked on before the introduction of the tool.

The institutions that guide behaviour and social action must be identified and analysed to examine the extent to which they constitute barriers or facilitators of adoption. Then, as necessary, the social processes which change institutions need to be initiated. It is beyond the scope of this book to define the appropriate change management processes, but in the face of so much adoption failure, we can use some of the ideas of this book to explore promising approaches for Web 2.0.

A simple way is to identify and articulate the postulates which influence people in their decision to use the tools to improve business outcomes. Postulates which might lead to rational *non-adoption* of Web 2.0 systems include:

- Managers can be deceitful: watch what they do, not what they say.
- It's best to keep doing things the way we have before.
- Keep things to yourself.
- Making mistakes leads to punishment.
- Only the group needs to know what the group knows.
- Only experts should express an opinion.

These norms and institutions can be changed over time: fear of speaking in public can be reduced when there is a culture that encourages asking questions, that having a go at something and failing is better than not trying, for example. These norms can be changed in organisations by leaders displaying these characteristics and enacting them in micro-interactions with staff over time. But it is a fragile process which can be easily destroyed by all-too-common leadership change, reluctant middle management, an unfortunate event or two where a question is ridiculed by a leader or a pack, and a general national culture which discourages 'stepping out' (also known as the *tall poppy syndrome*).

An institutional perspective helps. If the normative structure contradicts public contribution through norms of modesty and knowing one's place, vilification of mistakes or even vengefulness, and this norm is massive, reified and unspoken, then the scope of Web 2.0 should be tailored appropriately. Contribution might be better served by accepting the status quo and becoming expert and authority driven, with review and legitimation processes prior to publication, protected wiki pages, wikis of restricted scope and access and so on. This is unfortunate, and will suppress the wide participation, weak ties and network effects so crucial to Web 2.0 advantage, but it is likely that some Web 2.0 utilisation is better than none.

The institution of leadership

It is a cliché, but senior management commitment is very important to the success of Web 2.0 undertakings, as it is for most deliberate transformation initiatives. This is largely due to their direct, legitimate authority and their span of influence. Management will generally look to a business case for a set of tangible benefits, as they themselves are generally judged on such results. This kind of business case is often hard to find for Web 2.0, but the use of spaces and flows helps to nail it down. A strong business case will also help to maintain commitment if progress is not as exalted as anticipated.

Even where the amount of money (if any) to be spent on wikis, RSS or a blog system pales into insignificance against that spent on e-mail management, document control or ERP upgrades, someone will have to write a cheque at some stage, particularly in organisations where IT services are outsourced. Leaders must be convinced that the technology offers functional and productivity benefits or some other reason (such as staff attraction or workforce modernisation). Unfortunately, few managers devote the time to finding out what these benefits are.

But setting an example of using these systems and exposing one's opinion to criticism and feedback is a vital aspect of convincing the tentative to start using. What therefore influences the adoption of a technology by leaders themselves, other than financial commitment? Here are some thoughts to be considered:

- What constitutes leadership in the organisation: a dark suit, a serious manner, always being right, being paid significantly more or being part of a special society? If the in-group, institutional prototype for managers has characteristics which militate against the openness and level field of Web 2.0, it is unlikely that managers themselves will participate and inspire by active leadership.

- Managers may be less willing to expose themselves in a public forum. Managers can be very sensitive of the need to manage signals to their own workforce and their own image. They may be unwilling to participate in forums which are dynamic, interactive and broadcast universally.

- In organisations where managers move through roles in a matter of a few years, there is little incentive to implement strategic initiatives which bear fruit over the longer term. The building of organisational memory is an investment that is for the whole organisation and for the future, but management reward is often expressed through other forms of measurement.

- Managers themselves look upwards to their leadership. If the managers' manager is risk-averse, hostile to fluidity and dynamics, top-down and deterministic, then the manager will scarcely be inclined to take risk.

- Tolerance of dissent – the ideal collaborative environment is anti-hierarchical with little sense of role-based hierarchy and where knowledge rather than position determines authority. At 38 metres, the Hall of Supreme Harmony in the Forbidden City within Beijing was the tallest wooden structure in China for hundreds of years – no one was allowed to build a higher building than the Emperor. Does your organisation allow workers to have better ideas than the boss?

The locus of decision-making – business ownership

For many reasons, business involvement in technology projects is a critical success factor. This will be no exception in Web 2.0 projects – indeed it may be even more pronounced. The McKinsey July 2008 Report on Web 2.0 concludes with a critical and unambiguous indicator of Web 2.0 satisfaction: those companies with the lowest levels of satisfaction with Web 2.0 technologies were overwhelmingly provided with them on the initiative of the IT department (36 per cent of those dissatisfied compared with 11 per cent of those satisfied). Conversely, 25 per cent of those satisfied with Web 2.0 do this in a context where 'the business identified new technologies and brings them into the company without IT support'. While business involvement in IT projects is now received wisdom, this observation perhaps raises the stakes: lack of involvement by the IT department as a critical success factor! In all likelihood this reflects a strong readiness, leadership and feeling of perceived control over the technology in user departments.

The drumbeat of continuous improvement

There is no contradiction in a motivated or compliant workforce *not adopting* a useful tool. Even if the tool is understood by the protagonists to be useful and easily apprehended and learned, that workforce, although motivated to perform *well*, is not necessarily motivated to *improve*. An incentive to improve working methods is a different social object to the one which drives performance as measured by existing management criteria. In the absence of a salient norm which aspires to continuous improvement, the adoption of tools must be driven by some constraint which makes higher levels of performance clearly desirable – such as measured targets for performance improvement, regular increases in targets or decreases in resources to achieve the same targets. This makes non-improvement untenable.

Harvesting the benefits of improvement

In organisations where managerial positions change every year or two, the motivation of managers to introduce change (and 'rock the boat') which produces benefits which only materialise in the mid to long term may be low. Increasing levels of organisational memory using Web 2.0 tools is such an improvement that may only be useful to my managerial successor, so why expend effort? A fully internalised institution that motivates managers towards the greater good is required.

Privacy

Like the phobia of public speaking, to write in an open environment is a basic fear. In spite of the repeated observation that the younger generation places information of hitherto inconceivable privacy in public spaces, does this mean they will rush into corporate publication? Of course it doesn't! As observed in the Facebook News Feed fiasco, the otherwise unworried users resent being lifted out of the crowd and they do not like their data being used for purposes they did not themselves mandate. There would scarcely be a corporate environment in which users would be permitted to be anonymous, so every contribution to a wiki, blog or corporate Facebook will be associated with an identity. Secondly, most corporate environments consist of tribes who know each other well and have a passing acquaintance with other related tribes. Being revealed and exposed to ridicule by people you know or with whom you are acquainted because of an ill-considered contribution is a few keystrokes away, with the kind of consequences that may pursue a contributor for the rest of their career, should there be one.

It would seem that because of the scope and permanence of contributions to Web 2.0 software, public contribution might be a significant risk to one's identity and status in a corporate context. What ameliorates this risk perception? We need to understand this. Being a recognised expert would be one factor – in this instance what one writes is almost taken as gospel anyway. Being confident in one's knowledge would be another – as would be the case with well-educated scientists or engineers, for example. Being used to putting one's ideas in public would be another advantage – consider university academics who send in contributions to journals for ritual degradation in reviews, for example. Then there are those who just don't care what others think – quite possibly an inter-generational genetic defect we would all like to possess.

Power and participation

How is control created and exercised in your organisation? For Web 2.0, this is by no means a trivial question as the exercise of power is crucial in being successful with a technology which, to a large degree, is based upon the presumption of free and open expression and a volunteer ethos. It requires a form of work which does not necessarily measurably improve the performance of specific tasks, at least not in a way which can be mandated in advance. Further, it requires the changing of habits (i.e. from e-mail to wiki, from face to face to blog, from creating information to reusing information). Add to this the management fear of 'letting go' and allowing open use of Web 2.0 tools in the enterprise. But the systems will only become truly productive when power has shifted from the direct to the indirect and then to the institutionalised: when staff compel *themselves* to contribute their knowledge to wikis and blogs to conform to inner value constructs, in which case management control has increased substantially.

As we have seen, there are different dimensions to the issue of power. Let us first consider direct control, or the exercise of explicit authority and sanction for non-conformance. This has been tried with conventional knowledge management by providing rewards or promotion for measures such as the number of contributions to a forum. This has generally not been very successful and is unlikely to be successful with Web 2.0. However, the converse scenario looks different: if a leader instructs their group to use a wiki or a blog where there is a latent demand for such a tool, then this use of power to remove other forms of inhibition and legitimate participation can be very successful. This legitimation is even stronger where the leader leads by example and contributes actively to wikis or blogs or supports them with material or time.

Under these circumstances it would seem that the imprimatur of leadership and explicit power is a necessary but not a sufficient condition. So let us consider indirect control, which is the creation of an environment which has the secondary effects of facilitating or promoting contribution to and participation in open collaboration. The objective is to motivate participants to contribute through the power of social constructions and institutions to guide perception, thought and behaviour in a direction which is favourable to the development of a common good. These constructs are generally reified, having a life of their own, independent of the good sense or perception of the protagonists.

The power of the tall poppy

Many countries have an institution known as the 'tall poppy syndrome', essentially a behavioural norm that one should not get too far above one's station or ahead of others and thereby risk being cut down to size.[6] This ethos can be introduced into otherwise high-performing groups as part of the baggage of the wider society. And indeed, in open environments such as an enterprise wiki, I have encountered several instances of benign colleagues telling their peers (in a very nice way) who had been video-recorded for podcasts that they were 'glory seekers' or 'star struck': a cutting remark. The tall poppy syndrome is a power institution which will block adoption and use of Web 2.0 technologies, effectively slapping down people trying to 'do the right thing' (another power institution of course).

The cult of expertise

The institution of expertise enables holders of knowledge in discipline areas to wield influence within those areas, define what counts as knowledge and how one gets there and indeed how we should feel about ourselves vis-à-vis the knowledge we absorb. An examination of the learning process, levels of interactivity and proceduralisation will reveal how knowledge is conceptualised. Are relationships for future collaboration built by moving new people through the organisation or are there siloed walls, secret languages and rites of passage? The rituals that guide the protocols for knowledge exchange and creation vary and depend upon the institutionalised view of expertise. A cult of expertise will potentially scuttle attempts at participative and collaborative knowledge development but may lead to encyclopaedia articles of great depth, for example.

Repressive politeness

The language and rules of engagement on wiki sites generally are revealing. Reminders to stay polite are ubiquitous, and politeness is the generally accepted rule. Such formats constitute fertile ground for collaboration, co-creation and knowledge sharing. In the case of impoliteness there is generally immediate group sanction or even withdrawal of others' entries. The publicity of the forum, its permanence, enforces a public protocol with the highest common denominator of politeness and gravitas. Nevertheless, the power of institutions of politeness to create restraint may lead to a loss in signal richness and lead to an anodyne uniformity.

The power of special interests

The provision of software services within organisations is intimately bound up with money: the staggering rates of pay given to SAP module consultants and programmers and Oracle database administrators are a testament to the laws of supply and demand. The implementation of self-service freeware places service providers in a conundrum: how to justify the use of specialists who need to be charged out at $250 per hour to provide support for free software which users can adapt and configure themselves? It is not unknown to meet with downright hostility under these circumstances, resentment and a palpable sense of letting the genie of self-service out of the bottle of technological servitude. I have experienced multinational service companies deliberately 'going slow' on installing a freeware wiki until they 'had developed a policy'. So it is important to understand who will win and who will lose from the introduction of cheap or free ubiquitous software which requires no training or specialist support. In the case of Web 2.0 technologies, the Gartner Group states that many sceptical IT departments push back against Web 2.0, fearing loss of control, security issues and user empowerment.[7]

Power and influence – a summary

It may sound paradoxical, but the successful adoption of these democratic and anti-hierarchical technologies revolves around the exercise of power. To move people to behave in a new way which suits the institution of management, which suits the profit-making or governing organisation, requires the exertion of a force which overcomes natural momentum and inertia. This power to change can be exerted through direct control – by fiat, by order, by monitoring and by sanction, or by aligning the outcomes of the job with the products of the tool. It can be exerted by indirect control – incentives, performance measurement, the provision of a facilitating and motivating environment, and inspirational and exemplary leadership. Or the control can be exerted by the development and presence of a system of beliefs which make potential resistors unable to see the alternative: where the conceptual status quo becomes participation and where the matrix of actionable possibilities is determined by the internalised belief structures of the brave new way – a way which requires the collective intelligence and memory of the organisation.

Analyse the social groups

Organisations approaching Web 2.0 implementations strategically will often plan a 'rollout', a programme to spread awareness, provide usage scenarios, establish cells and allies, and argue the business opportunities to supervisors and managers. Given the highly variable propensities in groups to adopt the technology, an analysis of likely adoption based upon applicability, payback and the group prototypes is called for. Table 7.5 provides such a strategic approach.

Table 7.5 Analysing groups as potential adopters of Web 2.0

GROUP: Business need:	Very weak	Weak	Moderate	Strong	Very strong
Scope					
Using Web 2.0 will have a:					
• personal impact					
• group impact					
• inter-group impact					
• customer impact					
• all of enterprise impact					
Production efficiencies					
Using Web 2.0 will:					
• decrease costs greatly, moderately, slightly					
• increase group effectiveness					
People effectiveness					
Using Web 2.0 will:					
• improve speed to become effective in a role					
• minimise duplication and re-invention of the wheel					
• increase job satisfaction and staff retention					
• increase personal productivity					
Effort to achieve					
Implementing Web 2.0 will be easy:					
• the target group have no existing tools					
• the target group are readily available and accessible					

| Table 7.5 | Analysing groups as potential adopters of Web 2.0 (cont'd) |

GROUP: Business need:	Very weak	Weak	Moderate	Strong	Very strong
• the target group are motivated					
• the target group has an in-group prototype which encourages participation in Web 2.0-type tools					
Implementing Web 2.0 will be easy:					
• high open collaboration quotient					
• group values knowledge expression					
• low levels of secrecy					
• high number of young people					
Effort to sustain					
Sustaining Web 2.0 will be easy:					
• the target group are independent and autonomous					
• the target group are natural users of such systems					
• the target group have a clear and useful purpose for Web 2.0					

Notes

1. There is of course still a substantial amount of knowledge required to implement Web 2.0 in a robust user-friendly manner, but in general this will be the province of a few people within organisations. And in contrast to application and database technology, this knowledge is largely not 'technical': the people might be more accurately described as 'power users' or business analysts. This is not to say those with a particular vested view and interest may not insist on large teams of technical support ... Excellent books on Web 2.0 implementation which focus on technical and implementation aspects are Casarez et al. (2009) and Newman and Thomas (2009).
2. AIIM – The ECM Association (2008).
3. Dufft (2008).

4. Aberdeen Group (June 2008).
5. Bughin et al. (2008).
6. The term is sometimes attributed to the Roman historian Livy, who described how Tarquinus Superbus, a tyrant of Rome, sent a silent message to his son to eliminate the leaders of a conspiracy by cutting off the tops of poppies in a garden and telling the envoy to report to his son what he had seen: '[Death] cropt the heads of nations, as Tarquin struck off the Poppy-heads.' Institutionalising this as the resentment of peers is probably a far more powerful means of suppression than were the leader to exercise this power overtly.
7. Phifer et al. (2007).

8

Conclusion

Web 2.0 technology is social software. It has emerged into a digital-social milieu because it suits the modes of interaction favoured by the many that choose to conduct relationships on the Internet. These relationships vary greatly in type, content, intimacy and seriousness, but they are fundamentally social. Having evolved in 'Userland', the technology is easy, lightweight and free. The natural robustness that this technology has had to accumulate to withstand the nonsense, trivia, deviance and malice of the open Internet stands in laconic hipster contrast to the stolid belt-and-braces methods of much corporate information management. We have seen that the promise of this technology is quite remarkable, but not as remarkable as the resistance to it one encounters in the corporate world. Indeed, a clue to adoption might lie in the fact that the watchdog did *not* bark in the night.

Because the software is irreducibly social, social theory is required to appreciate it: that is the main thrust of this book. Orthodoxy has developed within the phalanxes of proselytisers for Enterprise 2.0, Library 2.0, Health 2.0 and Government 2.0 that itemises network theory, the strength of weak ties, networked collective intelligence and so on as the foundational arguments. Of course they are appropriate, but they are wish lists, not critical success factors. The momentum of this wave lies with social change and institutional trajectories: the purpose of this book is to understand that social world – and then to change it if that is the right thing to do.

The importance of space became clear to me when I had to explain the use of internal wikis and blogs to members of a large organisation in which I was vainly attempting to promote their use (of course this was to managerial baby-boomers – the X, Y and Net generation had already got it, but weren't managers or hadn't undergone 'management re-education'). Specific functional capabilities such as web page edit, change notification or discussion threads were easily understood, but rarely was there an unfulfilled need that e-mail, document management systems, electronic forums and so on couldn't handle. Then I began to formulate the potential in terms of space – encyclopaedia spaces, collaboration spaces, group spaces and learning spaces – and then the lights went on. The universal access, persistence and 'findability' of information became compelling when formulated in terms of an activity type that persists over generations and beyond individual groups of knowledge workers. This is because the institutions and purposes of these spaces as supportive of organisational business activities are clear: a *learning space* is where we learn ... an *encyclopaedia space* is where we place and seek authoritative knowledge ... a *group space* is where our group pools and shares information. A *flow* is a movement of this information towards the *purpose* of the space. The metaphor of the game can be used to great effect here. And the equipment for this game doesn't stand in the way of your work: it makes you independent of the IT department, it has a full audit trail and it makes it unbelievably easy to share information.

Once the very notion of *spaces and flows* has been internalised by decision-makers, we can consider what *kinds of knowledge* and *information* are going to be created and stored in a space. If we are creating an advisory space, will it contain *prescriptive knowledge*? If so, how will we make sure that it is true (because prescriptive knowledge *must* be true)? Or is our business process tolerant enough to reverse the occasional mistake? Will it be *expert, distinctive knowledge*? If so, how will we capture it from those cranky technophobes and upgrade it as the world changes? Is it *proprietary, general knowledge*? If so, how can we get the group (if there is one ...) to build it?

Then we come to consider the social interactions which will instantiate the *flows* of knowledge transformation, the dialectics of construction for a specific kind of knowledge. What is the best form of infrastructure to support the processes? If it is mostly externalisation of *prescriptive knowledge*, i.e. publication, then a blog or protected wiki is appropriate to create flows that push. If it is to be a *learning space*, then the socialisation of newcomers is important: flows that support *internalisation* of authoritative knowledge (mostly prescriptive or proprietary) but with opportunities for *externalisation* (to allow feedback and correction – learning opportunities) and *habituation*. But if it is a *collaborative or innovation space*, then the key dialectics of *internalisation, externalisation* and *objectivation* become important: creating new concepts requires flows that have a higher pulse, require asynchronous protocols to overcome space and time – Interactive Chat, RSS, Twitter or wiki pages come to mind.

Creating and sharing the knowledge is still not enough: awareness of the location, reliability and quality of knowledge types is essential. *Transactive memory*, the directories of organisational knowledge that contain metadata about knowledge, that tell us where to guide it, how to find it and how to retrieve it, is also crucial. All organisational memory must be embedded in a sustainable and ongoing transactive mapping process so that we can find what we need to know, when we need to know it.

Having decided the knowledge type, the space, the flows and the tools, we need to understand the *institutions* which determine action within the organisation: what are the mental models, the theories in use, the perceptions that guide whether and how people take the tools to hand? What norms dominate to legitimate and invite participation? Why would anyone move to a wiki from e-mail if the only advantage is to the organisation and not to the self? If the knowledge to be added is *expert and distinctive*, why would anyone 'give it away': are the usual suspects of self-realisation, reputation and renown sufficient motivators? If the knowledge is *proprietary* and general, why will anyone bother to put it on a wiki – it is common knowledge, except to those who don't know it ... and if it is *emergent knowledge*, who will take the time and the risk to volunteer novelties in the face of potential public ridicule? In considering the knowledge type, one needs to note that the very categories of prescriptive or proprietary knowledge are themselves institutions. If the self-concept of the organisation is not knowledge-oriented, how will such activity gain traction? And we can identify postulates to understand the logic of social action in the organisation, postulates that warn of potential non-adoption like 'we are a manufacturing organisation – we make stuff, we don't talk about it' or 'we laugh at people who get it wrong – we fire those who make mistakes'.

But organisations are not homogenous and we know that they have different constituencies. So we drill down to the level of the *group*: groups are guided by institutions specific to the *in-group prototype*. A company might have groups of scientists, groups of boilermakers, groups of managers, groups who work for head office. Some groups will be co-extensive with the organisation's formal boundaries, some groups will cross boundaries. Some groups will be remote from each other; others will form for a few weeks and then dissolve. The in-group prototype will be a good, but not guaranteed, indicator of the willingness of people to use public social software at work.

Why are theories of control and power important? For the simple reason that the effective adoption of these technologies is in the interests of the firm and to encourage adoption behaviour requires the exercise of power. This power comes in many forms, the most sustainable and effective of which is to *institutionalise* workers to the point where conformance is self-imposed. Fully internalised norms which equate personal recognition, collaboration and public innovation with self-actualisation and goodness are the most powerful methods for implementing tools and methods in the service of the organisation. These norms are by no means self-evident: consider cultural norms which militate against high performance – the tall poppy syndrome, modesty and restraint, belonging to a gang of no-hopers. The process of building and propagating institutions which are in the service of the firm has been a work in progress since industrialisation, so it is unlikely to be a quick fix, but it has a substantial momentum and very high payback.

So having understood the social reality around the creation of certain types of working knowledge, we come to the final hurdle: how to change it? Business transformation is notoriously difficult: most attempts to change do not work, and it is beyond the scope of this book to provide a guide – other than to offer some advice relevant to the context of implementing Web 2.0. The objects that guide decisions, the ontology of social action, cannot be sorted into a simple list of critical success factors. In some contexts they might suffice, in others more might be needed, in yet another none of them might be present in a successful project – human beings are odd like that. So creating the environment to maximise the chances for successful adoption and use of Web 2.0 tools *in a Web 2.0 way* will be a process of soft ontological design, not join-the-dots, architected 'change management'.

In some sense it would be helpful to adopt new language to describe what happens, or should happen, when we conceive of, design and implement Web 2.0 systems. We are constrained by language here, and Web 2.0 systems are different to many conventional applications when they are used as truly social systems. As part of 'letting go', perhaps we should move from software application to purpose, from information system to space, from business process to flow, from business rules to norms, from policy to behaviour and from compliance to consent.

And why should organisations bother? Because already the evidence is gathering that if you don't adopt these tools in the spirit of Web 2.0 – and the general statistics about technology say you probably won't – your organisation's performance will not be as high as it needs to be. The firms that adopt successfully, the knowledge-intensive firms for example, the adaptive enterprises, the firms with the right vision and leadership, will be lifted to higher levels of performance than firms that adopt semi-successfully. So you will need to change your carpentry *and* change your tools.

And academics – why should they bother to apply institutional theory, critical theory or constructivism – not to mention the thinking of Castells, Wittgenstein and Heidegger – to Web 2.0 technologies? Because it seems to me that the sheer width of these technologies and the range of the situations in which they can be applied make their management a social affair. Until technology researchers become social theorists to some degree, philosophers of knowledge, and learn to understand what is under the bonnet of knowledge creation, the great leaps forward will remain obscure to them.

Appendix: A case study[1]

This story is located in a fertiliser and sands processing company operating in central-north USA which exports most of its products to overseas markets, including China. It is a complex, enthralling and sometimes brutal environment, dominated by harsh geography and the unforgiving edges of the industry. The story straddles two epochs in a single year, separated by the schism of the global financial crisis of 2008. The first epoch was one of rapid, almost breathless, expansion in productive capacity to meet the world's hunger for natural resources: achieving 12 per cent annual growth in GDP, building a new city of 2 million persons each month, manufacturing half the world's televisions and most of its pillowslips, China was the locomotive of global growth. The worst imaginable sin for any processing company was to have any resource left in the ground or in the warehouse at the end of this orgy of expansion. Then within weeks, in September 2008, the financial crisis broke into the open, with global lines of credit disappearing, stock values collapsing, the US real estate and housing construction markets going into freefall taking consumer sentiment with them. Suddenly expansion projects in almost every such processing company around the world were being cancelled or frozen and contractors terminated. The talk of commodities' 'super cycles' and China's 'decoupling' from dependence upon the United States withered.

The two epochs reflected very different concerns and motivations. The core challenges of the expansionist epoch were project speed, production ramp-up, a skills shortage and high staff turnover, especially in the areas of trades people and engineers. After the crisis, the priority shifted to cost-control, controlled project quiescence, the maintenance of jobs, positioning for future growth and the management of uncertainty.

In retrospect, the Web 2.0 story is a very small part of this drama of course. But it had its moments of grand aspiration, when the participants could see what would happen if the tools were used to capacity and they were even prepared to suspend their natural pessimism. The project was observed closely by technical managers for its capability to 'add value' to the business and business managers could generally see the potential for shortening and simplifying communications processes. But the rapid adoption implied by the cheapness, simplicity, accessibility and patent *usefulness* of the technology did not eventuate, at least not in the short term. Indeed, in the post-crisis cost-cutting, this lag in quick payback may lead to the closure of a perceived non-core, social experiment. But the small story here has some big lessons and provides some insights which may serve to qualify expectations of the technology and impart ideas on how to make it work.

The company

The company is diversified into several types of processed product and each line of business is a profit centre, but head office provides investment funding, financial and managerial oversight, and policy in key areas such as safety, public relations, technology standards and industrial relations. Each line of business runs its own technology but connects through to the corporate networks to access centralised services. Strategy making and the setting of organisational objectives take place in regular cycles, with each level of planning breaking down into sub-plans for each organisational unit. Every goal is measurable, whether it be production figures, profit and loss or, in the case of the IT department, user satisfaction, help-desk response rates or project budgets.

The work model is largely based upon outsourcing and the use of specialists. This applies to the construction of production and processing facilities, the operation of resource collection, and much of the back office work such as surveying, geology and earth analysis. IT work, such as applications development, help desk, software maintenance and facilities management, is outsourced to a computer services company. Consulting services are used to develop information management strategies and specifications and to implement change management practices and so on. Most permanent personnel are at a head office site and most contractors work on sites in remote areas.

Organisational memory

Information and know-how within the company are stored in many places and in many forms. There is a very large volume of information used and produced to support the key business processes from exploration to assessment, planning, processing site construction, implementation and processing operations, logistics and marketing.

Prescriptive, normative information is found largely in procedures which direct staff in areas such as safety, equipment maintenance, equipment use, reporting, record keeping, administration, budgeting and so on. These are found in diverse areas, depending upon the specific group: networked drives, the business unit intranet, the corporate intranet and a variety of document management systems. Although the repositories differ, the process of developing, reviewing by experts and approving such documents by managers is largely similar. Other authoritative information to which this applies includes reports, published information and information for regulatory agencies. Finally there are the transaction processing systems which represent the state of the business and operations at any time. These are largely enterprise resource planning (ERP) modules which contain customer sales, production plans and actuals, maintenance plans, equipment profiles and histories, materials movements and locations. There are real-time data collection systems which record production, stockpiles, quality, locations and shipments and feed these into the ERP systems.

The non-prescriptive, *proprietary knowledge* – the 'way we do things around here' – is generally retained in the heads of staff: how to attack a problem, how to prevent problems recurring, what a particular job involves and so on. If a proprietary or common practice is deemed important by management, it is translated directly into procedures. There are procedures which prescribe post-project learning in the form of written reports, but these outcomes are not easy to find and so are not used.

There are several *deep experts* who have been with the organisation for decades. Their names recur when one is seeking advice about particular topics. Their knowledge is tacit although their expertise is sought after in the formulation of explicit reports and strategies. There has been no consistent attempt to capture their knowledge or pass it on through techniques such as mentoring or job-sharing. A common strategy to retain the knowledge of noted experts is simply to pay very well and convince them to delay retirement or departure. The large amount of contracting means that much on-the-job expertise departs when a contract is completed.

There is no explicit technological support for *emerging knowledge* apart from e-mail and desultory communities of practice using e-forum technology. As in any organisation, people meet, discuss and develop ideas and approaches to complete their projects and achieve organisational objectives. But solutions tend to be local and isolated as there is no way of overcoming problems of separation and anonymity. History and reasoning are not stored or shared and neither are the outcomes of conversations. E-mail management is of considerable concern to management, not because of the knowledge that is lost to the organisation in personal exchanges, but because of the potential for discovery and prosecution via the USA's Sarbanes-Oxley legislation.

Transactive memory

Knowing how to find information or advice is problematic and solutions are largely based upon an individual's ability to develop a *transactive directory* in personal memory and a network of contacts. There is no usable enterprise search function and information is scattered across disparate repositories in different parts of the organisation, so information is found by keeping local copies of documents or utilising personal networks to track stuff down. This reinforces the identification and application of local solutions.

Transactive directories, therefore, are kept largely in people's heads. The organisation chart is a highly used signpost and is available online, searchable and generated automatically from the SAP Human Resource system. The titles in the chart reflect an area of knowledge and contact details are precise and current in Microsoft Exchange. However, these titles are high level (a job title, a couple of words). As is to be expected, managers form transactive directory hubs: people will usually ask a project or group manager for advice on where to find something. Managers with longer tenure seem to have good memories of where something is or who did what and higher-level managers in the organisation seem to have directories with wider scope. Experts are also transactive hubs: they like to talk and will often remember that a certain report was done once and kept in someone's drawer or computer or that a particular system maintains assay information from a certain area.

The efficiency of *transactive retrieval* depends upon the completeness and accuracy of the transactive directory and the ease of then accessing the information or person. Using the organisation chart usually leads to a chain of interactions, when the first person recommends someone else and so on. Using a manager's or an expert's transactive directory allows a search intention to be articulated clearly and contextualised, and they can give a precise pointer to the information store. E-mail is often critical in the retrieval process: the first step is to a known transactive directory 'hub' and then tracking the information source down happens via e-mail and the Microsoft Exchange directory. The final step is often then a pleasant phone call, sometimes some travel, to actually obtain the desired information.

The *transactive allocation*, or the routing of information to a person based upon their 'need to know', is usually based upon a business process rather than a *transactive directory*. That is, information is generated in one place and sent to (or fetched by) a subsequent person because the business process workflow defines this. But information sent to a person based upon a transactive directory alone does not seem to be significant, although some routing of publications, reports, events and so on does occur. One symptom of poor transactive allocation seems to be scattergun information, that is telling a large number of people something in the fear of missing someone out. In fact, the converse of transactive information seems to be quite prevalent: people are considered themselves responsible for finding information and keeping current.

Transactive directory maintenance is performed in many ways. The main explicit and published directory systems, the organisation chart and Microsoft Exchange, are automatically updated through human resource processes. Documents generally contain the author's name which can be traced via these directories, for example. But below this there is a technology chasm where human transactive directories take over. Managers' and supervisors' personal, mental directories are kept up to date by the multifarious and wide-ranging interpersonal interactions they have. Expert directories are updated more slowly over time, as a long-termer will often have seen people come and go (often within the organisation). The personal directory of other staff is maintained through work interactions, being on various projects, social occasions, meetings and so on, where colleagues disclose information about themselves and what they know, which serves to build directories for future reference.

Institutional structures

This is a resources and basic processing company, front and centre: each manager wears virtual steel-capped boots; it is male dominated in most roles, although this is not the case in some areas such as human resource management, information and change management, health management or safety and some scientific areas. The company sees itself very much as a resources processing company, running a simple business that relies on the asset in the ground. The business is routine and repetitive and staff are driven by procedures and unambiguous work instructions, not innovation. The most important thing in this job is to work safely, and the company seriously does whatever it takes to be safe – and is seen to take safety seriously. As it is a hard business, with pronounced ups and downs, it's generally accepted that management have the right to make hard decisions, and that jobs are not secure, irrespective of your previous contributions. Because they outsource non-core, non-value tasks, the knowledge that contractors gain is dispensable. In terms of performance, success is primarily about production and financial budgets, is measurable and clear, and the value of activity is assessed by its direct contribution to production.

Power relations

Power in the organisation is largely explicit and coercive. It is exercised directly through hierarchy and rank. Job descriptions, personal goals and annual targets are set by managers largely to be measurable, and cover production, project completion, safety incidents, systems use, equipment downtime and so on. There are sanctions associated with underperformance, most commonly being fired or contracts not being renewed.

There doesn't seem to be a strong overall 'esprit de corps': the organisational mission and vision are clearly articulated, but it is a company one works, not lives, for. There is a social club, a health club, company breakfasts and share schemes, but the personnel generally conform to institutions of performance and direct control, not inner values of commitment to the company or the team.

Among the professional groups of scientists, geologists, managers and planners, there is commitment to the ethos of the profession, which extends the performance of these staff to beyond just what is required. People wish to do well to be good at their job, to establish their experience for their résumé and for future employment. These people subject themselves to the norms of their professions, which are largely about individual performance, the respect of colleagues and self-esteem.

Social identity types

In-group prototypes in the workplace generally revolve around job role and age. In such a complex organisation, there are many, widely divergent groups. There are scientists, marketing staff, maintenance engineers, geologists, accountants, surveyors, safety coordinators and so on. There are young people and mature staff in their sixties. There are those in groups in remote, tough areas and those in head offices in large modern cities. There are those who are company employees and others who are contractors.

The story

In the time of expansion, when the organisation was working flat out to bring new gathering and processing capacity online, the restless and innovative information manager, Katie, had initiated a slather of projects aimed at improving the management of information. This included documents which were prescriptive and which needed to be controlled: safety procedures, maintenance processes, reports – these were scattered in different repositories and network drives. The main impetus for improved control came from senior management concerned about legal liability if incorrect use of procedures led to injuries. If an electrical circuit was not isolated properly or a scaffold lacked safety mesh and a resulting injury investigation showed that a procedure was not used due to it not being 'found', managers became liable.

The company was not a 'knowledge management' company: it had little or no exposure to the discipline and little interest. But Katie knew it was important and that there were great efficiencies to be gained from improving the exploitation of the organisation's knowledge, but the exigencies of rapid expansion and the mindset of 'we collect it, process it and send it away – what's the big deal?' meant there were too many competing priorities and too little headspace for something as nebulous as knowledge. But the publicised war for talent and skills and the impending retirement of baby boomers added weight to the fear that the organisation would be left with a shallow, superficial and immature knowledge base.

So Katie was able to create a budget item to address this: she only needed a creative solution. This solution became a kind of Trojan horse for what is Web 2.0. While a simple interview and publish process for this knowledge may have satisfied the auditor, this was neither sustainable nor terribly useful. So the solution of a wiki, semantic web, social tagging, podcasting and blogs was introduced to carry the content of the knowledge capture: a Web 2.0 suite.

The solution worked as follows. Key experts were identified throughout the organisation. They were interviewed twice, once to establish the format and knowledge area of the interview and prepare the questions and a second time in which the questions were simply asked and the responses recorded. The questions were structured to provide self-contained 'learning objects' which were edited into individual video files and transcribed to text. Text and video were loaded into a wiki page with an appropriate title. The text, unlike the video, could be updated by other experts or business people going forward, either if it was missing something or as knowledge changed. The analyst conducting the interviews created a mini-ontology from the information, which was linked into an overall business process model. The ontology was used to tag the wiki article and one could find an article via search or navigation through the ontology. After interviewing about 50 experts, the wiki was evaluated by business managers, experts and users and, with some exceptions, found to be of sufficient potential to proceed with publication. The methodology for preparing and conducting interviews using video equipment was also tested by non-experts and found to be simple and the results useful.

Subsequently the content was published on the intranet using the TWiki software as a base. The initial installation of the freeware TWiki software on company servers provided diverting moments: according to procedures, it could only be installed on a server by the contracted outsourcing company (although it had been installed by the knowledge management consultant and running for months on his standard personal laptop for demonstration and testing purposes). This company was disconcerted by the notion of freeware with no visible means of support, and prevaricated heroically before providing a system programmer to download, install and configure all the software: a simple process lasting not more than two hours, with the programmer's manager nearby the whole time muttering darkly that 'it wasn't going well'. The TWiki freeware software supported 350 hundred users in its first six months of operation without a glitch, a prospect difficult for executives of large IT services companies to appreciate and enjoy.

Going live was low stress and simple: apart from not being immediately mission critical and not requiring simultaneous use by many workers, the system was simply very easy to use, robust and accessible. With no advertising at all, the system grew slowly but steadily: within four months there were hundreds of logged-in users. Of these, 50 per cent returned – a rate considered disappointing until Peter, the intranet manager, said he would give his right arm for a return rate like that on the intranet. The rate of editorial contribution was probably on the low side, reaching about 12 users actively contributing content.

The functionality within the overarching rubric of the wiki was substantial:

- There was standard wiki functionality – creating, editing, reversal and linking of information pages. Any user could upload videos, audio files, images, presentations or Adobe pdfs. To avoid conflict with existing document management facilities and version management, it was not permitted to upload 'editable' files such as MS-Word, MS-Excel or MS-PowerPoint formats. All training was in video-audio and screen capture format, available from within the wiki.

- An ontology, or semantic web, was made of the core business processes and concepts. These were linked together in a hierarchy as a 'category tree' and could be navigated to find useful articles which had been tagged with the standard concepts.

- Blogging was made available, although not using any specific blog software. Users were encouraged to use their own personal page as a blog, or simply to start a wiki page as a blog about a particular theme.

- Social personal pages were available where people could place personal interests, contact details, photos and so on. Initial interest in this was very high, particularly by young people who saw a reflection of Facebook in it, but actual contribution remained modest.

- Social tagging was made possible by allowing every user to tag any wiki page as they wished, but not allowing them to create formal category pages which linked into the organisational 'semantic web'. Tags without matching pages were reviewed regularly by the wiki administrator and, if found to be of general use, were given a category page and added into the organisational conceptual map.

- Every wiki page could create an RSS feed and personnel were free to use any RSS reader to subscribe. At this stage, there was no standard RSS reader available, but it was anticipated that the RSS reader within Internet Explorer 7 or Microsoft Outlook 2007 would become the standard reader, when the standard operating environment products were upgraded to those releases.

- Podcasting was documented and made available using the RSS feed capability. The intention was to use it for uploading training sequences and ad hoc training using the MS-PowerPoint narration capability or Windows Media Encoder, a free product to capture voice and screen dynamics.

To make it more accessible to lay users, many examples of good usage of the wiki and blog were given (such as a replacement for e-mail, collecting ideas, project discussion spaces, new personnel induction and so on) and the idea of wiki 'spaces' was developed. It was clear that the initial project (of interviewing experts with deep tacit knowledge) had been encyclopaedic in nature, but that the wiki could be used for a lot more. So four core wiki space types were explained to users:

1. Encyclopaedic – for collecting knowledge and expertise.
2. Collaborative – for developing ideas and analysing events.
3. Group – for organisational units or projects to manage their own information and provide a face to the rest of the organisation.
4. Learning – to provide information and orientation for new hires.

Several of these capabilities and spaces overlapped and therefore competed with existing software thus contravening the management mantra of tight cost control (minerals and natural resource companies are the lowest investors in information technology). A wiki, for example, can perform many of the publication functions of an intranet for group publishing but far more easily and immediately. The ability to quickly create a narrated PowerPoint presentation and upload it to a wiki for podcasting competed with SAP's Knowledge Warehouse, which is a highly structured collection of training courses which are directly related to the competencies defined in job roles with the SAP Human Resources module. The threaded discussion pages of a wiki were a dead-ringer for the threaded forums within the communities of practice – but far more open and accessible. The various portal offerings, such as those of Hummingbird or SAP, which create a web portal containing relevant applications for specific roles, could easily be usurped by personal or general-purpose wiki pages which bundle useful links and SOA functions. Selling the Web 2.0 story to management often met with the comment: 'We've already got one of those ... how are we going to know which system to go to?'

An explicit decision was taken to make all capabilities universally accessible through the single-sign-on mechanism. This meant anyone could upload or change text, with of course the knowledge that what they wrote would be clearly attributed to them, across the whole organisation. This was a risk. But the whole point (and all were agreed on this) was to make knowledge available wherever it might be needed and not to lock it up in private areas which precluded unanticipated use and promoted information hiding. Although the notion of private wikis and restricted blogs is attractive in many ways, in the view of all project participants and the steering committee it would be senseless to introduce another private content management system.

But it was clear from the outset that the systems could be used for a lot more than just posting videos and text contributions. Tom, a senior operations manager, was very preoccupied with ensuring that the prescriptive knowledge in safety and maintenance procedures was correctly stored and managed and insisted that the wiki not divert attention from this. Peter, a technology manager, was concerned with the arrival of 'yet another content management system', which overlapped with the document management system, the intranet and the communities of practice (all of which were performing poorly). Corporate policy-makers were introducing a mantra of technology simplification and reduction, in which a wiki fitted neither philosophically nor politically (there were too many 'similar' products). This led to a need to promote the wiki very quietly so as not to be cancelled immediately by one or other of these groups. The other side of the coin was that there was no one in a senior position who actively promoted the technology and no mandated, measurable targets for use or contribution.

However, the next part of the project, to acquire a more 'corporately appropriate package' than the TWiki freeware product and interview many business experts to load a substantial amount of content, was put on hold as the expansion epoch came to a shuddering halt. The managerial imperative moved from speed to cost reduction and project streamlining. The project was left without a formal change manager to promote it and the wiki moderator was left with the task of proselytising the solution without a budget or the capability to publicise widely. The strategy of 'viral contagion' had been adopted anyway, as being one which was recommended by the global consulting groups like Gartner, Forrester and McKinsey. This involved simply demonstrating the software to interested parties, talking through use-cases where productive wins could be gained and supporting people who decided to give it a go. No formal training was provided – education was all within the wiki as videos, narrated PowerPoint slides and live screen captures. Furthermore, the software was considered very simple. Significant amounts of information were posted about the potential savings, applications and advantages of the system.

The following paragraphs describe some examples of successful and unsuccessful attempts to tempt users and managers to adopt the system.

Deep expertise

There seemed to be all sorts of reasons to interview specialists, people considered to have deep knowledge of how to do things and why they had to be done. The results of the 50 interviews created a basic stock of very interesting, very useful, very extendible knowledge – all agreed on this. However, it was a bit like an encyclopaedia that stopped at 'D'. A plan had been worked out to complete interviews in all significant operational areas of the organisation before the axe fell on the funding. The knowledge was secured before experienced staff left, it was shareable across the entire organisation, it was cheap, easy and effective, all participants recognised the value, and only two people declined to participate. There actually appeared to be different types of interview to conduct: interviews about an operational area; analysis and discussion of lessons learned from projects and events; the services and skills offered by a particular group or division within the organisation. The experts themselves decided on what they wanted to talk about, based upon what they felt was important, what they kept getting asked and wanted to record once and for all, or what knowledge they felt was vulnerable should they leave the organisation – even what they thought was just nice to pass on, such as the tradition of an annual golf day between competing sites.

For example, there had been a problem with a certain piece of important machinery at one site that had held up production for some time. It had been incorrectly commissioned and then inadequately lubricated, leading to several days' breakdown where trucks could not be loaded. There were some simple but effective lessons learned that needed to be passed on to new maintenance engineers (an area of high turnover), so the manager of the maintenance section volunteered to be interviewed to see if using the Web 2.0 solutions could be used to record and post the lessons effectively. It was immediately clear that it was a good, cheap, easy solution, with a company vice president showing interest in promoting it. Further, the general maintenance area was struggling to achieve learning and consistency. However, the vice president left the organisation and momentum was lost. Some managers said that the best way to learn was to put the information into procedures. Others in the group said they enjoyed the video and had a bit of a friendly go at the manager for grandstanding and putting a video of himself up for public viewing.

Internal programmes

The company runs a number of general programmes, such as the Health and Well-Being Group, Workplace Safety and TQM Process Improvement. The Health Programme's job is to gather and disseminate hints on lifestyle and healthy living, to answer queries on common illnesses such as obesity, alcohol consumption and smoking, and to develop and publicise health events and programmes. This group quickly adopted using the wiki as it gave them a vehicle to very easily publish information and links, upload photos and commentary on events such as bike rides and walks, but also to receive comments back from staff and converse with them in an interactive forum. This reduced the number of e-mails, paper wastage and shared information very quickly across a broad front. The group manager was very supportive, progressive and encouraged the openness of the wiki. The nominated wiki support person, although not technical, was intelligent and receptive and picked up the necessary skills within hours.

In another example, a wiki page was developed for process improvement: a template was developed to publish and list lessons learned from projects to the wider organisational community. Previously the learning procedure had created paper documents which languished in drawers or in departmental network drives. This mini-system took 30 minutes to set up and allowed a group (which was usually physically dispersed after project close) to discuss a project wherever they were and immediately publish their findings into the standard format in a wiki page. The results were automatically tagged and findable via search. Although greeted enthusiastically by the responsible manager, they never used it.

The scientists

There was a group of scientists responsible for modelling, quality control, resource assessment, geochemistry and so on. They were distributed across many locations where they conducted their work, and were supported with the provision of scientific information, software and training about the specifics of the region from specialists in head office. Ian, the manager of the group, had been interviewed as an expert to create a wiki article on a specific area of geological interest. He had immediately seen the potential of the tool for his group: he was a devoted scientist, a lover of knowledge and very direct. He assigned his group's information and research manager, Simon, to set up an appropriate wiki area and support adoption. Simon, in a two-hour design session with the wiki administrator, set up the group's main site page, with useful, consistently sought information on the first page, and sub-pages for new hires, research documentation, who's who in the group and links to much needed (but carefully concealed) corporate information. Specialist areas were set up for the different areas of earth science and the specialists slowly built up pages to avoid having to repeat themselves. Instead of travelling to sites to educate new staff, they were able to narrate into PowerPoint presentations and upload those, although this did not happen often at first. New, young hires, particularly at sites, immediately understood how to use the system and the idea behind them.

One uploaded photos from social events, some less than dignified, and this prompted some quiet feedback from the wiki administrator on the need to consider the feelings of others ... But although initial use was not as regular or dynamic as was expected by Ian or Simon, it has increased over time.

The IT projects

Within the Information Services group itself there were varied responses to the Web 2.0 capabilities. Business analysts, for example, communicate with processing sites to resolve problems, establish areas of information need and explore solutions with users. These analysts must travel regularly to the sites for meetings, discussion and information exchange. Wikis are ideal for the communication and recording of ideas, solutions and agreements over distance and the difficulties of shift work. The corporate wiki was available across the business, equally to all people, but the analysts did not take it up, preferring to travel to the site and break up their routine.

On the other hand, a systems rollout staffed by contractors which affected personnel across the organisation prompted high usage. Divisions were being converted, trained and supported into the use of the new system one at a time, again a perfect opportunity for using the wiki to develop and refine a consistent message, for taking questions from users, for developing FAQs, for having discussions and resolving questions, even for uploading training and how-to information. A project wiki area slowly developed, with help documents and links being loaded, due largely to the pressure of one project participant. Information continued to be distributed by e-mails but nevertheless, over time, the project wiki area has become highly visited and now receives thousands of hits.

Finally, the programming department, again staffed mainly by contractors, was responsible for managing and fixing software bugs, discussing and planning extensions with business representatives, and generally keeping the production and transport systems operational. A large maintenance team, with wide areas of knowledge and relatively high turnover, was under constant pressure: their team leader identified architecture, service provision and requirements gathering as ideal (indeed urgent) areas of need for wiki use. The rapid, interactive nature of the work made wikis ideal – while maintaining a complete document record. However, Web 2.0 and wikis were not adopted in the short term, due in the most part to pressure of work.

One department, mainly based at sites, had the job of training staff across the organisation. They developed curricula for all types of situation and business role, which encompassed online training, advice, induction and follow-up. Their manager simply instructed them that they would use the enterprise wiki for their interactions wherever possible. After some initial business analysis, it was found that most of their tasks would be simplified by using the wiki. They found it cut down time and reduced travel to create curricula, identify problem areas and deliver follow-up advice to new starters. They created FAQ sections and uploaded media files for training, including photos of the natural environments.

Production

Within the operation, fertiliser and sands processing was also required. These were areas in the direct line of operation, where breakdowns affected production. The turnover in managers was fairly high, with actual leadership roles being, for skilled staff such as geologists and chemists, stepping stones to corporate careers. The perceived return on learning from a wiki was considered to take some time and, indeed, not be measurable with the current simple measures. A former manager of one of these plants was interviewed as an expert and some of his hitherto tacit knowledge was captured in audio-visual and text on how to optimise the capacity of these plants. The new manager also expressed interest in using the system to discuss and capture how to fine-tune and improve reliability in the processing machines, but did not take it further.

The system, along with a few interview videos with other old-timers, was demonstrated to one 'ageing' specialist, an expert in a large and critical piece of processing equipment, who had been fetched out of retirement at great cost. After watching the videos of others he said it would be perfect for their area: they spent a lot of time training new staff in how to optimise the truck positioning (factors like metal expanding and contracting in heat and cold, land incline and weight differentials, all leading to difficulties in positioning trucks precisely). After a long training period, especially when machines had been upgraded, there was fairly high attrition and fairly soon after this there was often complete team turnover. A video of an expert interview would set the scene for learning specific instrument use, give the bigger picture of the major elements to be considered, and be continually available for new staff. But the old-timer never returned subsequent calls.

Case study discussion

1. Identify and classify the barriers to adoption according to the following themes:

   (a) technology and usability issues;

   (b) business application and usefulness;

   (c) institutional and cultural barriers (expressed as postulates);

   (d) social identity and in-group prototypes of different participant groups;

   (e) the social dimensions of direct and indirect power and control;

   (f) the outsourcing model;

   (g) understanding how knowledge develops in groups.

2. What are the managers' concerns and how would you respond to them?

3. How could you use the concept of 'spaces' to design solutions and reduce the concerns of managers?

4. What would you do to make the systems a success?

Note

1. This story is a composite of several learning cases and I have chosen to embed it in a fictitious resource processing company. The intention is to allow the reader to practise their analytical skills and arrive at methods for analysing the receptivity of an organisation to a Web 2.0 solution and work out ways to secure adoption and productive use. The case has been created for metaphoric and educational purposes, is fictitious and does not represent or have any involvement with registered companies or people outside of this narrative.

Glossary of Web 2.0 terms

Please see Wikipedia.org for further explanations of these terms.

Blog – a type of website usually maintained by an individual person and displayed in reverse chronological order (from newest to oldest). It can contain postings on a theme, event or topic and contain video and image material as well as text.

Mashups – a mashup is a single web page which contains sub-sets of other web pages that can be conveniently placed together because it suits a particular purpose.

Metadata – data about data, that is it describes the form and structure of underlying data and information content.

Microblog – a form of blogging which allows small amounts of content to be loaded to a blogging website, usually at higher frequencies than a standard blog.

Ontology – a formal representation of a set of concepts which describe an area of activity or life.

Permalink – a URL that points to a specific blog entry.

RSS – Really Simple Syndication: a format for the publication of web feeds about specific topics which can be picked by an RSS reader and conveyed to the user as an indicator of a new event regarding that topic (a new news article or stock price change, for example).

Semantic web – a vision for enabling web content to be understood by software by developing a system of linked metadata which mirror underlying conceptualisations of human life and areas of activity. This metadata can be used to tag or interpret web content.

Social networking service – a web service which allows people to build communities based upon special interests or personal inclinations and share information with others with whom they form those communities.

Social tagging – the activity of creating, applying and sharing descriptive metadata (tags or labels) in order to annotate and classify content in web pages and documents. These tags can be created and shared via social tagging websites or using the functions of wikis, blogs or other website management systems.

Tag – a keyword or label assigned to a piece of information such as a document or web page.

URL – the Uniform Resource Locator is an address pointing to a particular resource (web page or file) somewhere on a network.

Web 2.0 – the second generation of Internet applications which make possible greater participation, interactivity and user control.

Wiki – a type of website, managed by wiki software, which allows the immediate creation, editing and linking of web pages. Wikis are usually used for the collaborative creation of information by multiple editors and contain many functions to improve information management such as linking, tagging and author management.

Glossary of terms from social theory

Please see Wikipedia.org for further explanations of these terms.

Cognitive system – the system of social institutions in an organisation which reflects the concepts which are material to production and service delivery and by means of which the world is interpreted.

Cultural postulates – logical premises or statements which express deeply held beliefs about the world within a group or organisation and which are generally common and shared within the group.

Direct control – the exercise of coercive power over individuals by which their conformance is enforced through directives, procedures and measurement.

Distinctive knowledge – knowledge which is owned by an expert and which is particular to that person.

Emerging knowledge – knowledge which is not yet externalised but emerges by virtue of it being brought out and combined in group situations and collaborations.

Externalisation – the process of expressing, by language or other symbolic acts, meanings and intentions to others.

In-group prototype – the conceptual template which describes and prescribes the attributes which are appropriate to signify group membership in specific contexts.

Indirect control – the exercise of coercive power over individuals by which conformance is achieved by aligning the distribution of rewards and indirect pressure, such as group norms, with the objectives of the organisation.

Institution – the perceptible structures of social order and patterning which indicate and determine how people in a given group should and do behave.

Institutional control – the exercise of power through the creation and inculcation of cognitive and normative ways of thinking which cause people to behave in the interest of the group or organisation.

Internalisation – the process of absorbing and understanding the symbols used in communication with others in a group.

Legitimation – the act of making an event, a concept or activity legitimate by attaching it to existing norms and values in society.

Normative system – the system of social institutions which contains values and principles which signify certain actions, methods or responses as the right thing to do.

Objectivation – the process of creating new common understandings of reality within social groups.

Organisational memory – the past experiences and learning within an organisation that can be brought to bear on current problems or tasks.

Proprietary descriptive knowledge – knowledge which is specific to an organisation that describes how things can be done or how they are usually done.

Proprietary prescriptive knowledge – knowledge which is specific to an organisation which prescribes how things must be done.

Regulative system – the system of social institutions which embodies the rules of routine action, procedure, roles and responsibilities.

Reification – the process by which a social concept or idea appears to exist independently of the social groups which create that concept.

Social identity – the sense of belonging and self-hood which is generated by being a member of a specific group.

Socialisation – the process of internalising and absorbing a group's culture, norms, routines and values in order to participate as a member of that group.

Transactive memory system – a way of explaining how responsibility for knowledge in groups can be shared by using information directories to track down or use the right source of knowledge when knowledge is needed.

Bibliography

Aberdeen Group (June 2008) *Customer 2.0: The Business Implications of Social Media*. Aberdeen Group at: *http://www.aberdeengroup.com*.

Ackerman, M. and Halverson, C. (2000) 'Reexamining organizational memory', *Communications of the ACM*, 43 (1): 58–64.

Anand, V., Manz, C.C. and Glick, W.H. (1998) 'An organizational memory approach to information management', *Academy of Management Review*, 23 (4): 796–809.

Anonymous (2009a) 'Ektron reports an increase in customers requiring a single solution for web content management and enterprise 2.0', 28 July. Retrieved 9 November 2009 from: *http://wwwektron.co/press release_enterprise20/*.

Anonymous (2009b) 'Herausfordernung Demografischer Wandel', *Der Mittelstand*, 1 (June).

Anonymous (2009c) 'Online playgrounds', *The Economist*, 25–31 July, p. 55.

Antoniou, G. and van Harmelen, F. (2004) *A Semantic Web Primer*. Cambridge, MA: MIT Press.

Argote, L. (1999) *Organizational Learning: Creating, Retaining and Transferring Knowledge*. Boston: Kluwer Academic.

Argyris, C. (1999) *On Organizational Learning*. Oxford: Blackwell.

Argyris, C. and Schön, D.A. (1978) *Organizational Learning: A Theory of Action Perspective*. Reading, MA: Addison-Wesley.

Argyris, C. and Schön, D.A. (1996) *Organizational Learning II*. Reading, MA: Addison-Wesley.

Asch, S. (1952) *Social Psychology*. Englewood Cliffs, NJ: Prentice Hall.

Ashby, W.R. (1956) *An Introduction to Cybernetics*. London: Chapman & Hall.

Attalli, J. (2009) *A Brief History of the Future*. Crows Nest, NSW: Allen & Unwin.

Barabási, A.-L. (2002) *Linked: How Everything Is Connected to Everything Else and What It Means for Business, Science, and Everyday Life*. London: Plume.

Barsh, J., Capozzi, M.M. and Davidson, J. (2008) 'Leadership and innovation', *McKinsey Quarterly*. Electronic version retrieved 11 November 2009 from: *http://www.mckinseyquarterly.com*.

Basso, M. (2008) *2018: Digital Natives Grow Up and Rule the World*, No. G00159053. Stamford, CT: Gartner Inc.

Bauman, Z. and May, T. (2001) *Thinking Sociologically*. Oxford: Blackwell.

Bell, M. (2004) *Leading and Managing in the Virtual Matrix Organization*, No. R-22-1959. Stamford, CT: Gartner.

Bentham, J. (1995) *The Panopticon Writings*. London: Verso.

Berger, P.L. and Luckmann, T. (1967) *The Social Construction of Reality – A Treatise in the Sociology of Knowledge*. London: Penguin.

Berners-Lee, T., Hendler, J. and Lassila, O. (2001) 'The Semantic Web', *Scientific American*, May. Electronic version retrieved 11 November 2009 from: *http://www.scientificamerican.com/article.cfm?id=the-semantic-web*.

Blaschke, S. (2008) 'Wikis in Organisationen', in P. Alpar and S. Blaschke (eds), *Web 2.0 – Eine empirische Bestandsaufnahme*. Wiesbaden: Vieweg+Teubner.

Boisot, M.H. (1998) *Knowledge Assets – Securing Competitive Advantage in the Information Economy*. New York: Oxford University Press.

Boje, D. and Winsor, R.D. (1993) 'The resurrection of Taylorism: total quality management's hidden agenda', *Journal of Organizational Change Management*, 6 (4): 57–70.

Braverman, H. (1974) *Labor and Monopoly Capital: The Degradation of Work in the Twentieth Century*. New York: Monthly Review Press.

Brickmann, C. and Ungerman, D. (July 2008) 'Climate change and supply change management', *McKinsey Quarterly*. Electronic version retrieved 11 November 2009 from: *http://www.mckinseyquarterly.com*.

Bruns, A. and Jacobs, J. (eds) (2006) *Uses of Blogs*. New York: Peter Lang.

Bryan, L.B. and Joyce, C.I. (2007) *Mobilizing Minds*. New York: McGraw-Hill.

Bucks Consulting (2007) *The Real Talent Debate: Will Aging Boomers Deplete the Workforce?* Secaucus, NJ: Bucks Consultants.

Bughin, J. and Manyika, J. (2007) How businesses are using Web 2.0: A McKinsey Global Survey', *McKinsey Quarterly*. Electronic version retrieved 11 November 2009 from: *http://www.mckinseyquarterly.com*.

Bughin, J., Chui, M. and Miller, A. (2009) 'How companies are benefiting from Web 2.0', *McKinsey Quarterly*. Electronic version retrieved 11 November 2009 from: *http://www.mckinseyquarterly.com*.

Bughin, J., Manyika, J. and Miller, A. (2008) 'Building the Web 2.0 enterprise', *McKinsey Quarterly*. Electronic version retrieved 11 November 2009 from: *http://www.mckinseyquarterly.com*.

Buhse, W. and Stamer, S. (eds) (2008) *Enterprise 2.0 – The Art of Letting Go*. New York: iUniverse.

Carter, S. (2007) *The New Language of Business: SOA and Web 2.0*. Upper Saddle River, NJ: IBM Press.

Cartwright, F. and Zander, A. (1968) 'Power and influence in groups: introduction', in F. Cartwright and A. Zander (eds), *Group Dynamics: Research and Theory*, 3rd edn. New York: Harper & Row, pp. 215–35.

Casarez, V., Cripe, B., Sini, J. and Weckerle, P. (2009) *Reshaping your Business with Web 2.0*. New York: McGraw-Hill.

Castells, M. (2000) *The Rise of the Network Society*, 2nd edn. Malden, MA: Blackwell.

Castells, M. (2001) *The Internet Galaxy*. Oxford: Oxford University Press.

Charman, S. (2006) 'Blogs in business: using blogs behind the firewall', in A. Bruns and J. Jacobs (eds), *Uses of Blogs*. New York: Peter Lang.

Chui, M., Miller, A. and Roberts, R.P. (2009) 'Six ways to make Web 2.0 work', *McKinsey Quarterly*. Electronic version retrieved 1 February 2009 from: *http://www.mckinseyquarterly.com*.

Coase, R.H. (1937) 'The nature of the firm', *Economica*, 4 (16): 386–405.

Coch, L. and French Jr, J.R.P. (1948) 'Overcoming resistance to change', *Human Relations*, 1: 512–32.

Cole, R.E. (1989) *Strategies for Learning: Small-Group Activities in American, Japanese, and Swedish Industry*. Berkeley, CA: University of California Press.

Columbia Accident Investigation Board (2005) *Report of Columbia Accident Investigation Board*, Vol. I, pp. 97–204. Electronic version retrieved 11 November 2009 from: *http://www.nasa.gov/columbia/home/CAIB_Vol1.html*.

Commerzbank (2009) *Abschied vom Jugendwahn? Unternehmerische Strategien für den demografischen Wandel*. Frankfurt am Main: Commerzbank AG, Zentrales Geschäftsfeld Corporate Banking.

Court, D., Farrell, D. and Forsyth, J.E. (2007) 'Serving aging baby boomers', *McKinsey Quarterly*. Electronic version retrieved 10 August 2008 from: *http://www.mckinseyquarterly.com*.

Cross, R. and Baird, L. (2000) 'Technology is not enough: improving performance by building organizational memory', *Sloan Management Review*, 41 (3): 69.

Davenport, T. and Prusak, L. (1998) *Working Knowledge: How Organizations Manage What They Know*. Boston, MA: Harvard Business School Press.

Deitering, A.-M. and Bridgewater, R. (2007) 'Stop reinventing the wheel: using wikis for professional knowledge sharing', *Journal of Web Librarianship*, 1 (39): 27–44.

Derven, M. (2009) 'Social networking: a force for development?', *Training and Development*, 63 (7): 58–73.

DiMaggio, P. and Powell, W. (1983) 'The iron cage revisited: institutional isomorphism and collective rationality in organizational fields', *American Sociological Review*, 48 (2): 147–60.

Drakos, N., Bradley, A., Gall, N. and Austin, T. (2008) *Tutorial: Social Context, Not Technology, Defines Social Software*, No. G00158294. Stamford, CT: Gartner Inc.

Dufft, N. (2008) 'Reality check enterprise 2.0: the state of play within German companies', in W. Buhse and S. Stamer (eds), *Enterprise 2.0 – The Art of Letting Go*. New York: iUniverse, pp. 140–9.

Dutta, S. and Fraser, M. (2009) 'When job seekers invade Facebook', *McKinsey Quarterly*. Electronic version retrieved 11 November 2009 from: *http://www.mckinseyquarterly.com*.

Ebersbach, A., Krimmel, K. and Warta, A. (2008) 'Auswahl und Aussage von Kenngrössen innerbetrieblicher Wiki-Arbeit', in P. Alpar and S. Blaschke (eds), *Web 2.0 – Eine empirische Bestandsaufnahme*. Wiesbaden: Vieweg+Teubner.

Efimova, L. and Grudin, J. (2007) *Crossing Boundaries: A Case Study of Employee Blogging*. Paper presented at the Proceedings of the Fortieth Hawaii International Conference on System Sciences, Los Alamitos.

Farrell, S. and Lau, T. (2006) *Fringe Contacts: People-Tagging for the Enterprise* (No. RJ10384). San Jose: IBM, Almaden Research Division.

Fleming, L. and Marx, M. (2006) 'Managing creativity in small worlds', *California Management Review*, 48 (4): 6–27.

Foucault, M. (1991) *Discipline and Punish*, trans. A. Sheridan. London: Penguin Books.

Frappaolo, C. and Keldson, D. (2008) *Enterprise 2.0: Agile, Emergent and Integrated*. Silver Spring, MD: AIIM – The ECM Association.

French Jr, J.R.P. and Raven, B. (1968) 'The bases of social power', in F. Cartwright and A. Zander (eds), *Group Dynamics: Research and Theory*, 3rd edn. New York: Harper & Row, pp. 259–69.

Friedman, T. (2005) *The World Is Flat*. London: Penguin Books.

Giddens, A. (1984) *The Constitution of Society: Outline of the Theory of Structuration*. Berkeley, CA: University of California Press.

Gillmor, D. (2006) *We the Media*. Sebastapol, CA: O'Reilly Media.

Granovetter, M. (1973) 'The strength of weak ties', *American Journal of Sociology*, 78 (6): 1360–80.

Gray, C.F. and Larson, E.W. (2003) *Project Management: The Managerial Process*. New York: McGraw-Hill.

Habermas, J. (1996) *Between Facts and Norms – Contributions to a Discourse Theory of Law and Democracy*. Cambridge: Polity Press.

Haseman, W.D., Nazaretha, D.L. and Paul, S. (2005) 'Implementation of a group decision support system utilizing collective memory', *Information and Management*, 42: 591–605.

Heidegger, M. (1962) *Being and Time*. New York: HarperCollins.

Hipp, D. (2009) 'Empfindliche Seele', *Der Spiegel*, 29 June, p. 51.

Hoebel, E.A. (1972) *The Law of Primitive Man*. New York: Atheneum.

Hollingshead, A.B. and Brandon, D. (2003) 'Potential benefits of communication in transactive memory systems', *Human Communication Research*, 29 (4): 607–15.

Huber, G. (1991) 'Organizational learning: the contributing processes and the literatures', *Organization Science*, 2 (1): 88–115.

Hutchins, E. (1995) *Cognition in the Wild*. Cambridge, MA: MIT Press.

Jackson, P. and Klobas, J. (2008) 'Transactive memory systems in organizations: implications for knowledge directories', *Decision Support Systems*, 44 (2): 409–24.

Janis, I. (1982) *Groupthink: Psychological Studies of Policy Decisions and Fiascos*. Boston: Houghton-Mifflin.

Klobas, J. (2006) *Wikis: Tools for Information Work and Collaboration*. New York: Neal-Schuman.

Klobas, J. and Jackson, P. (eds) (2007) *Becoming Virtual: Knowledge Management and Transformation of the Distributed Organization*. Heidelberg: Physica-Verlag.

Koller, P.-J. and Alpar, P. (2008) 'Die Bedeutung privater Weblogs für das Issue-Management in Unternehmen', in P. Alpar and S. Blaschke (eds), *Web 2.0 – Eine empirische Bestandsaufnahme*. Wiesbaden: Vieweg+Teubner.

Kosonen, M. and Kianto, A. (2009) 'Applying wikis to managing knowledge – a socio-technical approach', *Knowledge and Process Management*, 16 (1): 23–9.

Krippendorf, K. (1975) 'Some principles of information storage and retrieval in society', *General Systems*, 20: 15–35.

Kroski, E. (2008) *Web 2.0 for Librarians and Information Professionals*. New York: Neal-Schuman.

Lave, J. and Wenger, E. (1991) *Situated Learning: Legitimate Peripheral Participation*. Cambridge: Cambridge University Press.

Leadbeater, C. (2009) *We-Think*, 2nd edn. London: Profile Books.

Leary, M.R. and Tangney, J.P. (2003) *Handbook of Self and Identity*. New York: Guilford Press.

Lemert, C. and Branaman, A. (eds) (1997) *The Goffman Reader*. Malden, MA: Blackwell.

Leonard-Barton, D. (1995) *Wellsprings of Knowledge: Building and Maintaining the Sources of Innovation*. Boston, MA: Harvard Business School Press.

Lewis, K. (2004) 'Knowledge and performance in knowledge-worker teams: a longitudinal study of transactive memory systems', *Management Science*, 50 (11): 1519–33.

Li, C. and Bernoff, J. (2008) *Groundswell*. Boston, MA: Harvard Business School Press.

McAffee, A. (2006) 'Enterprise 2.0: the dawn of emergent collaboration', *Sloan Management Review*, 47 (3): 22–8.

McGregor, D. (1985) 'The human side of enterprise', in D. S. Pugh (ed.), *Organisation Theory*. Harmondsworth: Penguin.

McKinlay, A. (2005) 'Knowledge management', in S. Ackroyd, R. Batt, P. Thompson and P.S. Tolbert (eds), *The Oxford Handbook of Work and Organization*. Oxford: Oxford University Press, pp. 242–62.

Mader, S. (2008) *Wikipatterns*. Indianapolis, IN: Wiley.

Miles, D. (2009) *Collaboration and Enterprise 2.0*. Silver Spring, MD: AIIM – The ECM Association.

Milgram, S. (1967) 'The small world problem', *Psychology Today*, 2: 60–6.

Moorman, C. and Miner, A.S. (1998) 'Organizational improvisation and organizational memory', *Academy of Management Review*, 23: 698–723.

Moreland, R.L. and Levine, J.M. (1992) 'Problem identification by groups', in S. Worchel, W. Wood and J.A. Simpson (eds), *Group Process and Productivity*. Newbury Park, CA: Sage, pp. 17–47.

Moreland, R.L. and Myaskovsky, L. (2000) 'Exploring the performance benefits of group training: transactive memory or improved communication?', *Organizational Behavior and Human Decision Processes*, 82 (1): 117–33.

Moreland, R.L., Argote, L. and Krishnan, R. (1998) 'Training people to work in groups', in R.S. Tindale, L. Heath, J. Edwards, E. Posavac, F.B. Bryant, Y. Suarez-Balcazar, E. Henderson-King and J. Myers (eds), *Theory and Research in Small Groups*. New York: Plenum, pp. 36–60.

Morello, D., Kyte, A. and Gomolski, B. (2007). *The Quest for Talent: You Ain't Seen Nothing Yet*, No. G00153872. Stamford, CT: Gartner Inc.

Müller, C. (2008) 'Analyse sozialer Informationsräume zur Förderung des selbstorganisierten Wissensmanagement', in P. Alpar and S. Blaschke (eds), *Web 2.0 – Eine empirische Bestandsaufnahme*. Wiesbaden: Vieweg+Teubner, pp. 169–81.

Newman, A.C. and Thomas, J.G. (2009) *Enterprise 2.0 Implementation*. New York: McGraw-Hill.

Nonaka, I. and Takeuchi, H. (1995) *The Knowledge-Creating Company: How Japanese Companies Create the Dynamics of Innovation*. New York: Oxford University Press.

O'Reilly, T. (2005) 'What Is Web 2.0'. Retrieved 1 August 2009 from: *http://oreilly.com/web2/archive/what-is-web-20.html*.

Pfeffer, J. (2007) *What Were They Thinking? Unconventional Wisdom About Management*. Boston, MA: Harvard Business School.

Phifer, G., Smith, D.M., Bradley, A. and Abrams, C. (2007) *Gartner Predicts 2008: Web Technologies Continue to Drive Business Innovation*, No. G00153102. Stamford, CT: Gartner Inc.

Pink, D. (2006) *A Whole New Mind: Why Right-Brainers Will Rule the Future*. New York: Penguin.

Polanyi, M. (1973) *Personal Knowledge – Towards a Post-Critical Philosophy*. London: Routledge & Kegan Paul.

Postman, N. (1985) *Amusing Ourselves to Death: Public Discourse in the Age of Show Business*. New York: Penguin Books.

Prentice, S. and Sarner, A. (2008) *Defining Generation V: The Virtual Generation*, No. G00154114. Stamford, CT: Gartner Inc.

Ravas, T. (2007) 'Not Just a Policies and Procedures Manual Anymore: The University of Houston Music Library Manual Wiki'. Unpublished work, Pittsburgh, PA.

Rheingold, H. (1993) *The Virtual Community: Homesteading on the Electronic Frontier*. Reading, MA: Addison-Wesley.

Rigby, B. (2008) *Mobilizing Generation 2.0 – A Practical Guide to Using Web 2.0 Technologies to Recruit, Organize and Engage Youth*. San Francisco: Jossey-Bass.

Rogers, E.M. (2003) *Diffusion of Innovations*, 5th edn. New York: Free Press.

Rose, N. (1991) *Governing the Soul: The Shaping of the Private Self*. London: Routledge.

Rosen, E. (2009) *Buzz*. London: Profile Books.

Scott, W.R. (1995) *Institutions and Organizations*. Thousand Oaks, CA: Sage.

Scott, W.R. (2004) 'Reflections on a half-century of organizational sociology', *Annual Review of Sociology*, 30: 1–21.

Scott, W.R. and Christensen, S. (eds) (1995) *The Institutional Construction of Organizations: International and Longitudinal Studies*. Thousand Oaks, CA: Sage.

Seely Brown, J. (2002) 'Growing up digital – how the web changes work, education, and the ways people learn', *USDLA Journal*, 16 (2). Electronic version retrieved 11 November 2009 from: *http://www .usdla.org/html/journal/FEB02_Issue/article01.html*.

Senate Select Committee on Intelligence (2004) *U.S. Intelligence Community's Prewar Intelligence Assessments on Iraq: Conclusions, 4–7* (No. S. Rpt. 108-301): 108th Congress.

Sherif, M. (1935) 'A study of some social factors in perception', *Archives of Psychology*, 27 (187): 60.

Shuen, A. (2008) *Web 2.0: A Strategy Guide*. Sebastapol, CA: O'Reilly Media.

Sinclair, G., Klepper, S. and Cohen, W. (2000) 'What's experience got to do with it? Sources of cost reduction in a large speciality chemicals producer', *Management Science*, 46 (1): 28–45.

Smith, D.M. (2008a) *Key Issues for Web 2.0 and Beyond*, 1H08. Stamford, CT: Gartner Inc.

Smith, D.M. (2008b) *Web 2.0 and Beyond: Evolving the Discussion*, No. G00154767. Stamford, CT: Gartner Inc.

Smith, D.M., Gootzit, D., Raskino, M., Prentice, S. and Dulaney, K. (2006) *Predicts 2007: Web 2.0 and Consumerization Forge into the Enterprise*, No. G00143764. Stamford, CT: Gartner Inc.

Solomon, G. and Schrum, L. (2007) *Web 2.0 – New Schools, New Tools*. Washington DC: International Society for Technology in Education.

Stacey, R. (2001) *Complex Responsive Processes in Organizations: Learning and Knowledge Creation*. London: Routledge.

Stasser, G., Stewart, D. and Wittenbaum, G.M. (1995) 'Expert roles and information exchange during discussion: the importance of knowing who knows what', *Journal of Experimental Social Psychology*, 31 (3): 244–65.

Stein, E.W. (1995) 'Organizational memory: review of concepts and recommendations for management', *International Journal of Information Management*, 15 (1): 17–32.

Stein, E.W. and Zwass, V. (1995) 'Actualizing organizational memory with information systems', *Information Systems Research*, 6 (2): 85–117.

Stillich, S. (2009) 'Innovative Heinzelmännchen', *brand eins* (magazine), 6: 20–30.

Sunstein, C.R. (2006) *Infotopia – How Many Minds Produce Knowledge*. New York: Oxford University Press.

Suriwiecki, J. (2004) *The Wisdom of Crowds*. London: Abacus.

Tapscott, D. (1998) *Growing Up Digital – The Rise of the Net Generation*. New York: McGraw-Hill.

Tapscott, D. and Williams, A. (2006) *Wikinomics: How Mass Collaboration Changes Everything*. New York: Penguin Group.

Thompson, P. (1989) *The Nature of Work*, 2nd edn. London: Macmillan Education.

Walker, A.R. and Bittinger, S. (2009) *Findings: Recession Is Forcing Generation Y to Find Alternatives to IT Careers*, No. G00165778. Stamford, CT: Gartner Inc.

Walsh, J.P. and Ungson, G.R. (1991) 'Organizational memory', *Academy of Management Review*, 16 (1): 57–91.

Walther, T. and Krasselt, M. (2005) *Corporate Blogging – Chancen für den Dialog – Qualitative Studie und Umfrage bei 2700 Internetnutzern in Deutschland* (electronic version). Proximity. Retrieved from: *http://www.bbdo.de/de/home/studien.download.Par.0035.Link1Download.File1Title.pdf*.

Watts, D. (2004) *Six Degrees: The Science of a Connected Age*. New York: W.W. Norton.

Weber, M. (1930) *The Protestant Ethic and the Spirit of Capitalism*. Abingdon: Routledge.

Wegner, D.M. (1987) 'Transactive memory: a contemporary analysis of the group mind', in B. Mullen and G.R. Goethals (eds), *Theories of Group Behaviour*. New York: Springer Verlag, pp. 185–208.

Wegner, D.M. (1995) 'A computer network model of human transactive memory', *Social Cognition*, 13 (3): 319–39.

Wegner, D.M., Erber, R. and Raymond, P. (1991) 'Transactive memory in close relationships', *Journal of Personality and Social Psychology*, 61 (6): 923–9.

Wegner, D.M., Guiliano, T. and Hertel, P. (1985) 'Cognitive interdependence in close relationships', in W.J. Ickes (ed.), *Compatible and Incompatible Relationships*. New York: Springer Verlag, pp. 253–76.

Weinberger, D. (2007) *Everything Is Miscellaneous*. New York: Holt Paperbacks.

Weinberger, D. (2008) 'The risk of control', in W. Buhse and S. Stamer (eds), *Enterprise 2.0 – The Art of Letting Go*. New York: iUniverse, pp. 66–73.

Welker, M. (2006) 'Weblogs. Ein neues Werkzeug für Journalisten', in A. Picot and T. Fischer (eds), *Weblogs professionell – Grundlagen, Konzepte und Praxis im unternehmerischen Umfeld*. Heidelberg: dpunkt, pp. 157–74.

Whetten, D.A. and Godfrey, P.C. (1998) *Identity in Organizations*. Thousand Oaks, CA: Sage.

Wisse, B. and van Knippenberg, D. (2009) 'Power and self-construal', in D. Tjosvold and B. Wisse (eds), *Power and Interdependance in Organizations*. Cambridge: Cambridge University Press, pp. 52–66.

Wittenbaum, G.M., Vaughan, S.L. and Stasser, G. (1998) 'Coordination in task-performing groups', in R.S. Tindale, L. Heath, J. Edwards, E. Posavac, F.B. Bryant, Y. Suarez-Balcazar, E. Henderson-King and J. Myers (eds), *Theory and Research in Small Groups*. New York: Plenum, pp. 177–204.

Wittgenstein, L. (1958) *Philosophical Investigations*. Oxford: Basil Blackwell & Mott Ltd.

Zastrow, V. (2009) 'Der Aufstand der Massen', *Frankfurter Allgemeine Zeitung*, 28 June, p. 1.

Zhang, L., Tian, Y. and Qi, Z. (2004) *An Empirical Study on the Impact of Organizational Memory on Organizational Performance in Manufacturing Companies*. Paper presented at the Proceedings of the 37th Hawaii International Conference on System Sciences, Hawaii.

Zuboff, S. (1988) *In the Age of the Smart Machine*. New York: Basic.

Index